VOLUME EDITOR

... SCHMID is ... Professor of Philosophy at the University of Wisconsin-Rock County. His doctoral work was in philosophy of mind and his current research focuses on motivation in sport and education. Schmid has been playing in the mountains and on rock for more than 20 years.

SERIES EDITOR

FRITZ ALLHOFF is an Assistant Professor in the Philosophy Department at Western Michigan University, as well as a Senior Research Fellow at the Australian National University's Centre for Applied Philosophy and Public Ethics. In addition to editing the *Philosophy for Everyone* series, Allhoff is the volume editor or co-editor for several titles, including *Wine & Philosophy* (Wiley-Blackwell, 2007), *Whiskey & Philosophy* (with Marcus P. Adams, Wiley, 2009), and *Food & Philosophy* (with Dave Monroe, Wiley-Blackwell, 2007).

PHILOSOPHY FOR EVERYONE

Series editor: Fritz Allhoff

Not so much a subject matter, philosophy is a way of thinking. Thinking not just about the Big Questions, but about little ones too. This series invites everyone to ponder things they care about, big or small, significant, serious … or just curious.

Forthcoming books in the series:

Edited by Stephen E. Schmid

CLIMBING
PHILOSOPHY FOR EVERYONE
Because It's There

Foreword by Hans Florine

WILEY-BLACKWELL

A John Wiley & Sons, Ltd., Publication

Blackwell Publishing was acquired by John Wiley & Sons in February 2007. Blackwell's publishing program has been merged with Wiley's global Scientific, Technical, and Medical business to form Wiley-Blackwell.

Registered Office
John Wiley & Sons Ltd, The Atrium, Southern Gate, Chichester, West Sussex, PO19 8SQ, United Kingdom

Editorial Offices
350 Main Street, Malden, MA 02148–5020, USA
9600 Garsington Road, Oxford, OX4 2DQ, UK
The Atrium, Southern Gate, Chichester, West Sussex, PO19 8SQ, UK

For details of our global editorial offices, for customer services, and for information about how to apply for permission to reuse the copyright material in this book please see our website at www.wiley.com/wiley-blackwell.

Library of Congress Cataloging-in-Publication Data
Climbing – philosophy for everyone: because it's there / edited by Stephen E. Schmid.
    p. cm. — (Philosophy for everyone)
  Includes bibliographical references and index.
    ISBN 978-1-4443-3486-9 (pbk.: alk. paper) 1. Free will and determinism.
2. Liberty. 3. Risk-taking (Psychology) 4. Mountaineering—Miscellanea.
I. Schmid, Stephen E. II. Title: Climbing – philosophy for everyone.
  B105.L45C47 2010
  796.52201—dc22

                      2010006826

A catalogue record for this book is available from the British Library.

Set in 10/12.5pt Plantin by SPi Publisher Services, Pondicherry, India
Printed in Singapore

01   2010

To Beth

CONTENTS

FOREWORD

Climbers often claim, and it is often true, that it is about the journey, not the summit. Similarly, I suggest that the joy in philosophy is about pursuing the answers, not necessarily finding them.

As a professional climber and speaker, I have had the pleasure of interacting with a wide variety of strangers on the topic of climbing. I have fielded philosophical questions from the most ignorant city dwellers to the most experienced climbers: Why climb? Is solo climbing crazy or morally wrong? Is chipping a hold a bad thing to do? Are you scared of heights? How does one rate a climb or what does it mean to rate a climb? In answering these and many other questions, I am offering my considered opinion and, perhaps, am influencing the questioner's thinking on possible "answers." I am rarely providing a definitive answer. If I or anyone had *the* answers, then this book likely would not have been written. It is the posing of intriguing questions that makes philosophy interesting and exceptionally so when applied to the activity of climbing.

What a joy it is to sit back and let these champion philosophers influence our thinking on some of the most interesting philosophical questions in and about climbing. Some of the above mentioned questions and more are discussed with insight from experienced climbers and brilliant thinkers.

For example, here are two challenging issues. I am often asked whether I think people who solo are crazy. I have often responded with the question: "Do you think your father is crazy to climb a ladder in order to clean the rain gutters, or hang Xmas lights?" My follow up is that as a physical event, there is the same comfort level for many soloists as there would be for your father. This is usually not the end of my answer nor, I believe, is Mr. Agnafors' essay on the topic herein all that he has to say on the subject. Note that Agnafors addresses the *morality* of soloing while I was questioned on the *sanity* of a soloist. Another question I have been asked is whether chipping a ¼ inch hand hold is bad. In my opinion, more information about the specific case is needed to answer the question. I have glued holds on smooth cement walls. I have not glued holds on the smooth granite of El Capitan. Do I think manufacturing holds is okay? You'll need to track me down for tea to find out. In the meantime, Mr. Ramsey's essay on this very subject is a delight to read. Like these two, all the philosopher-climbers in this anthology have deepened my thinking on all the questions I think about and discuss with others.

By reading these essays, I have been further reminded that it is the careful pondering of the questions that is wise and prudent, not vesting in a single answer. It's a joy to be flexible and explore the tangents one follows when remaining open to other ideas. It is no surprise that the same flexibility is immensely useful when facing the challenges one encounters in the very act of climbing.

I have met high-level academics at the climbing gym and at the cliff. I have met accountants, lawyers, advertising agents, supermodels,[1] construction workers, and librarians, all of whom have that obsession with climbing that I have. There is something in climbing that feeds and satisfies a need in many of us. The physical aspect of climbing involves every part of your body, from the tip of your toe to the tip of your finger. You must truly mentally engage with the rock or mountain. You must inventory your strengths and apply what you have to the challenge in front of you. Often times, it is a matter of great consequence if you do not have your complete focus on the task immediately before you. Simply put, you are 100 percent focused on climbing. I call it physical meditation. You simply can't be thinking about the bills due or the office you must be at Monday morning at 8 a.m. *and* climb at the same time. Climbing is a great mental break from the "other world." You do not need to study any Western or Eastern meditation techniques to enjoy the benefits of climbing.

What is climbing to me? Before climbing came into my life, I was an athlete and a competitor (and I still am). I saw climbing initially as a sport. Quickly, I found one could adventure, explore, and play on wild terrain. It was just darn fantastic Huck Finn and Tom Sawyer-like adventure! I was smitten by climbing. Even in my twenties when my hormones were raging, I would choose a rock climbing outing over a date with a woman.

I loved the athletic movement involved and I loved the incredible places climbing took me. I would never have traveled to the places I've been if I were obsessed with swimming, basketball, or soccer. I went to Europe my first time and lived there some three months without going to a single tourist destination. I was climbing! It was not until my fourth year of visiting France that I made it to the Louvre. I'm known for my speed climbing – heck, I wrote the book on it! Make no mistake, I do not climb more to go fast. Rather, I go fast because I get in more climbing.

In the philosophical world, I will often take the stance of an Ayn Rand Objectivist (though I often take on world troubles personally as a Buddhist). Logical reasoning I often think of, as did Rand, as an unwavering tool one can count on to judge the merits of a philosophical argument and to guide one's actions and beliefs. Yet, some may think that to use logic to argue a position, either ethical or otherwise, in something as ridiculous as climbing may seem more ridiculous than the act of climbing itself. In most people's minds, I'm already guilty of illogical behavior. However, I can't think of a more rewarding and interesting "illogical" activity to ponder philosophically than climbing.

I have had immensely entertaining conversations about a single gear placement on a 1,000-foot rock route in Patagonia. I have had lengthy discussions about the ethics of rap bolting, chopping, drilling, and chipping the rock. People will try to pin you down on where you stand. They are either looking for a fight or knowledge. I've managed to avoid fights for nearly thirty years. Is climbing a worthy pursuit? Is applying philosophical discussion about climbing a worthy endeavor? At risk of a fight, I'll tell you where I stand on these two questions: Yes and Yes. As you will discover when reading these essays, all the contributors are on "my side." But if you have any doubts about climbing being a worthy activity, I encourage you to read chapters 2 (Charlton), 5 (Treanor), 6 (Sailors), and 7 (Ebert and Robertson).

By reading the following essays, if you are not a climber you might well give it a try. If you are a climber, you will likely find yourself reading statements you have made or at least thoughts you've had about climbing. You might well find you are rethinking how and why you climb. You may find you are a little more flexible on and off the rock. In the end, you may just enjoy climbing a little more.

Speed be with you.[2]

NOTES

1 Hans is married to retired supermodel Jacki Adams, who is an accomplished climber herself (see www.jacquelineflorine.com).
2 "Speed" derives from the old English word *spede*, which means success and prosperity.

ACKNOWLEDGMENTS

Thank you to each of the contributors for your excellent essays, commitment to the journey, and willingness to endure my ceaseless edits. While most of you I know only through email, it has been a pleasure to work with you on this collection. I look forward to talking story over beers after a day of climbing together.

Thank you to Hans Florine for contributing the foreword.

Thank you to Fritz Allhoff, Jeff Dean, and Tiffany Mok at Wiley-Blackwell for your guidance and support.

Thank you to Daniel at rockclimbing.com for permission to use your climbing terms as a reference for the contributors and as the source for this volume's glossary.

A special thanks to climbing partners and friends: Katie Devine, Chris Durand, and Doug Hemken. Your advice and comments at various stages of this project were invaluable and greatly appreciated. An additional thanks to Doug for sharing your keen insights on the essays.

Finally, thank you to all those readers who share our passion for climbing and philosophy.

Stephen E. Schmid

STEPHEN E. SCHMID

PHILOSOPHIZING INTO THE VOID

An Introduction to *Climbing – Philosophy for Everyone*

"Because it's there," George Mallory is said to have responded to a reporter's question about why he wanted to climb Mt. Everest.[1] Arguably, these are the most famous words in climbing. The reporter, in asking his question, was undoubtedly expressing a common sentiment – why would you participate in this seemingly meaningless, useless, life-threatening pursuit? Surely, there is more you can do with your life than that! Perhaps the enduring allure of Mallory's answer can be attributed to what it implies more than what it says. In light of attempting Everest, one can discover in Mallory's answer a call to expand the limits of human possibility and greatness – the answer inspires us to act on our dreams and ascend to great heights; it challenges us to face the unknown void; and it reminds us that there may be no other reason for our quest than the challenge, adventure, and fun of climbing.

Like climbing, those who venture into the philosophical void will discover similar sentiments and revelations. Contemplating the value of philosophy, Bertrand Russell writes:

> Philosophy is to be studied, not for the sake of any definite answers to its questions . . . but rather for the sake of the questions themselves; because these questions enlarge our conception of what is possible, enrich our intellectual imagination and diminish the dogmatic assurance which closes the mind against speculation; but above all because, through the greatness

of the universe which philosophy contemplates, the mind also is rendered great, and becomes capable of that union with the universe which constitutes its highest good.[2]

So the philosopher, when asked "Why philosophy?" might find him or herself answering like Mallory: "Because it's there."

In the last several decades the connection between philosophy and climbing has become pronounced. This is especially so in the area of ethics, a branch of philosophy that is concerned with defining the principles that should govern our behavior. The seminal essay on climbing ethics is Tejada-Flores' 1967 "Games Climbers Play," which originally appeared in the American journal *Ascent* and was later anthologized in a collection of climbing essays. This essay revealed a new way of thinking about climbing. Tejada-Flores showed how the sport of climbing is a collection of different games, each with its own set of rules and playing fields. From the bouldering game to the expedition game, the seven climbing games Tejada-Flores identified provided a means of talking about climbing ethics. Climbing ethically, he writes, "means respecting the set of rules of the climbing-game that one is playing."[3] With a means of determining ethical climbing, Tejeda-Flores equates climbing with style to ethical climbing. A climber with good style deliberately climbs according to the rules of a climbing game. Better style arises when the climber follows a more restrictive, more difficult set of rules to accomplish his climbing game (for example, using trad rules to climb a big wall). Today, this way of framing climbing style and ethics is part of the fabric of climbing discourse and is expressed in everything from climbing magazines to fireside debates. In mapping the terrain for climbing games, Tejada-Flores' essay did what all good philosophy does – force us to rethink and understand our world anew. Ten years after its initial publication, Ken Wilson wrote that Tejada-Flores' essay still provided a useful mechanism for understanding climbing.[4] If the philosophical essays in this volume are any indication, Tejada-Flores' essay is as influential now as it was more than forty years ago.

In another significant essay published seven years later, Yvon Chouinard and Tom Frost rail against "mad bolters" and warn against the loss of adventure and mystery in the vertical wilderness, as trips once venturing into the unknown become just another routine gym workout.[5] Their call for individual restraint and responsibility emphasizes that success is defined by how you climb and not what you stand atop. Their call to climb simply with as little impact as possible has become the predominant style and guiding ethic of many climbers.

2   STEPHEN E. SCHMID

When reading the essays in this volume, you will notice the measured impact these two early treatises bring to current philosophical discussions of climbing. The essays within acknowledge and pay tribute to these early forays into the philosophical void. At the same time, this anthology traverses new ground, touches on sensitive ethical debates heard around the camp fire, explores classic philosophical questions, and has fun in the process. Whether budding boulderer or weathered mountaineer, these essays will hopefully help you answer two important questions: "Why climbing?" and "Why philosophy?"

In the second part of this introduction I want to offer you a summit view of this volume and briefly survey the terrain each essay will cover. There are four parts to this book: "Tying In," "Quest for the Summit," "Cutting the Rope," and "Mixed Climbing." The first three parts focus on a different aspect of climbing or philosophical method, while the topics in the last part are more diverse. In addition to the essays, you will find a glossary of climbing terms at the end of the volume to assist you during your journey.

Part one, "Tying In: Why Risk Climbing," addresses what, for many, is the most obvious aspect of climbing – the risk. Both climbing and philosophy are serious business. However, committing a mistake in philosophy won't kill you. In climbing, even simple mistakes can be life threatening. Given the inherent risks in most climbing games, why risk tying in? What does the risk bring? Given the risks, are we ever justified in tying in? And why do so many non-climbers find the risks inherent in climbing so unacceptable? The authors of this section's essays address each of these questions in turn.

First to tie in, Kevin Krein examines an apparent paradox in many forms of climbing. For many climbers, their love of climbing results from, among other things, the feeling of freedom it produces. At the same time, climbing can be a very confining, restricting activity. Pinned down by storms in a wind-whipped tent or frozen between delicate moves on a tricky climb is far from our typical notion of liberation. Examining ancient Stoic philosophy, Krein argues that risk and other inherent features of climbing provide a unique opportunity for a climber to experience freedom. The Stoic conception of freedom arises when one is able to understand and conform to one's environment. The simplicity and limited options inherent in climbing, further limited by its risks, provide the climber with unique opportunities to align his will with the opportunities the mountain affords. At these times, the climber feels free.

Many who have been climbing for a while know someone who has died from a climbing accident, whether the result of their own error or due to uncontrollable events. In the next essay, Paul Charlton considers the risks of climbing against the backdrop of the death of his longtime climbing partner and friend. Since the risks associated with climbing are more present than in daily life, Charlton argues that we must weigh the costs of climbing against its benefits if we are to justify these risks. For some, the rewards – pleasure and personal growth – will outweigh the costs of climbing – from frivolous expenditure of resources to death. Charlton leaves it up to each climber to determine whether the risks of his or her climbing pursuits are worth the rewards.

When answering the question "Why climb?" Joe Fitschen takes a different route than Charlton. Instead of considering how one might justify climbing and its attendant risks, Fitschen proposes a broader explanation. To adequately explain why climbers do what they do, Fitschen suggests we ask a more general question: "Why do people climb?" In phrasing the question this way, Fitschen asks a question about our species and sketches an evolutionary explanation for why we climb. Climbing is in our genes; the urge to climb is as natural as any other human endeavor. The pleasure that many of us naturally feel in exerting ourselves and overcoming vertical challenges only reinforces our evolved dispositions.

In the final essay, Heidi Howkins Lockwood asks why an astronaut's risks are considered acceptable when the risks faced by climbers are seen as unacceptable. Lockwood notes that many people disapprove of the risks that climbers take, while at the same time approving of equally dangerous activities. Lockwood examines two underlying assumptions motivating this disparity in attitudes about risk takers and their risky activities. The first assumption is that we ought to avoid risk-taking activities that might require a costly or dangerous rescue. The second assumption is that risk taking is unacceptable because the risk taker ignores the possible impact his actions have on family and friends. Building from her own personal experiences on expeditions to the world's highest mountains and drawing from climbing and non-climbing tragedies, Lockwood argues that both of these assumptions fail to justify the disparity in how people treat risk-taking activities. While Lockwood thinks the risks in most climbing activities are acceptable, she argues that taking extreme risks simply for the risk itself is not acceptable.

Part two, "Quest for the Summit: Cultivating the Climber," focuses on the character traits climbing develops and what characteristics are most

   STEPHEN E. SCHMID

valuable in the quest for the summit. The first essay starts by continuing the question from the previous section, "Why climb?" Brian Treanor answers this question from an Aristotelian perspective when he argues that climbing helps cultivate important virtues. In particular, he shows how climbing can cultivate the virtues of courage, humility, and respect for nature. While Treanor acknowledges that these are not the only virtues climbing has the potential to cultivate and that not all climbers exhibit these virtues, he thinks developing these virtues is particularly important in our modernized, coddling, and risk-adverse world. Climbing, then, serves a certain practical value – it may help develop the traits and virtues that allow one to flourish and live well in our non-climbing world.

Pam Sailors discusses the value of dangerous sport by examining the approaches and characters of two types of climbers: summiteers and mountaineers. The difference between the two hinges upon what motivates each type of climber to stand on top of a mountain. The summiteers, she proposes, are motivated to reach the summit at all costs – the value of climbing is found in affirming to oneself one's ability to accomplish a challenging goal. Mountaineers, on Sailors' account, are motivated by the climbing itself, where the desire to reach the top of the mountain is secondary to the experience of being on the mountain. As Sailors notes with passages from famous climbers, the motivation to experience the mountain leads to one moving beyond one's own interests to a sort of spiritual connection with the mountain. Many of the moral failings that have been witnessed in high-altitude expeditions, most notably Everest 1996, Sailors traces to the difference in the motivations of climbers. The desire to summit at all costs may explain why some climbers have failed to offer assistance to ailing climbers, leaving them to die on the mountain. While Sailors' essay focuses on high-altitude climbing, the basic points of her essay apply equally well to other forms of climbing.

Ebert and Robertson argue that a fundamental value of mountaineering is self-sufficiency, and the more self-sufficiently one climbs, the more laudable the climbing achievement. Using Hermann Buhl's 1953 solo ascent of Nanga Parbat as their core example, Ebert and Robertson argue that self-sufficient climbing increases the climber's commitment to the dangers and risks of mountaineering. The less a mountaineer depends on others or technology to assist him in his climbing endeavors, the less guarantee there is for success. It is because the climb is harder or riskier when done self-sufficiently that self-sufficient climbing achievements are more valuable. While Ebert and Robertson's claim is an evaluative claim, in that it gives one a means for saying which climbing achievements are better than others, they also think their thesis carries normative weight. The normative claim is that one ought to climb as self-sufficiently as one can, relying on one's own skills and abilities to ascend and descend a mountain, given the objective difficulty of the mountain. They defend their thesis against several criticisms, including the claim that self-sufficiency can lead to foolhardy actions.

Before reading the next essay, you might want to put down your greasy burger and fries. Levey's tasty take on sport climbing as analogous to eating fast food compares two different climbing games and the values each produces. Just as all meals are not the same, all climbing games are not the same. Sport climbing, like a ready meal, is quick and cheap. Trad climbing, Levey proposes, is like haute cuisine: it is slowly executed using expensive ingredients and is more committing. Sport climbers might not like this analogy and its implication that slow food tops fast food. As Levey readily admits, we all eat both. He agrees that a more authentic "dining" experience is had with trad climbing, and trad climbers possess a more authentic climbing style. However, this conclusion does not come out of a fast-food box. To make this final point, Levey uses Hegel's master and slave distinction to argue that trad climbing reflects the situation of the slave, which for Hegel is the more authentic relationship. From this influential distinction, Levey concludes that the trad climbing game is more authentic than its fast-food variant. So, what's for dinner?

Leaving the Western traditions, the final essay in this section shifts to a Zen perspective on climbing. Being in the moment, in the zone, or going with the flow are common experiences in climbing. The capacity for climbing to produce these immersive, Zen-like experiences is one of the lures of climbing. Eric Swan elaborates on many of the Zen-like qualities of climbing. He also demonstrates how the discipline of climbing parallels many of the same trainings used in Zen philosophy to train the mind toward Nirvana: the physical work involved in climbing or preparing for a climb, the active meditation found while on a route, the problem solving that is intuitive and physical and not logical, and the instruction received from Zen masters. The final section of his essay focuses on two modern climbing masters – Derek Hersey and Chris Sharma – and how their climbing embodies Zen-like mindfulness through the disciplining of mind and body.

Part three, "Cutting the Rope: Climbing Ethics," plunges into the realm of moral principles. The first essay stems across the previous section into

  STEPHEN E. SCHMID

the ethics debate by examining the ethics of three climbing games arising from the values of climbers in dialogue with their climbing community. Dane Scott takes us on three different climbing excursions, each representing a distinct ethic and value arising within their respective climbing communities. The first trip is to Tuolumne Meadows' classic Bachar-Yerian, where John Bachar's ground-up ethic embodies the Nietzschean values of mastery and commitment. In contrast to this climb, Scott heads next to Smith Rock and the home of sport climbing. Here, Alan Watts and the test-piece To Bolt or Not to Be provide the backdrop for Scott's highlighting of the values of individual liberty and freedom and their relationship to sport climbing. While these two routes and their famous originators were part of a debate about climbing ethics, Scott looks at a young pioneer, Sonnie Trotter, who combines the ethics, style, and values of both traditional and sport climbing games. Scott concludes his tour in Canada at The Path, where Trotter's new route reflects an awareness of the community and traditions which have defined trad and sport climbing. Scott emphasizes that the dialogue between climbers and the larger climbing community helps define and ground the rules or ethics of climbing games.

The next essay ventures into contentious territory. Rock climbers climb routes that have been developed by some other ambitious climber – cracks are cleaned, bolts are placed, and unstable rocks are removed. While most rock climbers find such route preparations acceptable, most of these same individuals would find it unacceptable, if not unethical, to chip holds into the rock to make the route climbable. Why is the manufacturing of holds wrong? William Ramsey examines the justifications surrounding our condemnation of hold manufacturing and finds these justifications lacking. While Ramsey is not suggesting we go out and start chipping holds, he does challenge us to be consistent in our ethical reasoning.

Some consider free solo climbing, that is climbing without protective gear, to be one of the purest forms of climbing. Undoubtedly, it is one of the riskiest climbing activities. Despite the risk or because of it, some of the world's elite climbers have practiced the activity, adding to its allure. Should you free solo? While many would argue that they have a right to do as they wish, it is not clear that an appeal to personal liberty will itself provide an ethical justification for free soloing. Marcus Agnafors looks at several reasons given for free soloing and weighs these reasons on their ethical merits. As Agnafors notes, the question of whether free soloing is morally permissible is a complex question. So, should you free solo? Agnafors' essay will help you answer that question.

The final essay in this section looks at the issue of environmental degradation. If you've been to a popular climbing destination, then you have noticed it – climbers' trails snaking across the terrain, trash littering the trail and campsites, vegetation trampled at the base of a climb, or human excrement oozing from under the rock you decided to sit on for lunch. Climbers negatively impact the environment. What is ironic is that many of us climb in part to be in nature and to escape the chaos, noise, and pollution of the city. What those climber trails, garbage, and indelible marks on the rocks remind us is that others, many others, have traveled these trails before us. Even low-impact travel in the backcountry is impact. So, when does the impact of any one climber result in degradation of the environment? A single footstep on a lichen-covered rock won't make a notable difference, but with enough foot traffic, rock and vegetation will give way to a trail. Dale Murray's essay examines the challenge of determining when environmental degradation occurs and provides a practical solution to limiting our impact. It may be, Murray suggests, that we have to accept limits on our behavior in the form of climbing quotas, different climbing practices, and maybe self-imposed abstention from certain types of climbing to preserve our climbing habitat.

In part four, "Mixed Climbing: Philosophy on Varied Terrain," we look at a range of philosophical topics related to climbing. Suppose the next time you went to your favorite climbing crag or stepped up to your favorite trad route that there, standing in front of the route, was the person(s) who established the route. You know, the person who first found the line, cleaned it, bolted it, and wrote it down. Now, suppose Joe Routesetter asks you to pay him to climb the route he established. "After all," he says, in response to your surprised look, "I spent weeks and hundreds of dollars putting up this awesome route you are about to enjoy. It's only fair that you compensate me for my efforts!" One of the kinder responses to his demand would be to inform Joe that that's not how it's done around here. But Joe is simply acting on the prevailing norm in capitalistic society – one should be compensated for one's efforts, especially if others are going to benefit from those efforts. This hypothetical case is foreign to the climbing community. It simply is not part of climbing culture. Debora Halbert's essay examines how climbers and the climbing community operate as a gift economy. Climbers (not Joe) gift their time, energy, and resources to develop routes that they freely share with the larger climbing community. It's hard to imagine climbing without such a gift culture.

The next essay transitions from climbing culture to a climber's personal, felt experience. Nothing seems more certain than the elation and satisfaction of pulling through a challenging problem that one has been working on for hours, days, or weeks. However, Stephen Downes argues that climbers might be mistaken about the very experiences they cherish. Just as we might be mistaken about our visual experiences of the world or misremember what we had for breakfast, so too our knowledge of climbing experiences, feelings, and abilities might be mistaken. While simple, everyday lapses in our self-knowledge may be acceptable, lapses in self-knowledge about our climbing experiences may be more significant and result in us overestimating our climbing ability, putting ourselves and others at risk, or unethically scoring our comp card. Given that we might not be the best judges of our own climbing abilities, you might think twice the next time you are picking up a partner at the local crag to have some fun – you might wonder whether your new partner really can climb as hard as he says.

The final two essays discuss wildly different aspects of climbing and use different philosophical approaches, but both attempt to advance the same basic thesis. Many have claimed that beauty is in the eye of the beholder. Like one's preference for Brussels sprouts, whether one finds some object pleasing is a matter of taste. Or is it? A common assumption is that aesthetic judgments are purely subjective. And, since they are purely subjective, our preferences really don't say anything true about that object. Richard Graziano's essay argues that climbing grades are not subjective but that they are real properties of a route. Using a classic distinction, Graziano argues that climbing grades are dispositional properties; they are real features of a climb that have the power to challenge us in certain ways. Rating systems, like the Yosemite Decimal System, are our way of labeling the objective climbing grades. After considering Graziano's thesis, you may top out on a route and wonder about another aspect of climbing. Coiling your rope after the climb, you exclaim to your partner, "That was a beautiful route!" "Yes, it was," he responds. Are you both agreeing that the route you just completed was beautiful because you both have the same preferences and tastes? Gunnar Karlsen argues that when we make an aesthetic judgment about a route's beauty, we are making a claim about the objective features of that route, not simply about our personal tastes. We discover these objective features when we climb. The features of the rock, placement of holds, and the types of moves the rock forces us to make are perceived in our body's movements through space. We "see" through our bodily movements to the aesthetic qualities of the route, just as we see through our blue visual experiences to perceive the blue sky.

So it's no wonder that both you and your partner made the same aesthetic judgment, since the route produced in both of you similar experiences.

As these essays demonstrate, there's a close and rich connection between climbing and philosophical reflection. Perhaps John Muir was right: "When we try to pick out anything by itself, we find it hitched to everything else in the Universe."[6] I hope you enjoy the journey.

NOTES

1 Mallory's response appears in a 1923 interview in the *New York Times*, "Climbing Mount Everest Is Work For Supermen," March 18, 1923, p. xii.
2 Bertrand Russell, *The Problems of Philosophy* (Oxford: Oxford University Press, 1997), p. 161.
3 Lito Tejada-Flores, "Games Climbers Play," *Ascent* 1 (1967), reprinted and quoted from Ken Wilson (ed.) *The Game Climbers Play* (London: Diadem Books, 1978), p. 24.
4 Ken Wilson (ed.) *The Game Climbers Play* (London: Diadem Books, 1978), p. 13.
5 Yvon Chouinard and Tom Frost, "A Word," *Chouinard Equipment Catalogue* (October 1974).
6 John Muir, *My First Summer in the Sierra* (Boston: Houghton Mifflin, 1911), p. 110.

  STEPHEN E. SCHMID

PART I

TYING IN

Why Risk Climbing

CHAPTER 1

CLIMBING AND THE STOIC CONCEPTION OF FREEDOM

There are moments on high cold mountains, life enhancing moments . . . they are fragile transient times, when the borders between living and dying seem to overlap, when the past and future cease to exist and you are free.

Joe Simpson[1]

Why climb? For the natural experience; for the danger that draws us ever on; for the feeling of total freedom; for the monstrous drop beneath you. It is like a drug.

Herman Buhl[2]

I'm in love with climbing because of the beauty of the moves, because of the sensations it gives me and the feeling of freedom I experience. And this is even more the case, the higher up I am!

Pietro Dal Pra[3]

The pursuit of freedom is often cited as a reward of climbing. Even a little thought, however, shows that it is difficult to make any sense of the idea that a person could be more free when climbing than they are in other aspects of their life. Most people would not consider themselves free in the situations in which climbers routinely find themselves – on small ledges or steep slopes, often tied to someone else or an anchor just a few feet away, where any kind of movement is constrained by a number of factors and where serious injury or death could result from even a small mistake. In this essay I attempt to explain how, even under such conditions, climbers can experience a rare and profound sense of freedom. In fact, I will argue that climbers experience the freedom they do in part because of the constraints imposed on them and the dangers they face while climbing.

One place to start is by asking what people usually mean by the term "freedom." As a rule, when people say that they are free, they mean that they are unrestricted. That is, they have possible options that they can choose between as they wish. Often, the more options that exist, the freer a person is considered to be. But rather than talking in completely general terms, normally, people discuss more specific types of freedom. For example, one can have freedom of action or movement. A person who is free in this sense may go where he or she pleases and do what he or she wishes. To the extent that this is not the case, we say that a person is not free. A person who is trapped, injured, or is limited in his or her actions in any other way lacks freedom in this sense.

A second type of freedom that people often talk about is political freedom. In this context people are considered free if government or social controls do not inhibit them. It is worth noting that a person may lack freedom in the above mentioned sense (freedom of movement or action) but still be politically free. For instance, I have a friend who is currently spending time on the couch recovering from an ankle injury suffered while bouldering. While his freedom of movement has been reduced, so that he is not able to climb or ski, his political freedom has remained untouched.

A third context in which we speak of freedom arises primarily in philosophical discussions of free will and determinism. This is generally considered to be a metaphysical problem concerning whether or not human beings really make free choices, or are determined, either by mechanisms of physical causation or otherwise, to act exactly as they do. It is often said that people are free in this sense if, given a circumstance, they could act, or could have acted, other than they actually do or did.

As for the first sense, freedom of movement or action, when one is climbing, his or her options are more limited than in most situations in life on horizontal ground. Right now, I can get up, walk in any direction, decide to visit friends, go for a run, or even head out to go rock climbing. Once on a climb, however, my options are generally limited to a few possible ways of going up (if I can), going down, or staying put (for as long as I can). Part of climbing is putting oneself in situations where one's movements or actions are limited, sometimes to the extreme.

In terms of political freedom, while there are rare cases in which a person might use his or her climbing skills to escape an oppressive government, in general, one is no more politically free on a mountain than in one's home. It is even true that some climbers claiming to be seeking freedom travel from places where people enjoy extensive political freedom to places that are far less politically free in order to climb. It is fairly clear that the freedom associated with climbing is not political.

As for freedom of the will, it certainly seems to be the case that humans either have free will or do not. So, it is difficult to see how being immersed in a climb could have any influence at all on whether a being is free in this sense.

In fact, according to any understanding of freedom that requires many possible options, we are less free while climbing. Oddly enough, it is often when climbers have the fewest options that they claim to experience the most freedom. In the quote from Pietro Dal Pra above, he says that the higher up he is – where his actual options are most limited – the freer he feels. Often, it is when climbers talk about fully committing to a particular route – moving past the point where they have the option of retreating, and onto the portions of routes where the risks are commonly the greatest – that they claim to really feel free.

We might look at this situation and say that climbers, like many athletes, are just not very good at expressing themselves. When they say that they feel free, they mean that it feels good to do what they do. I don't think that this is the case and will spend the rest of this essay trying to explain the sense in which climbers can be free. In order to do this, however, I will turn to a way of looking at freedom that is different from the common, contemporary understanding of it. The Stoics of ancient Greece and Rome had a conception of freedom that I will argue explains what climbers are trying to express. In order to present this conception of freedom, I am going to abandon talk of climbing for a short while and turn to Stoic philosophy.

Stoicism developed in Athens in the fourth century BCE and was one of the most influential philosophical schools in Greece and Rome. The school takes its name from the fact that its founder, Zeno of Citium, chose to meet on a particular *stoa* (porch or colonnade) overlooking the large public area in Athens. After Zeno, the next two heads of the school of thought, Chrysippus and Cleanthes, continued to develop Stoic ideas. These three philosophers formulated the foundations of the general positions of Stoicism.

Unfortunately, while the three principal Stoics produced books that were well known (Chrysippus is said to have completed 165 works), none of those books survived beyond the classical period. We know what the early Stoics thought because other philosophers, historians, and commentators whose work did survive paraphrased and quoted Stoic texts. Scholars have collected these fragments and have pieced together Stoic philosophical positions.[4] Figuring out the details and development of early Stoic theory is a bit like trying to figure out what happened to Mallory and Irvine on Everest or to Maestre and Egger on Cerro Torre. Some events are generally accepted and agreed upon, others are the subject of much debate. And, every once in a while, someone digs around a bit more and a new piece of evidence is found. The topics I address in this essay are among those generally agreed upon.

The early Stoics felt that they were working out a complete philosophical system in which all parts were interconnected and consistent. So, in explaining the Stoic idea of freedom, I will also, by necessity, cover various other aspects of Stoic philosophy.

One thing that is very clear is that the Stoics were strict determinists – they held that every event in the universe is physically caused by the events preceding it and that things could not happen in any other way than they do. In an illustration that might make some climbers uncomfortable, the Roman philosopher Cicero explained that according to the Stoic position, "The passage of time is like the unwinding of a rope, bringing about nothing new and unrolling each stage in its turn."[5]

What needs to be shown is how it is, according to the Stoics, that one can be free, though the events of his or her life could not turn out other than they do. And, for this essay, of course, what needs to be explained is how it makes sense to talk about feeling free when one is well above that last piece of pro and can barely make the next move, or one is pinned down by wind and unable to leave a tent for several days. My hope is that the answers to both of these questions will be fairly clear once I have provided more information on Stoic metaphysics.

Although the Stoics were determinists, they also felt that every event in the world occurs according to a divine plan or direction. The Stoics understood God to be that which guides all events in the universe to occur in accordance with reason. But rather than existing outside of nature and directing it, they held that God *is* reason and *is* contained in nature. Chrysippus is said to have claimed that "divine power resides in reason and the mind and intellect of universal nature" and that "God is the world itself."[6] And, importantly, the *logos* (reason or rationality) of

  KEVIN KREIN

humans is not entirely separate from the universal reason or *logos* of God, the determining force governing events in the universe. In fact, the early Stoics saw the rationality of humans to be part of the rationality that constitutes God. It is in this relationship of the reason of individual humans to universal reason that the Stoic notion of freedom can be developed.

Chrysippus held that the stated goal of the Stoic philosophers was "living in agreement with nature . . . which is in accordance with the nature of oneself and that of the whole."[7] Living in accord with oneself and the universe, they argued, was the result of living completely according to reason. Because the universe is governed by reason, living by reason will lead to the individual living a life in harmony with the events of the world. Stoics refer to a person whose understanding is in harmony with the flow of events in the universe as a wise man or sage. For the wise person, there is no inner conflict because his or her will is governed by reason, and no outer conflict because the world is also so governed.

With no conflict, the wise person only wants to do that which universal reason allows. Thus, while every event is determined, the wise person is free in the sense that his or her desires are not inhibited in any way. The world is governed by reason and the wise person acts in accordance with reason, so he or she can do all the things he or she wants to do. It would be difficult to say that a person who can do whatever he or she wants to do is not free. We can see why, then, the Stoics would claim that "Besides being free, the wise are also kings, since kingship is rule that is answerable to no one; and this can occur only among the wise."[8]

In a classic illustration of the Stoic idea of freedom that is generally attributed to Chrysippus, we are asked to consider a dog that is tethered to a wagon. As the wagon moves along, either the dog may move along with the cart, in which case the dog's will and necessity unite, or the dog may struggle against the motion of the cart. In either situation, the dog will move along with the cart. In the latter case, while the dog struggles, it is pulled along anyway, and the Stoics claim that it is not free. In the former case, though tied to the wagon, it is, according to the Stoics, free.

But it is important to remember that, according to the Stoics, the dog is not free because it has simply accepted its bondage and resigned itself to following wherever the cart goes. It is free because its will is in accord with the will that steers the cart, so that its own volition takes it to the same place the cart is going. In such a case, the tether becomes irrelevant, as the dog can and will go exactly where it wants.

If we take the cart to represent the flow of events and the dog to represent an individual human, the wise person is like the dog that moves along with the cart. With this in mind, the Stoic claim that only the wise person is free and all others, regardless of their political position, are slaves, makes sense.

We can also see a comparison to the world of climbing. As a climber moves up a route, he or she encounters changes in weather, various types of terrain, equipment failure at times, and different objective hazards. The climber who understands, acknowledges, and accepts these things, and willingly chooses to act in accord with his or her situation, can be said to freely choose his or her path. The climber who does not understand the situation he or she is in, or attempts to act without regard to the various aspects of his or her environment, will be restrained by these features anyway. In this case, like the tethered dog who fights the direction of the cart, the climber is not free.

While I think that there is wisdom in Stoic philosophy, my goal in this essay is not to convince readers that the Stoic worldview is correct. Instead, I focus on using the Stoic understanding of freedom to explain the freedom experienced in climbing. In addition, I will suggest that the activity of climbing, and the risks inherent in the activity, create settings that are conducive to the experience of that freedom. If my explanation is correct, Herman Buhl, Pietro Dal Pra, and Joe Simpson experience a type of freedom similar to that discussed by Zeno, Chryssipus, Cleanthes, and Epictetus.

There are times in climbing when all of the correct moves are obvious. Things go smoothly and everything feels solid. It feels, at these points, like everything works. But a large part of that success is in not attempting things that will not work – seeing the right moves rather than the wrong ones. In this situation, the climber becomes free in the sense that he or she is unrestricted – whatever he or she attempts, he or she can do. What a climber needs to do in order to experience freedom of this sort is to align his or her will with the relevant features of the mountain environment. Freedom in climbing is about knowing oneself and one's environment well enough that one desires to do exactly what one can. This, then, is the basis of the climber's freedom. As Chrysippus may have put it if he had been a climber: one may achieve freedom by climbing in accord with the mountain, that is, in accord with one's own nature and the mountain's nature. Like the Stoic sage, the climber who understands the mountains and his or her self, and whose will is in harmony with the mountain environment, is free.

  KEVIN KREIN

But the freedom does not result from having many options; instead, it is a result of desiring precisely those things the mountain allows.

This explains as well why it is only climbers who feel free in the kind of conditions I have been describing. Anyone who does not know the environment, techniques, and equipment of climbing will not understand the relevant features of that particular world. The non-climber's will is not likely to be in accord with the mountain environment and the non-climber is not likely to see the appropriate responses to given situations.

On the other hand, it is more experienced climbers who will tend to feel free the most often. Experience generally means having a better understanding of the mountains from a climber's perspective. Knowing mountains better, and knowing how to respond to changes in weather, snow, rock, and ice, allows one to do more – to push things closer to the edge. This knowledge also allows one to remain in harmony with the mountain environment under a broader variety of conditions.

The experience of freedom I am describing is precious and difficult to achieve. What is particularly interesting about climbing is that the mountain environment has certain features that almost seem designed to help climbers experience the Stoic type of freedom. The first of these is the simplicity of the climber's world. The Stoics describe a way of being in which a wise person moves through life seemingly unimpeded by the things that cause distress to others. This is the result of coming, through reason, to a state of being in harmony with oneself and the world. Achieving this state is rare because the world is such a complex and difficult place.

But the world of climbing is a much simpler place than the world experienced in normal life. Or, to put it more precisely, while climbing, the relevant features of the world with which one must interact are greatly reduced. In comparison with life in general, the goals of climbing are very straightforward and the distracting features with which one must deal are eliminated. In most of our lives, we juggle long-term plans and short-term goals, finances, relationships, and careers. None of those things are particularly relevant in the middle of a difficult climb – they are not part of that world. In the simplified world of climbing, it is often absolutely obvious what one's options are and which option is the best. When a climber is on, he or she knows exactly how to react and wants to do exactly what he or she should do. It is easier, I claim, for the climber to be in sync with relevant aspects of the environment than it is for any person to even take in most of the relevant aspects of normal life.

As well, the risks associated with climbing may play a role in helping put climbers in the right state of mind to experience freedom. Climbers simply must attend to issues of the moment, such as when and where to set up a camp, where the next gear placement will be, or just making sure the next footstep is solid. If climbers are not focused on their immediate situation the results can be disastrous. The danger of the climbing environment persistently encourages climbers to enter into a greatly simplified mental existence. This in turn helps climbers be in accord with themselves, at least for certain periods of time. Add to this as well that, given the isolated nature of climbing and ethos of self-sufficiency, there is often little room for lamenting one's situation rather than accepting it and acting. Once one understands what action is required, it is clear that there are no acceptable options other than simply attempting to accomplish what needs to be done.

So, as the Stoic sage sees events and understands what the appropriate response is, when a climber is in the right state of mind, he or she is in harmony with the mountain and sees what must be done when and how. At these times the climber is in accord with the events of his or her world. Achieving freedom, in this case, is not the result of having many choices, but of the fact that the climber's mind and world are relatively straightforward and easily harmonized.

The approach to freedom I consider above is a product of early Stoic thinking. While I think that it adequately addresses the question of how climbers in an extremely restricted environment might be free, I will also consider a second, slightly different, Stoic approach to freedom that I think is relevant to a more complete understanding of freedom and climbing.

Roughly four centuries after Zeno founded the school, the Stoic philosopher Epictetus argued that if freedom is found in getting what one wants, desiring only what one can control is a way of achieving freedom. Epictetus was a slave in the early part of his life and started to study Stoic doctrine in this position. He later gained his freedom and established his own school. For much of his life, he lacked freedom of movement and political freedom, yet he argued that this did not deny him freedom in the most fundamental sense.

Like the early Stoics, Epictetus held that true freedom means being able to do what one wants to do. He also pointed out that there are some things that are always in our control, namely, our own mental states and our attempts to do things. He argued that if we recognize

this and limit our desires to those things that are within our power, we can be free. As Epictetus put it:

> Some things are under our control, while others are not under our control. Under our control are conception, choice, desire, aversion, and, in a word, everything that is our own doing . . . things under our control are by nature free, unhindered, and unimpeded.[9]

No matter what our political position, be it emperor or slave, there are many things outside of our control and if we do not recognize this, Epictetus argues that loss of freedom will result. As Epictetus advises, "Remember, therefore, that if what is naturally slavish you think to be free . . . you will be hampered, will grieve, will be in turmoil, and will blame both gods and men."[10]

I argued above that the climbing environment is particularly ripe for putting people in situations in which they might experience freedom. It is simple and it promotes the kind of interaction that leads to aligning one's will with the environment. But it also is a prime ground for developing the kind of attitude Epictetus claims we should cultivate. There are few environments we encounter in which it is so clear that things which influence our fortunes are out of our control. Storms, wind, failure of partners, or even our own bodies, are often beyond our control. On expeditions, at least, it seems that much of what it takes to be successful is keeping oneself in the right frame of mind as one's situation changes. In climbing, more so than in other aspects of life, there is a stark contrast between what is in our power and what is not. If giving advice on climbing, Epictetus might recommend that one take an attitude of the following sort: "If conditions warrant, I would like to ascend, and if conditions do not allow it, I would rather not." If success is based on mental strength, composure, responses to changes in the environment, and other things in the climber's control, the climber can act freely in all conditions. Time spent attempting to control things that one cannot leads to the feeling of being hindered or enslaved by the mountains rather than freed by them.

While I have argued that the freedom of climbing is related to that of the Stoics, it is clear as well that there are differences. According to Stoic understanding, the wise man does everything well and is free in every aspect of life. They are said to have maintained that this "is a consequence of his accomplishing everything in accordance with right reason and in accordance with virtue, which is expertise concerned with the whole of life."[11] The perfectly wise climber is always successful because he or she attempts to do only what the mountain allows. At the same time, such a climber sees possibilities better, and thus seems unimpeded by obstacles that stop others. Still, unlike the freedom of the Stoic wise man or Epictetus, the freedom of the perfectly wise climber is limited to the activity of climbing. Many people who experience profound freedom while climbing find it nowhere else. Anyone who knows a lot of climbers can name several who, although free while climbing, feel hindered, trapped, or enslaved in all other aspects of their lives. So, for anyone who cannot spend all of his or her time climbing, the freedom offered by the activity is limited. On the other hand, the sense of freedom is repeatable and, though rare, much more commonly attained than the Stoic wise man's state of mind.

If my general claims are correct, then there is a legitimate sense of freedom connected to climbing activities that does not require that athletes have many possible options from which to choose. The mountain environment can be unforgiving, and spending time in the mountains exposes climbers to very real risks. The climber's freedom is a product of acting in accord with oneself and with the harsh mountain environment. When a climber can do this, rather than presenting obstacles, the mountain presents opportunities to ascend – in that time the climber becomes profoundly free.

NOTES

1 Joe Simpson, *This Game of Ghosts* (Seattle: Mountaineers Books, 1993), p. 227.
2 Quoted in Reinhold Messner and Horst Hofler, *Herman Buhl: Climbing Without Compromise*, trans. Tim Carruthers (Seattle: Mountaineers Books, 2000), p. 71.
3 "Pietro Dal Pra: The Mountain from all Perspectives," online at www.planet mountain.com/english/special/people/dp/dalp2.htm.
4 All of the fragments I quote in this essay were collected and translated by A. A. Long and D. N. Sedley in *The Hellenistic Philosophers*, Vol. 1 (Cambridge: Cambridge University Press, 1987). Long and Sedley provide a section number followed by a letter as a way of cataloging fragments. For all quotations, I will list the primary source followed by Long and Sedley's identifying number and letter.
5 Cicero, *On Divination*, Book 1, Section 127 (Long and Sedley, 55O).

 KEVIN KREIN

6   Cicero, *On the Nature of Gods*, Book 1, Section 39 (Long and Sedley, 54B).
7   Diogenes Laertius, *The Lives and Opinions of Eminent Philosophers*, Book 7, Sections 87–9 (Long and Sedley, 63C).
8   Ibid., Book 7, Sections 121–2 (Long and Sedley, 67M).
9   Epictetus, *Manual*, In W. A. Oldfather, *Epictetus* (Cambridge, MA: Loeb Classic Library, 1966), p. 483.
10 Ibid.
11 Stobaeus, Book 2, Section 66 (Long and Sedley, 61G).

CHAPTER 2

RISK AND REWARD

Is Climbing Worth It?

Charlie was a climber's climber: he climbed hard, well, and constantly. Whatever life trajectory Charlie had while growing up in the Midwest changed when he came out West for college. He found his passion in climbing, and climb he did – hundreds of routes every year, on rock, ice, and in the mountains. He owned almost nothing except climbing gear and fully lived the climbing life.

Charlie was my main climbing partner and we had climbed together for years. On an April day when I was abroad, Charlie was with another talented climber and close friend topping out on the alpine ice route Super Couloir in the Canadian Rockies. The ice was in great shape and they cruised the route. At the end, Charlie had to tunnel through a cornice to reach the ridgeline. He poked his head back through and looked at his partner with a huge grin – another great day, another great climb.

He belayed his partner up to his perch on the ridgeline. Efficient as always, he stashed one of the ropes and the technical gear in his pack, shortening the remaining rope between them for what they expected to be a simple descent of snow slopes on the backside of the mountain, with only a few short rappels. His partner quickly started down the ridge. As the rope between them came tight, Charlie pulled his anchor and followed in his partner's boot tracks down the ridge. A few steps later they were both swimming in a sea of sliding snow, having triggered an avalanche that swept them over cliff bands and 3,000 vertical feet down the mountain.

Charlie was killed by trauma during the fall. Miraculously, his partner survived the fall and lay atop the snow at the bottom of the avalanche runout with a shattered right femur, crushed left knee, and chest trauma. Hypothermic and hallucinating, he spent three nights and four days lying there, slipping in and out of consciousness, before a phone call from back home eventually led to a helicopter flyover that spotted them. Charlie's partner was rescued and, after a year of intensive surgeries, made almost a full physical recovery.

Why?

Why do people climb? Why do we intentionally go out of our way to expose ourselves to these sorts of risks? Many of us dislike these questions. They are uncomfortable. The answers we sometimes hear reflect this discomfort: "Because I like climbing," "Because it is fun," "Because the mountain is there." Though these answers may be true, they are not sufficient in themselves. In order to live ethical lives, we need to have solid reasons for why we do what we do. Those other answers – I like it, it's fun – are good enough only if the decision is ethically justified.

Can one justify climbing? Yes. But the bigger issue goes deeper than that: Are there ethically justified reasons why we should climb?

Attempting to live ethically is not simply contemplating what actions we should prohibit in our daily lives. It is a much more profound endeavor that concerns how we fill our lives and how we fulfill the promise of our lives. Charlie chose to fill his life through climbing. He embraced what climbing offered. Why?

We often don't think of climbing as ground zero for tough ethical decision-making. Yet climbing is not a mere recreational activity. Instead, it is an ethical decision, and a weighty one at that. When painful events transpire – like Charlie's accident – we are reminded that we aren't joking around with this. To fail to take the ethical dimension of climbing seriously is disrespectful and belittles ourselves and other climbers. The decision to climb is not one to take lightly.

Climbing is illustrative of the ethical decision-making that we are forced to undertake in all arenas of our lives. In this essay I look at how this decision-making functions, with the aim of helping all of us – climbers and non-climbers alike – become more thoughtful in our ethical reasoning throughout our lives. Ethical challenges similar to those found in climbing confront all of us, from pilots to policemen, soldiers to stock-brokers. When should we voluntarily enter activities with risk? How do we know if it is worth it? I return to risk soon, but consider this claim as you read:

> Taking on a risk blindly is not only irresponsible but also ethically unjustified.

What makes taking on risk acceptable is doing so deliberately because it is the most justified decision in that particular context. This is what we'll explore.

Justifying Climbing

Charlie's death was a crushing blow to many lives. The pain and long-term damage it caused have left huge gaps in the lives of his friends and family. His fiancée described how the loss created a reluctance to trust because of apprehension about going through such an ordeal again. And beneath all of this, there is the nagging thought, "He didn't have to do this. . . ."

Climbing is a voluntary activity. Because we choose to climb – and we choose what, how, and how much we climb – climbing enters the ethical realm. Ethics is the branch of philosophy concerned with a number of related questions: What shall I do? What sort of life should I lead? What ideal should I emulate?

I use the utilitarian ethics of English philosopher John Stuart Mill (1806–73) to weigh the costs and benefits of climbing. Mill was a hedonistic utilitarian. He argued that happiness is the highest good and that the morality of any act is to be measured by its consequences, not by our intentions. Our ethical mandate is to choose actions that maximize the amount of pleasure in the world and minimize the amount of pain. Out of all the options available to us at any one time, we must select that action which creates the greatest amount of happiness for the greatest number. We cannot only consider ourselves. The impacts (good or bad) of our climbing on others must be taken into account objectively, without prioritizing any one person's interests over another's.

Mill recognized that people define pleasure in different ways: an off-width crack makes some of us quiver with excitement, others scowl with disgust. While some philosophers[2] were comfortable considering each person's distinct conception of pleasure to be of equal value, Mill wasn't satisfied with this approach.

For Mill, quality matters. He believed some forms of pleasure are better than other forms of pleasure, an idea he famously captured by suggesting, "It is better to be a human being dissatisfied than a pig satisfied; better to be Socrates dissatisfied than a fool satisfied."[3] There are higher pleasures (Socrates') and lower pleasures (the pig's). But how do we know what those higher pleasures are? Mill said we know through the informed opinions of those who have experienced multiple types of pleasures and are thus able to make a direct comparison between them. While discussions between knowledgeable sources over what constitutes the highest-value pleasures will undoubtedly continue long into the future, I accept Mill's point that the quality of the experience must be measured alongside the quantity.

The utilitarian calculation that Mill used to determine the morally proper action is this: formulate the different options available to us; determine what consequences are expected to follow from each act, impartially considering all who will be affected; weigh the cumulative pleasures and pains for each option; then, act on the option that in sum produces the greatest pleasure or least pain. Simple, right?

Simple, maybe. Easy, no. Mill sets a high standard. All of our decisions, all of the time, are to be evaluated and scrutinized through our ethical lens. There is no time-out, no recess from living ethically. All of our decisions in life are ethical decisions because every choice we make has consequences for ourselves or others.

This takes us back to our voluntary decision to climb. Should we risk climbing? To answer positively, we must be able to argue that climbing produces more total benefits than any other choice I could make. This is a serious task indeed. To see whether we can achieve this, we first need to lay out the costs and benefits of climbing.

Costs of Climbing

While there are numerous potentially negative consequences of climbing, many of the possible costs are captured in three criticisms commonly voiced against climbing. One criticism is that climbing is a frivolous and misplaced attempt to find pleasure. There are different qualities of happiness, and perhaps climbing brings only lower-quality happiness. The time, energy, and resources spent on climbing should therefore be redirected to more meaningful pursuits such as academic learning, religion, commitment to a career, or social service. Obviously, being a climber does not preclude one from doing other things with one's life. One can be a climber and a philosopher – indeed, some are. But many of us recognize that our climbing has involved sacrifices in other arenas of our lives. Climbing can derail our focus on other, possibly more beneficial pursuits.

A second criticism is that climbing is an activity that has little social value and only serves the climber's self-interests. In our focus on climbing, we may neglect responsibilities to our families, communities, and societies. Whether it is annual expeditions to the Himalaya, frequent weekend climbing trips, or simply the amount of gym time required to climb hard rock, climbing involves a lot of focus on oneself. We are often reminded that we ought to consider more than our self-interests when acting.

A third criticism is that climbing is overly dangerous. Granted, there is a broad spectrum of risk associated with different climbing disciplines. Gym climbing doesn't hold much risk, while alpine-style climbing on remote mountains can hold a good deal of risk. There are also important distinctions between climbs with objective risks (dangers we have little control over, like a serac collapsing) and subjective risks (dangers we have more control over, like tiring and falling from a route). Moreover, non-climbing life is filled with risks, too. Far more climbers die of cancer, from old age, or in car accidents than die climbing, so we aren't comparing a risk-filled climbing life with a risk-free non-climbing life. However, people who don't climb don't face the particular risk of climbing accidents. In other words, anyone may get cancer, but only some people put themselves at risk of dying in an avalanche. It's this additional risk and its potential for real consequences that must be weighed.

I mentioned earlier that blindly accepting risk is unjustifiable. Engaging in risky behavior for no reason at all, oblivious to the ramifications of our behavior, is indefensible. If the risks I take climbing start to resemble Russian roulette, and I can't give a solid, well-reasoned justification for why I am assuming this risk, then I need to call the Moral Mountain Rescue Squad.

But justifying risk is complicated because accurately predicting the outcomes of our actions can be hard. Charlie didn't make his decisions on Super Couloir intending to die in a fall. In fact, he was one of the most deliberate and conservative climbers I've ever known. People can make their best guess as to what will transpire from a certain act, but assessments and intentions do not always match the actual consequences.

This makes the task of assessing risk quite challenging. Risk, by definition, means the possibility that a negative outcome may arise. Some risks seem relatively easy to anticipate (climbing K2 will be dangerous), while other risks are harder to plan for because they seem beyond reasonable prediction (I could be run over by a rogue Vespa tomorrow). In hindsight, we can often be harsh in our judgments of a decision that didn't turn out well. We may lament, "I never should have taken that risk." Yet we do not have the gift of foreknowledge at the time we are confronted with hard decisions. During our actual decision-making processes, correctly calculating the likelihood of an outcome is notoriously difficult. This makes risk hard to grasp.

Some propose approaching risk in terms of weighted probabilities, a logically coherent approach that considers both the value of a potential outcome and the likelihood that it will occur. But splitting hairs about probabilities may be trumped by an imprecise way of deciding how much a particular experience is worth to us. Is the experience of climbing K2 more valuable than the experience of climbing Mt. Rainier? If yes, then how much more valuable is it – 10 times more valuable? 1,000 times more valuable? Using numbers to define inexact, subjective value borders on absurdity. Yet when we try to weigh which risks in our life are worth it, how much we value something becomes critically important. Is 30 years of high-quality life more valuable than an *anticipated* 40 years of lower-quality life? Than 50 years? Than 70 years? Utilitarianism says that whichever situation creates the most overall good (measuring both quality and quantity) is the morally correct choice. Higher-risk decisions, therefore, demand greater rewards in order to be justified. Because climbing can shorten lives, the amount of value we find in climbing really matters.

So the moral concern is that our climbing and everything that goes along with it might unintentionally damage ourselves and damage those connected to us. This fear that the damage of climbing is so great that it may not be justified is disturbing because it is, at least, plausible.

Benefits of Climbing

Having explained some potential costs of climbing, what are some of the benefits that can emerge from climbing? I divide these into the categories of the intrinsic value found in climbing and the instrumental value found in climbing.

Intrinsic value

The intrinsic value of climbing refers to those forms of happiness that are found directly in climbing itself. Recall that our ethical mandate is to maximize happiness. The intrinsic value of climbing is its ability to directly produce happiness. So, the first obvious intrinsic value of climbing is the pure joy that it brings to many of us. The immense satisfaction of climbing a splitter hand crack hundreds of feet above the deck can be an awesome experience. Successfully finishing a pitch that taxed our abilities to the utmost, watching the sun rise high on a mountain – these are significant sources of happiness in our lives. The quality of our happiness is important, and climbing can bring high-quality joy to our lives. Anyone who has climbed will attest to that.

Alongside this is the happiness associated with close friendships fostered in the mountains. The bond between climbing partners is unique, tempered as it is by intense, challenging trials. Years of experiences in the mountains with Charlie created a friendship that brought – and still brings – immense joy to my life. Climbing can foster a type of closeness with another human being that becomes a lifelong source for happiness.

Finally, we should not overlook the aesthetic value found in climbing. The happiness found in experiencing sublimely beautiful environments is again a high-quality form of happiness that stands out in today's world. It is only through climbing that you have the aesthetic experience of looking out from the top of a peak onto the sea of mountains in the Karakoram or in the Alaska range. How much happiness we get from that experience will vary, but many of us think that the quality of that happiness is indeed very high.

Instrumental value

Beyond intrinsic value, climbing offers instrumental value. The instrumental value of climbing is that it can be a vehicle for finding happiness in another realm of life or at another time in life. In this case, climbing is not the direct source of happiness. Instead, it cultivates virtues that down the road will be a greater source of happiness. Though easy to overlook, this personal evolution may be one of the most important benefits we take from climbing. So what are some of those instrumental values, and how might they lead to personal evolution?

Instrumental value 1: The cultivation of human excellence

Climbing can expand our individual human potential. Resilience and self-empowerment emerge from our experiences surmounting fear, adversity, and our own mental and physical barriers. This enables climbers to accomplish greater achievements in their activities outside of the mountains than would have been possible otherwise. Through its lessons, climbing can inspire individuals and society to extend the limits of what is possible.

I was awed by Charlie's attitude and work ethic. When difficulties arose – in climbing and outside of climbing – he met them head on. It was in large part because of climbing that Charlie came to welcome challenge and hardship as avenues to cultivating human excellence. We need to value what is conducive to our flourishing as human beings – and that includes toughness for overcoming the difficulties life presents.[4] Charlie found that 30 feet above your last ice screw with burning calves and forearms is good training for this.

Many climbers are quite familiar with hardship. Alpinists routinely joke about the misery of their most rewarding climbing experiences: "It doesn't have to be fun to be 'fun'." But suffering isn't the goal in itself. Rather, suffering is often something we must experience as we work toward our most meaningful goals in life. If we are to seek great achievements, then we must learn not to be afraid of the difficulties that will accompany the process.

What do Edmund Hillary, Greg Mortenson, John Muir, and US Supreme Court Justice William O. Douglas have in common? Each of them mentioned in their writings how climbing played a large role in the contributions they later made to society.[5] Many people, no matter what their ethical orientation, feel that they are most fulfilled when they do things that go beyond themselves. Towards this end, the discipline, self-reliance, and courage that emerge from climbing can expand what we view as our individual human potential and leave us better equipped to contribute to our societies. Climbing can evolve the core of who we are and what we can offer the world.

Instrumental value 2: Psychological growth

Climbing can also nurture empowering psychological growth. By teaching us how to better focus our energies, embrace challenge as a valuable force for personal development, and competently manage risk, climbing can improve the quality of our lives.

Charlie loved rock climbing because it was an activity structured to allow him to seek out, train for, and succeed at a challenge that taxed his abilities to the utmost. When he came to hard routes at the top of his skills, he was mentally and physically 100 percent focused on the task at hand. No distractions, no extraneous thoughts, nothing but this focus. Almost all of us have experienced this focus while climbing, and almost all of us have experienced the resultant exhilaration when we succeed.[6] Learning how to create happiness through embracing challenge is a skill that can help us find greater satisfaction in all of our endeavors.

The challenges inherent in climbing help us become more competent at managing risk. Like it or not, risk is everywhere in life. In order to succeed at any activity, we must be able to navigate the risks along the way. Climbing helps increase our abilities in this domain because climbing at its core is a structured activity of managing risk. A major aspect of our development as climbers is progressively getting better at assessing, mitigating, and responding to the risks found in our climbs. Learning how to effectively manage risk with existential consequences can leave us better equipped to face down the challenges in our work and personal lives.

Instrumental value 3: Reprioritizing lives
Engagement with genuine risk in the mountains can be transformative and lead us to reprioritize our lives in beneficial ways. If we are self-reflective, we may see that our encounters with risk provide us with valuable perspective on life.

In 1963, Willi Unsoeld and Tom Hornbein left a camp high on the West Ridge of Mt. Everest, the first two humans ever to venture on that ground.[7] At a time when few people had stood atop the world, their goal to complete a new route to the summit left them committed with little knowledge of what to expect. When they later reached a difficult section of cliff bands from which there would be no retreat, they did not descend but went up instead. Forging through to the summit, they endured an open bivouac above 28,000 feet on the descent, but ultimately survived to complete the first traverse of the mountain. This accomplishment of Hornbein and Unsoeld is a defining example of risk.

Willi Unsoeld, a philosopher himself, advocated that we embrace the benefits of risk in our lives. He argued that risk is good for our souls, that it helps us to achieve higher-quality, more fulfilling lives. The transforming encounter with risk, in this view, is actually the primary point of climbing. Risk awakens our potential and makes us truly alive. Unsoeld lived and died pursuing this idea.[8]

Genuine life-and-death risk is a component of many climbing endeavors. Ice climber Laura Waterman describes a situation with which most climbers are familiar:

> Oddly enough I wasn't scared but in a state beyond fear. Our precarious situation was so patently obvious that I felt an immense calmness and clear-headedness that comes only when you know you are on the thin edge between living and dying.[9]

We may not walk away from such encounters as the same person. Risk and misfortune can awaken us to our potential in life and change how we view our lives. Charlie and I shared thought-provoking experiences in the mountains involving risk and decision-making that prompted us to make positive changes in our personal relationships and in how we prioritized our commitments. Some of this reprioritization took years to manifest. Thus, we should be wary of judging the encounter with risk merely on its immediate consequences. Even Charlie's death, while it offered no positive consequences for his own life, was a positive catalyst for some of those affected by his death.[10] Because we often do not immediately comprehend the long-term impact of experiences that can arise through our climbing, what initially appear to be negative events can ultimately serve to transform lives in positive ways.

The Balance

So now, morally speaking, our cards are on the table. We've outlined some of the common costs of climbing – the diverted energy, self-focus, and danger. We've seen some of the intrinsic values of climbing – the pure joy, close friendships, and aesthetic beauty. And we've noted some instrumental values leading to personal evolution – expansion of our potential in life, empowering psychological growth, and reprioritization of our energies.

With the pros and cons laid out before us, we weigh all these factors as they apply to our situation in order to justify the risks of climbing. The quality of each component makes a difference, so we must determine not only the quantity but also the quality of the happiness and pain created by each component. We do our best to predict short-term and long-term outcomes, and we consider how all others will be affected by each of these factors. Ultimately, we carry out this sort of evaluation for each of the options available to us in our lives, then choose that option which maximizes total happiness. If climbing is not the option that maximizes total happiness, then we should not choose it.

Not all of these risks or rewards will be present for all climbers. People will add and subtract other costs and benefits to the mix. By laying things out in front of us, we may find that up to now we haven't been deliberately cultivating some of the values that can be found in climbing. We may realize that we haven't been purposeful in how we climb, why we climb, or what we climb.

In order to justify our climbing, we need to be reflective and thoughtful about the ethical impacts of our actions. If we are not thoughtful, our climbing could easily become a harmful, destructive activity. Here is the challenge – Mill set the bar high. In order for our climbing to be justified, it must produce the most overall happiness out of *anything* we could do with that time and energy.

I've laid out a rosy picture of climbing. The good of climbing might seem to easily outweigh the drawbacks. All we have to do is justify climbing through these somewhat abstract and idealized philosophical concepts, right? Hardly.

This isn't just abstract theorizing. People die climbing. Charlie is gone because of decisions he made about climbing. Nothing will fill that gap created by his demise. Some affected by this will never forgive climbing for what it took away. But this stark reminder that climbing has consequences should not lead us to turn away from the tough ethical terrain surrounding these decisions. Instead, it should prompt us to be thoughtful and reflective as we weigh the options before us.

Conclusion

Earlier, I mentioned that it is unjustifiable for us as climbers to continue in a dangerous activity oblivious to its consequences. If we are blindly assuming risk through our climbing, we need to change that. However, risk accepted with deliberation can be ethically justified. When we utilize Mill's framework, we may find that it pushes us in new directions. It opens up how we understand climbing and what we seek to cultivate through the experience. Climbing can bring about tremendous amounts of happiness. Moreover, it can positively transform the lives of climbers, leading to valuable personal evolution that greatly enriches their lives and what they can contribute to the world. We cannot overlook that.

Charlie was a deliberate and reflective climber. We had spoken at length regarding the justifications of climbing. While I can never know what he thought when making his decisions on Super Couloir, he had considered the consequences of the climbing he did and made choices that he was morally comfortable with. Charlie knew that he might ultimately die climbing, but he still felt that the moral measurement weighed on the side of climbing.

What does this tell us? It tells us this is serious business. Can climbing be justified? Yes. The rewards of climbing can outweigh the costs. Now it is up to each of us, in our particular situation, to determine if they actually do.

NOTES

1   I am grateful to the friends and colleagues who provided valuable feedback on earlier drafts of this essay. I offer special thanks to Glenn Kessler and Kristina Mustacich for sharing insightful conversations on these topics over the years – I hope Charlie would be proud.
2   Namely Jeremy Benthan, Mill's intellectual predecessor in utilitarian philosophy.
3   John Stuart Mill, *Utilitarianism*, ed. Roger Crisp (New York: Oxford University Press, 1998), p. 57.
4   For further reading on suffering and challenge, see Friedrich Nietzsche, *Beyond Good and Evil*, trans. R. J. Hollingdale (London: Penguin, 1990).
5   See Edmund Hillary, *Nothing Venture, Nothing Win* (New York: Coward, McCann, and Geoghegan, 1975); Greg Mortenson and David O. Relin, *Three Cups of Tea* (New York: Viking, 2006); John Muir and William Cronon, *John Muir: Nature Writings* (New York: Library of America, 1997); William O. Douglas, *Of Men and Mountains* (Guilford: Lyons Press, 2001).
6   For more discussions on this, see Mihalyi Csikszentmihalyi, *Flow: The Psychology of Optimal Experience* (New York: Harper and Row, 1990).
7   Thomas Hornbein, *Everest: The West Ridge* (San Francisco: Sierra Club Books, 1966).
8   Unsoeld was killed in an avalanche on Mt. Rainier in 1979, at age 52.
9   Thomas Jenkins, "Perfume in the Ozone," *Summit* (June–July 1979): 167. Quoted in Richard Mitchell, *Mountain Experience* (Chicago: University of Chicago Press, 1987), p. 29.

10 Maria Coffey captures this sentiment when she writes of how the awareness of death that comes with climbing can positively affect others associated with climbers: "Ask mountaineers why they climb and invariably they say that it makes them feel alive. It allows them to live in the moment. Ask those bereaved by climbing accidents if anything positive has emerged from the tragedy and, in one way or another, they usually echo the climber's sentiment. If they love someone, they tell him. If they have a gift to give, they give it now . . . just in case. They take nothing for granted. 'I can tell you what Death has taught me,' says Terres Unsoeld in her one-woman play *Making My Way in the Dark*. 'It's taught me to hold on to life and make each moment count.' Her 21-year-old sister, Nanda Devi Unsoeld, died on her namesake mountain. Three years later, when Terres was twenty, her father, Willi Unsoeld, was killed in an avalanche on Mount Rainier. And what did she do after these double tragedies? 'I started living life with a vengeance.'" See Maria Coffey, *Where the Mountain Casts Its Shadow* (Seattle: Mountaineers Books, 2003), p. 229.

PAUL CHARLTON

CHAPTER 3

WHY CLIMB?

 When I was a lad learning to climb I read all I could about climbing. *Annapurna* told me about one price of success – Herzog's and Lachenel's loss of toes from frostbite. I also learned of the tragic deaths following the first ascent of the Matterhorn and the disappearance of Mallory and Irvine in the clouds of Everest. I found the most sensational account in the pages of *Argosy*. The writer related in gruesome detail the deaths of four Austrians while attempting to climb the North Face of the Eiger in 1936. Why did they do it? For the glory of *der Fuerer und der Fatherland*, according to the article. Perhaps, but in my experience climbers are not very nationalistic, let alone Nazis. But the question of why people climb remains, especially in the face of the potential costs.

When asked why he climbed, the English explorer and mountaineer George Mallory famously replied, "Because it is there." On the surface, it is easy to take his answer as an attempt to get rid of annoying interviewers. I think there is more to it than that, but some ground must be prepared. When asked why he climbed, Chuck Pratt, one of the top climbers in Yosemite Valley in the 1960s, replied, "Because I am too short for basketball." Pratt was five feet five. Such answers are of a piece with Miles Davis's answer when asked, "What is jazz?" Davis responded, "If you have to ask, you'll never know."

As a rule, people do not ask why others engage in a particular sport, but climbing seems to invite the question the way talus attracts falling rocks. A friend who is a fencer has told me that he has been asked the question, perhaps because fencing doesn't leap to mind when one thinks of American sports. We may suppose that Cyrano knows. But climbing can't inspire the question simply because it is a somewhat unusual sport. One suspects that there is something about how climbing is perceived that leads to the dialogue.

How can philosophy help? Ordinarily, "why climb" would be a question for psychologists or psychiatrists, since it would seem to be a matter of motives. Was Pratt compensating for his short stature? Has anyone considered Mallory's mother as a source of his adventurous soul? There is, however, an approach to philosophy – analytic philosophy – that seeks to clarify difficult concepts and issues and that may be of use here.

An analytic philosopher might want to know what "Why do you climb?" means. What kind of answer would satisfy the interlocutor? Probably not Mallory's or Pratt's. In a superficial sense, we could be asking the question in the same way that we ask about other, quite ordinary activities, and we would expect answers like "It's fun," "It's challenging," "You get to meet interesting people of the opposite (same) sex in the climbing gym (on the crag)," or "My boyfriend (girlfriend) needed a belayer." While such answers might be quite honest, they tell us more about the person responding than they do about climbing. Suitably modified, answers like this can be given about many other sports, especially outdoor sports like skiing, kayaking, or tennis.

The writings of climbers suggest that they interpret the question along the lines of "Why do you climb? Are you nuts?" The vision of great discomfort, the prospect of Lionel Terray's "conquest of the useless," and the genuine risk of injury or death no doubt contribute to such a view, and these aspects of climbing often occur to the climber as well. What the climber needs, therefore, is a justification of climbing. Climbers have talked about their intimate relation with Nature, the testing and mastery of the self, the play on a field that has ultimate consequences. There is something to such justifications, but not as much as many climbers would like. From my experience with climbers, I have to conclude that, given their normal range of virtues and vices, it is unlikely that climbing has made them significantly better people. Rather, climbing has been the stage on which the good and not so good aspects of their personalities have been played out. After all, I doubt that we would be inclined to say that being an artist or a scientist or a movie star has

   JOE FITSCHEN

made anyone a better person even though we might admire a particular artist, scientist, or movie star. If a climber claimed that the sport improved the quality of his or her life, I would readily agree (at least, up to the point of death), but such a justification could be offered for almost any voluntary human endeavor and therefore doesn't speak much to the question of *why climb?*

Justifications, while often called for, are not very substantial. We might ask a professional football player why he is willing to suffer the weekly punishment and the real possibility of long-term physical injury, and he may say he does it for the money. Whether or not we accept that as a justification depends on our own attitudes toward pain and money – what we think is worth what. If he says he does it for the love of the game (a more noble attitude), there is still nothing that forces us to accept the justification. On occasion, we might also suspect that the person offering the justification is deluding himself. Children's justifications can be prime examples of this.

Suppose we ask, why do people climb? By generalizing the question we strip away the tics and traits of individual climbers. Put this way, the question asks for an explanation rather than a justification and a deeper explanation than that given at the superficial level. By deeper I do not mean more profound, only that the explanation is more encompassing in the way that quantum theory is deeper than atomic theory. Here I must switch from being an analytic philosopher to being a speculative philosopher, an approach probably more in keeping with the common conception of what philosophers do. This is tricky ground because the analytic approach was developed to clear away the cobwebs spun by the speculators, particularly the Idealists like Hegel (1770–1831) and Schopenhauer (1788–1860).

Evolution and Climbing

The explanatory framework I want to explore is evolution. The advantage of such a framework is that, like other scientific theories, it offers naturalistic explanations. It may seem these days that evolutionary theory is trotted out to explain just about everything. While this speaks to the underlying power of the theory, there are, no doubt, limits. The following, therefore, is meant to open up a line of inquiry rather than to provide definitive answers. That is to say, it is philosophy, not science.

When I was young the number of peak baggers in the United States was small and the number of rock climbers smaller still. There were probably fewer than a hundred who had a love for the sport. Even now it is clear that most adults have no particular urge to climb. But children do. Recently, I was walking with my two-year-old grandson; I was on the sidewalk, he on the grass strip between the sidewalk and street. At regular intervals young trees had been planted, and a mound of mulch girdled each tree. My grandson didn't go around the mounds. He gleefully went over them, and soon I engaged him in a chant, "Up the mountain, down the mountain." Great fun until we ran out of trees, but then he pointed to a flower-covered bank on the other side of the sidewalk and said, "More mountains." A visit to any neighborhood park will reveal kids climbing on whatever apparatus is provided. They climb ladders and chain nets and swing from bars and rings – just like monkeys, one is tempted to say. Even in an often-visited playground, the children seem to be exploring the terrain, and the exploration is vertical as well as horizontal.

Darwin held that all the forms of life on earth are related and that the relations can be represented in a vast bush-like structure. Under certain conditions, new species would differentiate themselves from existing species, forming, as it were, a new branch of the bush. The main mechanism for such branching was natural selection. In a given environment, some traits would be more likely to contribute to survival and procreation and so would be passed on to future generations. The standard evolutionary picture for human development is that long ago our ancestors moved from a life in the forest to one on the plain, that we subsequently walked upright, and that we eventually made and used tools and developed language. But the transition from something ape-like to something humanoid is not like the transition from caterpillar to butterfly. Rather, it is reasonable to expect that certain physical and psychological traits and tendencies carry over from one life form to another, such as the way the whale takes along the five prongs of bone in his flipper and a pair of lungs when he returns to the sea. From our simian ancestors we have a remnant of a tail and certain social inclinations. While climbing can't be said to be a mode of life on the plain like it was in the trees, the ability and desire to climb, inherited from the past, could still have utility. There is food in trees, and trees and crags offer a better viewpoint to look for game or distant habitat or potential dangers. Not everyone has to be able to climb, but a group with some climbers has an advantage in many habitats, such as palm-tree studded islands, and an individual who is both agile and not afraid of heights has a niche in the group.

We should wonder at this point whether or not this is only another just-so story; that is, a seemingly plausible explanation that won't hold up in the long run. To increase the plausibility I would return to Mallory's explanation. Suppose he was serious. Suppose that the existence of the mountain was all that was needed to trigger in him the urge to get to the top. Such an urge is far from universal in humans, but it is very real in some and it need not involve mountains. People like to get up high. They go to the top of the Empire State Building, they labor up the seemingly interminable spiral staircases of St. Peter's Cathedral in Rome, they take the tram to the Aiguilles du Midi in Chamonix. When I was young, like many other kids, I climbed trees. When I was older I switched to mountains and rocks, and, as far as I can tell, "because it is there" was all the reason I needed. In fact, in many situations it was the only reason I had, not that any reasons were called for. For some climbers, the urge to get to the top can seem obsessive, but for others, if the opportunity presents itself and the energy is available, the path leads upward as naturally as for a brown creeper working its way up an oak tree. Once on top, we might enjoy the view, take pleasure in sinews well used, congratulate ourselves for some kind of success, but none of these was a necessary reason for undertaking the climb. "Because it is there" isn't much of a reason, but it will do.

Fallacies and Evolutionary Theory

Philosophers are supposed to be good at detecting fallacies (mistakes in reasoning), so before considering other evolutionary aspects of climbing, I should discuss a few fallacies that arise when people aren't used to an evolutionary point of view, namely, teleology and universality. Teleology looks at the world in terms of goals or purposes, and many (but not all) explanations of human behavior are therefore teleological insofar as our behavior is guided by intentions. But nature (even Mother Nature) is not intentional. Contrary to those who believe that we humans are the *summum bonum* at the top of the tree of life, we are the result, but not the goal, of natural processes. So it would be a mistake (a fallacy) to think that a particular feature, trait, or tendency came into existence or was developed *in order to* solve some particular problem. Rather, the feature arises and *happens* to solve some problem of either survival or sexual reproduction and is therefore favored in future generations. As Stephen

Jay Gould pointed out, the panda's problem of stripping leaves from bamboo shoots would have been better solved if it had, like us and our cousins, developed a thumb for the purpose.[1] Mutations involved in the evolving structure of pandas didn't lead to that line of development. Instead, the enlargement of another bone, one corresponding to our wrist, happened to do the trick, although not very well. Compared to some other animals, we aren't very well adapted for climbing steep rock or ascending to high altitudes. We make do with the body and mental attributes that we have. Whether or not our climbing abilities solve, in some circuitous way, the problem of sexual reproduction is outside the scope of this essay.

The fallacy of universality occurs when people assume that because a particular feature, trait, or tendency is widespread it must be common to all members of a class, particularly if the feature is regarded as one that defines the class. Ludwig Wittgenstein's (1889–1951) analysis of concepts like "game" showed that there need not be a defining feature behind every concept. Rather, there could be a constellation of features, some of which could be found in any particular case. Wittgenstein likened these to family resemblances whereby we can identify members of a family even though not all members share Uncle Bob's large nose or Aunt Betty's winsome personality. But we like our categories neat. We may be surprised when we come across a person with clearly Asian features who speaks idiomatic English with an American accent (if she was born in the States, what else would she speak?). Or we may have trouble adjusting to the notion of ambiguous gender, especially when in our adolescence we tried so hard to be really male or really female. And we may still regard those who are different from ourselves as belonging not only to a different class but also as being in some way inferior. In the case of evolution, the germane class is the species, but showing that certain members of a species lack a particular trait, a love of heights or a talent for off-width jam cracks, for instance, says nothing against the evolutionary roots of such traits.

In addition to these fallacies, there is considerable confusion about the status of scientific theories and the theory of evolution in particular. For the moment, I will just point out that scientific theories are constructed primarily to coordinate a body of facts with a view to explanation and prediction. Such theories stand or fall on how well they are able to explain the natural facts that need explanation and how well the predictions derived from the theory conform to subsequently obtained facts. Also, these theories are not cast in stone but change as additional information

    JOE FITSCHEN

requires more explanatory power. Evolution doesn't do anything by itself. Instead, it provides a framework for natural selection, sexual selection, and, as has been shown more recently, genetic drift. These processes, operating at the level of the gene, repeatedly have been demonstrated to produce changes that modify the organism and, given the right environment, the organism may become a new species.

Climbing and Evolution and Pleasure

Back to "Why climb?" Well, I like climbing. Isn't this just another answer of the superficial kind? Not in the sense I intend. I want to call attention to the pleasure(s) involved in climbing, whether physical, aesthetic, emotional, or intellectual. With regards to the last, those who don't climb may not think of climbing as an intellectual activity, but difficult rock climbing, especially, requires a lot of problem solving. I well remember experiencing more brain fatigue than physical fatigue at the top of some climbs. With regards to pleasures, we may pursue them, indulge them, experience them, delay them, but we can't choose them. What pleases us often varies over time. We acquire certain tastes and become sated by others. But in the here and now, an action or a stimulus either pleases us or it doesn't. In either case, it can be a motive for further actions or experiences. All this should be obvious. What is not so obvious, perhaps, is the source of our pleasures. Again, I would suggest evolution. If one takes pleasure in sexual activity, one is more likely to reproduce. If one takes pleasure in physical activity, one is more likely to be physically fit. If one likes the warm feelings of friendship, one is more likely not to face the world alone. Prudential considerations can lead to the same results, but the pursuit of pleasure often trumps prudence as any moralist (and any hedonist) knows. What pleases us seems to be built in, to be a function of our genetic heritage and therefore subject to evolutionary mechanisms. In contrast, prudence comes from experience. Some people have a built-in fear of snakes, but few in the West take prudent steps to avoid mambas or cobras.

In a general sense, the pleasures of climbing can be found in other activities. Athletes of all stripes, for instance, probably experience some kind of physical pleasure in their sport. But I would maintain that the character or quality of the pleasures is different. Here I want to consider rock climbing, although similar considerations could be developed for mountaineering or high-altitude climbing as well. As usually practiced, rock climbing is probably the slowest of physical sports. A given move may take minutes (even if successful), and a climb can take days. I well remember one pitch of about 120 feet that took my partner, Royal Robbins, ten hours to lead (that amounts to five minutes for each foot of elevation gained). That happened to be a pitch that required difficult direct aid, but free climbing often proceeds slowly as well. A sudden move may cost the climber her slim purchase on a foothold. A careless move may move the climber's center of gravity away from the rock and into space. And, as mentioned above, the climber may spend many minutes just trying to figure out the sequence of moves that will lead to success.

As it happens, this snail-like movement can be a source of pleasure, probably not too different from the movements and pleasures in the adagios of a ballet. In most sports, the action happens quickly (even in baseball). Reaction time is critical; execution must rely a great deal on the formation of good habits. But in climbing, the climber has time to experience the muscular contraction or relaxation of each muscle, and that can feel good. It doesn't feel so good when the fingers tire and open, so the climber learns to use muscles efficiently. Matching the body's resources to the demands of the particular section of rock also feels good. The particular kinds of moves that a climber can use to get higher are many and varied, but among them, hanging from a hold and then pulling up on it can be especially pleasurable. More rare, but even more fun, is the dynamic move where the climber more or less leaps, gibbon-like, from one hold to another. An offshoot of this move is the pendulum traverse where the climber, held by the rope, swings back and forth across a rock face to achieve a distant hold. Particular climbers will favor some moves over others, often because their physiology makes those moves easier, but the physical pleasure is a constant. It can also be fun (pleasurable) to move quickly over easier ground, taking delight in the rhythm of constant but varied motion.

The sources of aesthetic pleasure vary widely from individual to individual, but in climbing it largely comes from the field of play, the natural environment. It is easy to think of vast vistas, soaring peaks, jutting crags – something along the lines of the paintings of the nineteenth-century American landscape artists. There is, however, pleasure to be found in the small, the close at hand. The planes of granite can form abstract shapes that, if transportable, could find a home in MoMA. Small flowers bloom in solitary niches. Pleasure can even be found in the quality of the air on a climb – a difficult quality to describe, but it's not the same as the air in the valley floor.

Emotional pleasure is difficult to separate from the aesthetic and even the physical, but its special quality often is connected to the intensity of the climbing experience. Joy, happiness, glee, and relief can all be found in overcoming difficulties, and the difficulties of climbing can sometimes be extreme. Climbing, though, can lead to an emotion not often found in other sports – serenity. This often comes from the slow pace of climbing and is probably experienced more by the belayer than the climber, or it may waft over the climbers at the end of a climb. In my experience, at least, it is an emotion that lasts longer than the negative emotions that also often accompany a climb: "Yes, I was afraid and frustrated and even angry at my ineptness (and perhaps at my climbing partner), but in spite of all that this was where I wanted to be; I felt as if I could stay here forever, felt as if everything I wanted was at hand. 'Tis a pity we had to come down." Individual climbers will no doubt add and subtract from my list of pleasures, but the point remains that such pleasures are part of our individual genetic heritage. What else could explain why I like honey but not horserad-ish, Titian's women but not Twiggy, telling stories around a camp fire but not at cocktail parties? Since we don't know what future environ-ments will be like (especially these days), we can't say whether or not a particular trait or pleasure-guided tendency will find favor in the game of natural selection. All I am proposing is that some of the traits that were well suited for an arboreal life proved not to be disadvanta-geous for life on the plain. I have suggested that they may even have some utility, but even if they don't they have not been selected out in all gene lines.

Ethics

When ethics is mentioned, some people envision a little old lady with dour mien, seemingly held together by starched lace, perched on the very edge of her chair. Others will look to a priest or rabbi, minister or imam. Both approaches are grounded in authority and tradition. Ethics is one of the oldest philosophical concerns, and the philosopher wants to base the study of right and wrong, good and bad, on reason. To do this, it is not enough to derive ethical conclusions from certain principles.

The principles themselves must be justified. Such reasoning and justification is usually called normative ethics. There is also a branch of ethics called descriptive ethics that, rather than saying what ought to be done (or not), talks about how ethics functions in human affairs and how certain principles might have come to be favored. It is through this approach that I want to consider climbing ethics as arising from evolutionary roots.

We have evolved as social creatures, and, although solo climbing has its virtues and adherents, most climbing is done in small groups. Consequently, ethical issues arise both within and between groups. One big chunk of ethics concerns justice or fairness, but, apart from the fraudulent claim of a first ascent, justice doesn't seem to be a major concern in climbing. Most climbing disputes center on climbing style: to bolt or not to bolt, to use a power drill or not, to attempt the climb in one push or establish camps, to hire a guide or find a partner, among others. More recently, climbers are at odds on the issue of just where the "top" of a climb is – the summit or the end of difficult climbing.

If the various pleasures available to the climber are her chief motivation, then it follows that she would not appreciate the practices of other climbers that lessened those pleasures. Coming across any fixed protection might do so, but encountering unnecessary bolts, pitons, or slings (not to mention garbage) could take the sheen off an otherwise glorious day. Further complications arise when one climber's necessary protection is deemed unnecessary by another. Overcrowded climbs or crags could also mitigate the climbing experience (although we are social creatures). And crags dotted with white chalk marks might be objectionable, not only on aesthetic grounds but also because, by identifying holds, the chalk can reduce the intellectual challenge.

But pleasure isn't the only motivator. A sense of achievement or accomplishment can also motivate, and not only in someone vying to be an alpha male. Pleasure operates in the moment, but someone may do a climb that offers no pleasure at all and still feel good about what she has accomplished. Such satisfaction can last long after the misery of the climb has faded. Complications from an ethical point of view arise because of different assessments of what has been accomplished. The pride of the master bolter is not likely to be lessened by the disparagements of those who prefer to climb free. If getting to the top is all that matters, then all means are acceptable. If doing a first free ascent is what matters, then any techniques that lead to that result are acceptable for the climber. But if such means and techniques are not necessary for other climbers, then they are likely to raise questions of ethics. Some climbers may even make the case that the climb should wait to be done by those who can do it in better style.

Lito Tejada-Flores, in a seminal article, introduced the notion of climbing games.[2] Each game, from bouldering to big mountain expeditions, had rules (established by common practice, not Lito) that functioned to define climbing style and maintain a sufficient level of challenge. As an overall descriptive account of climbing ethics, the article still seems germane today. But climbers who don't find the informal rules of a particular game to their liking still show up at the base of climbs.

Not only are certain pleasures (and fears) part of our genetic heritage, but our sense of self, our ego, is as well. Other primates seem to have some self-awareness, but ours was greatly enhanced with the development of language through which we map out not only the world but our place in it. One might note the large number of sentences, especially in oral communication, that begin with "I."

At bottom, the main ethical problems that arise in climbing can be seen as pitting a climber's ego against the value of an experience as an experience (the pleasure principle), which is perhaps why such problems persist so long without any resolution on the horizon. The world of climbing has the social character of a Western. Ranchers and cattlemen compete for limited goods, and the arm of the law is not very long. The custodians of our public lands have stepped into the bolting controversies, but otherwise there is no one to adjudicate the disputes.

In the 1950s, when climbers were few in number and generally uncomfortable in the usual social milieus, the climbing ethos was that of the tribe. Disputes arose mainly when someone from a different tribe (or no tribe at all) decided to leave his mark on our territory. Even then, other tribes such as the Vulgarians in New York and later the Stonemasters in California shared our core ethical values which primarily stressed relying on technique rather than technology. Nevertheless, ego and pleasure can compete within the same soul. If ego wins, you do what it takes to complete the climb. If pleasure has the upper hand, you retreat and come back another day.

But enough of such weighty matters. (Philosophy by definition is always weighty.) I shall close with a little light verse that provides a coda to the speculative themes I have developed.

Gibbons
Of all the animals at the zoo
I like the gibbons best, don't you?
They move in pure parabolas with grace
Unmatched by any other race.

If I were a gibbon I'd fall flat
Trying to catch what they catch at.
Over, under, around and down,
They're most like us when on the ground.

"Man has descended," Darwin decrees.
We should have stayed up in the trees.
With mind and body one, not two,
The gibbon's my idol of all the zoo.

NOTES

1　Stephen Jay Gould, *The Panda's Thumb* (New York: W. W. Norton, 1980).
2　Lito Tejada-Flores, "Games Climbers Play," *Ascent* 1 (Sierra Club, 1967).

CHAPTER 4

JOKERS ON THE MOUNTAIN

In Defense of Gratuitous Risk

 To what extent, under what conditions, and for what reasons should we view unnecessary risk taking as permissible? As participation in so-called "extreme sports" has increased, questions about the permissibility of recreational risk have led some to believe that gratuitous risk taking, as exemplified by extreme sports such as climbing, is somehow more problematic than other currently accepted forms of risk taking. It is often held, for example, that while it is permissible for an astronaut to take various significant but necessary risks in order to further our scientific knowledge, there is something less acceptable about a mountaineer taking comparably significant but unnecessary risks, say, by knowingly traversing a dangerous avalanche-prone slope, in order to further his or her self-knowledge, or merely to have fun. I will call this the *asymmetry thesis* because its advocates believe that there ought to be a difference between our attitudes toward activities that involve unnecessary and avoidable risk and our attitudes toward pursuits that entail only necessary or ineliminable forms of risk.

Is the asymmetry thesis true? Should we view some risks as acceptable because they are deemed necessary, while viewing unnecessary, gratuitous risks as unacceptable? If so, what reasons do we have for arguing that there ought to be a difference in our treatment of gratuitous risk versus other forms of risk? My aims in this essay are (1) to examine two common defenses of the asymmetry thesis and argue that both are flawed; and (2) to offer an alternative explanation of the intuitive plausibility of the asymmetry thesis, which may, under certain conditions, be invoked as a defense of the thesis. Taken together, these arguments suggest that, while there are some forms of gratuitous risk taking that may be justifiably banned or restricted, in most cases climbing should not be censured simply on the grounds that it involves risk.

The Rule of Rescue

One common defense of the asymmetry thesis, the thesis that some types of risk are justifiable and other types are not, suggests that we have a *prima facie* obligation to follow some version of the *Rule of Rescue*. The term "Rule of Rescue," coined by A. R. Jonsen in 1986, is used in bioethics to describe the widespread view that we have an obligation to rescue or comfort identifiable individuals facing imminent death, even when such rescues involve the expenditure of potentially limited resources and/or significant risks for the rescuers. Paradigm cases include earthquake victims pinned underneath the debris of a school, a child suffering from visible malnutrition or deformity, and the final hours of a person facing an unavoidable death. "Our moral response to the imminence of death," Jonsen observes, "demands that we rescue the doomed. We throw a rope to the drowning, rush into burning buildings to snatch the entrapped, dispatch teams to search for the snowbound."[1] In relation to the asymmetry thesis, the Rule of Rescue implies that if a costly rescue would be mounted in response to imminent death, then individuals have an obligation to avoid unnecessary risk-taking activities in which such a rescue would be required. In short, risky activities that might require expensive or equally risky rescues are unacceptable.

In the annals of climbing and mountaineering search and rescue efforts, the Rule of Rescue plays a prominent, if implicit, role. Rescue teams – often involving dozens of rangers, mountain rescue staff, pilots, spotters, and medical personnel – are assembled to respond to the distress of even a single person. The cost of such rescues is significant and well documented; in 2008 the United States National Park Service spent nearly $5 million on search and rescue efforts. And although rescuer fatalities are relatively rare, each search and rescue mission poses a very real risk to the pilots and climbing rangers. One particularly well-publicized accident in North America was the crash of an Air Force Reserve helicopter which suddenly lost altitude during a rescue and rolled 1,000 feet down Oregon's Mount Hood. In the news coverage following the incident, ABC News commentator Sam Donaldson gave voice to a clear defense of what I have called the asymmetry thesis based on the Rule of Rescue, noting that activities such as climbing are "purely optional" and that "it is unreasonable for us to set about doing something potentially dangerous that we don't have to do . . . and then take it for granted that others should risk their own lives to save us."[2]

The urge to respond based on an implicit Rule of Rescue is not limited to professional rescuers or the non-climbing public; it is felt equally by climbers themselves. The chief duty of a guide, for example, is and always has been to keep clients safe and, if necessary, provide rescue, even at the expense of his own life. Guides who returned from a climb without their clients in the Alps during the nineteenth century were likely to face a judicial inquiry, and guides who sacrificed their own lives in a successful effort to save those of their clients were elevated to iconic status. Perhaps the most famous example of this was the story of Jean-Antoine Carrel, an Italian guide who died of exhaustion at the base of the Matterhorn after having successfully guided his clients down during an unusually severe storm. In his eulogy for Carrel, British climber Edward Whymper extolled the virtues of making the ultimate sacrifice, saying Carrel "recognized to the fullest extent the duties of his position, and in the closing act of his life set a brilliant example of fidelity and devotion."[3] More recently, journalist and climber Jon Krakauer, reflecting on events immediately after the 1996 Everest season, valorized the same aspects of guide Rob Hall's final performance:

> Rob was bringing up the rear. . . . He was with [two climbers] who . . . kind of collapsed. And Rob stayed with them, as a good guide should, and that cost him his life, I have no doubt.[4]

Even independent climbers – including those who might be considered the highest risk takers – feel a strong urge to rescue or comfort others facing an imminent death. A case in point is the efforts by a group of climbers to save the life of Basque climber Iñaki Ochoa de Olza on Annapurna, one of the world's fourteen 8,000-meter peaks, in May 2008. On descent from the summit attempt, Ochoa had a seizure and collapsed at an altitude of approximately 7,400 meters, well within the proverbial "death zone." With apparent brain damage complicated by pulmonary edema, he was semi-conscious and unable to continue the descent.

Ochoa's climbing partner refused to leave him, struggling through three additional nights at Camp 4 without supplemental oxygen, food, or fuel to melt snow for water. Climbers from other teams responded to the radio call for help by heading up the mountain with emergency altitude medication and oxygen, stopping only to melt snow for water, and, in the case of two Swiss climbers, climbing without high-altitude gear.[5] Swiss climber Ueli Steck ultimately reached Camp 4 on the fourth day and continued to try to comfort and revive Ochoa until he died. He was later awarded the 2008 Eiger Award, the equivalent of an Oscar for alpinists, for his actions. Steck predictably denies that the rescue efforts were heroic: "We simply helped two comrades. A matter of course."[6]

There are clear and compelling reasons, then, to believe that the Rule of Rescue applies equally to search and rescue staff, the non-climbing public who fund the rescues, and climbers themselves.[7] An interesting question is whether the rule is a moral rule with normative force, or merely an empirical fact about the ways in which we humans tend to behave.[8] For my purposes here, however, this question is irrelevant; either way, the question is, do individuals have an obligation to avoid unnecessary, risky activities which might require a potentially costly rescue? Some legislators in the United States apparently think the answer is "yes"; over the past 15 years, various fees, bans, and restrictions have been imposed on climbing. "This bill is about those jokers up on the mountain," declared Oregon Representative Bob Tiernan in introducing House Bill 3434 (the predecessor of the so-called "Beacon Bill"), a 1996 piece of legislation which makes climbers in Oregon liable for a portion of the search and rescue costs if they fail to register for a climb and carry a mountain locator unit, a cellular phone, or a two-way radio.[9] In an era of budget cuts and the privatization of welfare and service programs, legislators in Washington, DC have painted the US National Parks Service multi-million dollar mountain rescue strategy as an expensive program to subsidize an international youth counter-culture of climbers.

Leaving aside the question of whether and in what sense the risk or activities of climbers are in fact gratuitous, I want to show that, despite initial appearances, the Rule of Rescue does *not* provide adequate justification for the position that gratuitous risk is less acceptable than other forms of risk. My argument is threefold. First, I will demonstrate that the Rule of Rescue is not required for justification or explanation of the thesis that gratuitous risk taking is more problematic than other forms of risk taking. Second, I will argue that there are also cases in which unnecessary risk is retrospectively justified due to the success of a mission,

  HEIDI HOWKINS LOCKWOOD

despite the fact that the Rule of Rescue would have applied had there been a life-threatening situation. This suggests that the Rule of Rescue provides insufficient explanation for our intuitions regarding the asymmetry thesis. Third, I will argue that a justification of the asymmetry thesis based on the Rule of Rescue would have strongly counterintuitive consequences.

So far, the stories we have considered have all been cases in which a rescue is possible. This is not the case for all forms of climbing, or, indeed, for all forms of risk taking in extreme sports. A good example is the practice of free soloing, the game of climbing multi-pitch routes without partners, ropes, harness, or any of the usual accoutrements. Free soloists typically climb routes well within their ability range, but are susceptible to uncontrollable risks such as loose rocks and sudden changes in weather. A fall from a multi-pitch route is invariably fatal – so certainly "terminal" that it does not necessitate a rescue of any kind. The Rule of Rescue, in other words, is not a concern for free soloists. Although one might argue that there are costs associated with body recovery, it is reasonable to think that those costs can be minimized and involve little or no additional risk. And yet the risk taking involved in free soloing and other guaranteed lethal climbing games is criticized as roundly – perhaps even more so – than the risk taking involved in traditional climbing. One of the more surprising examples of this was an editorial piece in *Outside Magazine*, which depicted legendary free soloist Dan Osman's new game of controlled falling as a "Stupid Pastime," a term reserved for "the alarming, ever-expanding roster of outdoor activities that . . . meet the following criteria: (1) they seem silly at first glance, and (2) they seem idiotic at second glance."[10] In short, free soloing is seen as an unacceptable risk even though the Rule of Rescue does not apply. What this and similar criticisms (or even bans placed on high-risk, no-rescue sports) clearly suggest is that the Rule of Rescue is not a necessary factor in the explanation of intuitions regarding the asymmetry thesis.

Nor is the Rule of Rescue a sufficient factor, as can be seen in examples of climbs in which risk is retrospectively justified due to the success of a project, despite the fact that the Rule of Rescue would have applied had there been circumstances in which a rescue was required. One prominent example of an expedition in which climbers accepted additional (arguably "unnecessary") risk, yet earned widespread public acclaim was Tom Hornbein and Willi Unsoeld's 1963 traverse of the West Ridge on Everest. While several of their teammates elected to summit via the "normal" Southeast Ridge/South Col route, Hornbein and Unsoeld opted for a truly daring traverse of the unclimbed West Ridge. In doing so, they completed the first traverse of a Himalayan peak, and became (along with their teammates) the first Americans to reach the summit of Everest. Among the accolades received by the team was the Hubbard Medal, the National Geographic Society's highest honor, presented by President John F. Kennedy. Had Hornbein and Unsoeld failed to return from the climb or encountered difficulties on the route that necessitated a rescue attempt by their teammates, the public most likely would have responded with criticism and perhaps even allegations that their bold venture placed the entire team at risk, rather than praise for their visionary success. In other words, the grounds for the censure of gratuitous risk do not lie in the mere fact that a climb might, under certain circumstances, prompt others to undertake a risky rescue.

Lastly, the Rule of Rescue justification of the asymmetry thesis leads to counterintuitive consequences. In particular, risk takers who accepted the justification would have reason to think that (ideally) acceptable climbs are solo endeavors in remote regions where no rescue is possible, with no known itinerary, no media coverage and no means of communication. Such monastic ventures are not non-existent, but they certainly run against the norms and mainstream culture of the climbing community. The "climbing code" detailed in the most widely read mountaineering handbook in North America, *Mountaineering: The Freedom of the Hills*, explicitly indicates that climbers should climb in a party of at least three "unless adequate prearranged support is available," and "leave the trip itinerary with a responsible person."[11] These guidelines demonstrate that climbing is not and never has been an elaborate suicide game. Even more troubling is the message implicit in the idea that the only acceptable climbing risks are those that are remote and unsupported, with no possibility of rescue; it is as if the value of those climbers' lives is somehow not worth the cost or risk of a rescue. This message is at best puzzling and at worst incongruous with the value placed on rescuing individuals.

The Argument from Compassion

A second defense of the asymmetry thesis holds that gratuitous risk is reprehensible because the risk taker is failing to consider the possible impact of the risky activity on others. The effect of climbing on spouses, partners, and children is explored in depth via a wide range of interviews

   HEIDI HOWKINS LOCKWOOD

with family members of climbers in Maria Coffey's book, *Where the Mountain Casts Its Shadow*. One of the common threads in the interviews is a mixture of admiration and exasperation with their risk-taking loved ones. "Climbers are very single-minded and unspeakably selfish," laments one of the wives.[12] Others talk about the pain of separation in the weeks prior to an expedition, the difficulty of reuniting, the challenge of attending events at which excesses of adulation are bestowed on the climber-hero, the perception that the bonds between climbing partners are closer than ties with family, and, above all, the difficulty of coping with the specter of the possibility that the partner or parent won't return.

These hardships are of course not unique to the families of climbers. They are also experienced by the families of any person who engages in an unusually risky pursuit that requires a single-minded commitment and long absences. Astronauts are a case in point. Sarah Cuddon, producer of *The Astronaut Wives' Club*, a documentary that examines the hardships faced by families of astronauts in the 1960s and 1970s, reports that carefully concealed depression and alcoholism were common. "The Apollo program," she reports, "provoked a relentless and remorseless media frenzy. Wives of astronauts had to maintain their composure for a worldwide audience at some of the most stressful moments in their lives."[13] One of the wives interviewed by Cuddon remembers being overwhelmed by the challenge. "[My husband] was a complete workaholic. The space program was all he thought about. I knew he would never be able to show me the love I needed or make me a priority and I became suicidal," she reports. Much like the families of climbers, the families of astronauts apparently often feel marginalized, underappreciated, and abandoned. And yet, despite the obvious parallels, there seems to be no mention in books, blogs, or interviews of words such as "selfish," "irresponsible," or "immoral" in connection with astronauts involved in NASA programs.

The differential treatment of astronauts and climbers is perhaps most striking in the media coverage of climbers who are mothers and astronauts who are mothers. The accomplished British high-altitude mountaineer Alison Hargreaves, for example, was pilloried by the media when she died in a sudden storm on K2 in 1995, leaving behind a husband and two children, ages four and six.[14] Despite the fact that her expedition to K2 was motivated largely by the desire to provide basic financial support for her family, Hargreaves was criticized by both the press and the public for her irresponsibility and lack of good judgment as a climber and mother with young children. I, too, have experienced the media preoccupation with the perils faced by a mother who climbs. While on tour between my own expeditions to K2, Everest, and other 8,000-meter peaks, I was frequently challenged about my motivations and asked direct questions about the combination of risk and motherhood. Much of the support for my climbing came from the National Geographic Society, which sponsored my expeditions not because I was a single mother who climbed, but (in part) because I argued that the concept of wilderness cannot be defined in the absence of a perceiver. This leads quite naturally to the idea that "wilderness" describes not just a specific type of place, but the way in which we interact with a place. The frontiers of the next millennium, I insisted, lie not merely in the exploration of physical spaces, but in understanding our relationship with the world. That said, the fact that I had a child was an apparently irresistible tag line. When NBC aired a National Geographic Explorer piece with Matt Lauer to promote the show's move to CNBC, for example, the special was billed as featuring "rattlesnakes, sharks, and a mother who climbs."

The experiences of Hargreaves and myself stand in stark contrast to, say, the media treatment of Christa McAuliffe in the wake of the Space Shuttle *Challenger* disaster. McAuliffe applied to the Teacher in Space Project in the mid-1980s, noting that she had always had an interest in space exploration and viewed the program as "a unique opportunity to fulfill my early fantasies."[15] She was selected out of an applicant pool of more than 11,000 teachers and after months of training boarded *Challenger* with the other six crew members. Seventy-three seconds into the flight, the shuttle broke apart. McAuliffe left behind a husband and two children, ages six and nine, who were watching the launch. After her death, dozens of schools, scholarships, conferences, and even planetary craters were named in her honor; in 2004 she was posthumously awarded the Congressional Space Medal of Honor. Nowhere – in any of the news articles, books, or other media coverage – have I been able to find any suggestion that boarding the shuttle as a mother with two young children might have been an irresponsible or selfish decision.

Why, we might wonder, is there such a salient discrepancy between the perception of climbers and the perception of astronauts? Why are the negative consequences of risk permissible for astronauts, but not climbers? On what grounds can the *argument from compassion* be invoked as a defense of the asymmetry thesis? There are, I think, at least two natural responses. One is that a job as an astronaut provides a reasonable income for a partner or family, thereby offsetting the negative effects of the risk. The intrinsic risk is an unavoidable consequence of the career, much like

  HEIDI HOWKINS LOCKWOOD

the risk of careers in logging, active military service, or any of the other fields that make the US Department of Labor's annual "top 10 most dangerous jobs" list. Climbing, on the other hand, is rarely considered a career or source of stable income, unless one is working as a guide or a member of a full-time mountain patrol. Another possible response – and perhaps the most invoked – is that, whereas the research conducted by astronauts in space offers clear and tangible benefits to humanity, the allegedly self-centered nature of the climber's game lacks an obvious value to society. Let's consider each of these in turn.

The first response is simply misinformed, based on an erroneous perception of the relative pecuniary status of astronauts and professional climbers. Although it is true that there are far fewer climbers who are in the enviable position of being able to make a living from their passion, it is *not* the case that the typical professional climber is indigent or unable to provide a respectable level of support for his or her family. According to the NASA jobs site, salaries for civilian astronauts range from $65,140 to $100,701 per year.[16] The income range of professional climbers is much broader, but certainly comparable. The typical strategy is to maintain a diversified portfolio of sponsors who will provide gear and financial support in exchange for product promotion, images, and sometimes assistance with product development. This base income can then be supplemented by speaking engagements (ideally, two to three keynote or corporate gigs per year, plus an outdoor retailer tour with poster or book signings and a fundraiser for a charity), and an occasional book contract. In my experience, sponsors are willing to provide anything from $1k to $70k per annum, depending on the size of the company and the level of commitment. Book advances are typically $10–50k. The fees for keynotes and corporate speaking engagements vary. The speaker fee for Ed Viesturs (the first American to summit all fourteen of the world's highest peaks) is $10–20k; Joe Simpson (best known as author of *Touching the Void*) commands £7,500–18,000; and Erik Weihenmayer (a blind climber and excellent speaker, with Everest and many other impressive ascents to his credit) receives $20–30k. In other words, even with the expense of expeditions and the cost of insurance, it is entirely possible for professional climbers living in many countries to make a living within or even well beyond the range of an astronaut's salary. To do so of course requires a certain resourcefulness and persistence; but then, so does climbing.

The second response is more interesting. Here we essentially have an argument that the risks taken by astronauts with families are permissible because the potential positive consequences of the activity outweigh the potential negative consequences of the risks. In other words, the risks taken by astronauts are an unavoidable by-product of the process of furthering our scientific knowledge. The risks taken by climbers, on the other hand, fail to provide a tangible benefit to the larger community. We might try to counter this response by insisting that climbing *does* have value for society. The world needs risk takers to inspire, challenge, cross the boundaries of the possible, enter the realm of the mystical, dare to make huge leaps into the unknown. Even those who perish in the attempt provide us with modern-day versions of the myth of Icarus. The problem with this objection is that it pins the value of climbing to the value of the lore, the written and verbal record of the experiences. Climbers would, on this view, have an obligation to capture and relay their experiences via words, photos, film, or other media. But this can't be right; to suggest that the value of climbing lies in the value of the stories is to conflate the activity with the lore.

A more promising line of thinking is to question the *structure* of the justification, that is, to question the grounds for thinking that the risks climbers take are gratuitous because they fail to provide a positive or neutral net value to society. The justification goes something like this: (1) the risks climbers take are gratuitous because they fail to provide an overall good; (2) they fail to provide an overall good because they fail to (aim to) provide a positive benefit to society; (3) they fail to provide a benefit because (the aims and purposes of) climbing is not valued by society; and (4) the aims and purposes of climbing are not valued by society because they are viewed as gratuitous. This chain of reasoning is clearly circular. Rather than providing an explanation *why* we should think that risks taken by climbers are gratuitous or frivolous or reprehensible or any other value-laden adjective, we have simply been given an unenlightening value-laden string of synonyms: gratuitous risks are reprehensible because they fail to produce a positive or neutral net good, because they're not valued, because they're gratuitous. And without further justification for the sameness of these terms – without some explanation of *why* we should think that gratuitous activities should not be valued – the second response does not provide an adequate defense of the asymmetry thesis.

An External Justification

In the preceding two sections I have argued that neither the Rule of Rescue nor the argument from compassion provides adequate justification for

  HEIDI HOWKINS LOCKWOOD

our differing attitudes towards gratuitous risk. I am equally pessimistic about the prospects for other arguments which attempt to show that the asymmetry thesis can be defended by claiming that there is some essential feature of gratuitous risk which singles it out for different treatment from other forms of risk. But if we reject these arguments, are we forced to conclude that our intuitions about the asymmetry thesis are unfounded? Can we justify bans and rescue fines or fees, and continue to censure the "jokers" on the mountain, without either claiming that gratuitous risk is intrinsically reprehensible, or providing a defense based on considerations such as the Rule of Rescue or argument from compassion?

In this section I want to argue that the best defense of the asymmetry thesis is on external grounds. Gratuitous risk taking is not *ipso facto* irresponsible. But it is irresponsible given certain commonly accepted background assumptions. It is these assumptions, I believe, that are tacitly driving many of the arguments against taking unnecessary and avoidable risks; to the extent that such assumptions are justifiable (or objectionable), the asymmetry thesis will also be justifiable (or objectionable).

The best case to use in making this point are the intuitions we have regarding the participation of parents in climbing or other risky sports. In this case, there is an interesting dual asymmetry: the asymmetry we examined earlier between attitudes towards climber–mothers and astronaut–mothers, and the asymmetry between attitudes towards male and female climbers who are parents. Both of these asymmetries can, I believe, be explained by the presence of background gender inequalities.

Despite the various improvements and gains women have won over the past fifty years, gender inequality remains pervasive in our society. Wage disparities are the most commonly cited evidence of the inequity; according to 2009 data for the US, the average full-time working woman's earnings are only 78 percent of her male counterpart. Women are 42 percent more likely to live in poverty than men, and most of the work done by women in our society remains in fields associated with the "traditionally female" role of caring for others: service and clerical work, domestic labor, teaching, nursing, and so on.[17]

Given these inequities and other background assumptions about both the extent to which women will assume responsibility for childcare and domestic work and the unique bond between mothers and their children, it is perhaps not surprising that the death of Alison Hargreaves on K2 provoked moral outrage in the media. Polly Toynbee, an influential liberal commentator in the UK, provided a particularly revealing remark in her criticism of Hargreaves' career choice. "What is interesting about Alison Hargreaves," she wrote, "is that she behaved like a man."[18] Risk taking, she argued, is a prototypically male choice, fueled by testosterone and the culture of machismo. Hargreaves' behavior was "appalling" because she was a woman who violated the norms of social acceptability in making the decision to leave her family and risk her life to reach the summit of K2, an option traditionally reserved for men. The treatment of male high-altitude climbers in the international media at the same time as Hargreaves – fathers who, like Alison, were taking huge risks on difficult routes – provides good evidence of the attitude that while it is objectionable for a woman who is a mother to take risks in climbing that can ultimately lead to death, it is morally acceptable for a man who is a father to do the same. As Hargreaves' biographers note, there was a remarkable bias in the media's posthumous condemnation of her dual role as mother and climber: "A few days before Alison disappeared, Paul Nunn and Geoff Tier, both talented British mountaineers and both fathers, died on a mountain called Haramosh II, close to K2 . . . many commentators believed that a mother taking such risks was morally more culpable than a father doing the same."[19] As I mentioned earlier, my own experiences with the media corroborate this asymmetry. While I was almost invariably asked frank questions about the effects of my climbing on my daughter, the other high-altitude climber supported by my primary equipment sponsor was rarely questioned about his children. As a rule, the fact that some male climbers with children opt to take risks that can lead to incapacitation or death is not generally viewed as problematic or even examined by the media.

It is not hard to make the case that the asymmetry in the treatment of male and female climbers is based on background assumptions about gender inequities. But what about the other asymmetry discussed earlier – the differential treatment of astronauts who are mothers and climbers who are mothers? In this case, both are female. So how could the difference be due to gender inequity? In order to understand how assumptions regarding gender enter the picture in this case, we need to look a little more closely at the descriptions of the activities undertaken by female climbers and astronauts. In the case of Hargreaves, the media depicted her as a climber who was driven by commercial gains, a woman who placed her career before her children. In the case of contemporary female astronauts such as Laurel Clark, a mother who died in the 2003 *Columbia* disaster, the media portrayal is that of a woman dedicated to scientific research. A moment of reflection reveals that the latter is well within the scope of the traditional female role of service, whereas the former is not. Although women continue to be underrepresented in both the sciences and space exploration, there is nothing about the role of working as a member or even a leader of a scientific research team that runs strongly counter to the traditional role of women as compassionate devotees dedicated to furthering the goals of a higher power – in this case NASA and the pursuit of scientific knowledge. Women whose primary goal is financial gain, on the other hand, are often vilified by the media and even their own peers. We are distinctly uncomfortable with females whose ambitions are to dominate and capture, rather than to support and cultivate. In the male-dominated world of high-altitude climbing, Hargreaves was as ambitious and single minded as any male climber. She also needed to make a living as a climber to support her family. Her ambition was treated as surprising but marginally tolerable; it was the profit-making goal that placed her beyond the bounds of social acceptability and earned her the moral opprobrium.

I take it for granted that there is something objectionable about gender inequality, and therefore view the argument from gender inequality not as a defense or justification of the asymmetry thesis, but rather as a plausible explanation of the intuitions behind this particular (errant) application of the thesis. But might there be another, uncontroversial background assumption that could serve as a justification for other applications of the asymmetry thesis? The answer, I believe, is yes. Although I have focused just on the background assumptions related to gender inequality here, it should be clear that there are other assumptions that might serve as external justification for the asymmetry thesis. Let's take a closer look, for example, at Representative Tiernan's remark about the "jokers" on the mountains in connection with the Oregon House Bill 3434. At the first committee hearing held to debate the bill, Representative Montgomery, the bill's sponsor, described the bill as a piece of legislation designed "to recoup . . . money from people who go up there and act like a bunch of fools." Another member of the committee, Representative Grisham, dismissed climbers' opposition to the bill by insisting that climbers are opposed to the locator devices just because they're not macho: "I mean, how can you go out and wrestle with the wilderness . . . and enjoy it if you're carrying something that is supposed to protect you?" he asked facetiously.[20] Jokers. Fools. Machos. Wrestling with the wilderness. The image here is quite clear: climbers are cavalier adrenaline junkies who are either addicted to danger or out to prove something.

And the implicit background assumption is equally clear: whereas climbers are risk-mongers who are inexplicably hooked on that peculiar, chalky taste of fear, the rescue personnel who take huge risks to save them are extraordinary heroes valiantly facing unavoidable danger in the interests of the betterment and protection of humanity. To seek risk as a mere end is, in a word, irresponsible. To accept it as an ineliminable means to some other goal is not.

I don't think that most climbers are cavalier. Or adrenaline junkies. Or macho fools. It *is* undeniable that risk and real danger are important parts of the climbing game; there is something essential about the possibility of real loss, even death, and without the presence of danger many climbers would quit. But risk is not ordinarily viewed as the sole end or primary *objective* of climbing. The way climbers climb is (typically) calculated to maintain a certain acceptable level of risk and uncertainty. "Style" is the word that is usually used to describe this process. Using an aluminum ladder to scale an indoor climbing wall, for example, would be considered "bad style." It would simply be too easy. But using ladders to climb the Khumbu Icefall on Everest is considered standard practice. The icefall is so dangerous and difficult that you may die anyway, with or without ladders. At some level, the style process plays a role in almost all the risky games we play – climbing the career ladder, driving a car, developing relationships. It's just easier to recognize in climbing, where the risk is overt and the rules that help maintain the uncertainty of the outcome are easier to identify.

I say that "most" climbers aren't macho fools and that risk is not "ordinarily" viewed as the objective of climbing because there are clearly some exceptions to the rule. One measure of this is the extent to which a climber portrays himself as in control of the unpredictable elements of the game. To depict the survival of a fall or avalanche or other near-fatal incident as an "accomplishment" is to exhibit a form of machismo. And risk is arguably an element of the goal itself when a climber's goal is to attempt one-time stunts for which there is no way to reasonably practice.

I accept the assumption that there is something objectionable about seeking risk as a *mere* ends, as opposed to accepting risk as a means or ineliminable feature of an experience. It is this assumption, I believe, that provides grounds for questioning the permissibility of gratuitous risks under certain circumstances. While it does not provide a defense of, say, the Oregon Beacon Bill or the "special use" fee for climbing on Denali, it *does* potentially provide a defense for the recovery of rescue costs on a case-by-case basis when climbers show intentional or reckless disregard for personal safety.[21] In short, I think it is the belief that there is something wrong about pursuing risk as an end itself that motivates the asymmetry thesis and leads some to condemn climbing as a risk-seeking activity. However, this condemnation is based on a misperception of the activity; climbing and mountaineering have never been, at least for me, about seeking risk as an end in itself.

And so, in conclusion, we have what I believe is a reasonable justification for a limited application of the asymmetry thesis, based on an external assumption about the appropriate role of risk in human endeavors. In general, whether or not the intuitions that we have regarding a particular application of the asymmetry thesis have normative force – whether or not gratuitous risk taking ought to be viewed as morally reprehensible under specific circumstances – depends on whether the external norms that serve as a basis for those intuitions are ethically defensible. This of course leaves many questions open. Should we, for example, place a higher value on investigations of the external, physical world than exploration of our *relationship* with the world? Should we apply differential standards to climbers of different ages? I have strong opinions on these and similar questions, but I leave the task of puzzling through a philosophical defense to others.

NOTES

1   A. R. Jonsen, "Bentham in a Box: Technology Assessment and Health Care Allocation," *Law, Medicine and Health Care* 14 (1986): 174.

2   Lloyd Athearn, "Climbing Rescues in America: Reality Does Not Support 'High-Risk, High-Cost' Perception," May 19, 2005; online at www.angband. org/~gary/MReal.pdf (accessed December 8, 2009).

3   As quoted by Jonathan Simon, "Risking Rescue: High-Altitude Rescue as Moral Risk and Moral Opportunity," in Richard V. Ericson and Aaron Doyle (eds.) *Risk and Morality* (Toronto: University of Toronto Press, 2003), p. 384.

4   Noah Adams, "Survivor of Everest Catastrophe Discusses Climb: Interview with Jon Krakauer," *All Things Considered*, National Public Radio, May 16, 1996, transcript number 2215–13.

5   The Swiss pair's boots, mitts, and down suits were inaccessible, stored at a camp on their intended route on the south face.

6   See http://blog.mountainhardwear.com/2008/06/on_annapurna.html#more for an English translation of the rescue as related by Ueli Steck to Edi Estermann, originally published in *Schweizer Illustrierte* 23 (June 2, 2008).

7   Or at least climbing partners and independent climbers climbing in areas in which there are no guides or rescue services. Much has been written about the Everest 2006 season, during which two dying climbers were ignored by other teams as they continued to the summit. Given the prevalence of guided climbing on Everest and the fact that communication with climbers during the summit bid is often orchestrated via radio by team leaders, it is reasonable to think that the climbers in question viewed their role on the mountain as that of the client, rather than guide or fellow climber.

8   For interesting discussions of this question, see Simon, "Risking Rescue."

9   As quoted by Lloyd Athearn, "Jokers on the Mountain: When Politics and Mountain Rescues Collide," *American Alpine News* (January 1997), originally published in *Climbing Magazine* 163 (1996).

10   "The Outside Prognosticator: Really Quite Stupid," *Outside Magazine* (January 1996); online at www.outside.away.com/outside/magazine/0196/9601frqs.html (accessed November 30, 2009).

11   Ed Peters (ed.) *Mountaineering: The Freedom of the Hills*, 4th edn. (Seattle: Mountaineers Books, 1982), pp. 6–7.

12   Maria Coffey, *Where the Mountain Casts Its Shadow: The Dark Side of Extreme Adventure* (New York: St. Martin's Press, 2003), p. 54.

13   *The Astronaut Wives' Club*, BBC News, November 8, 2007; online at www.news.bbc.co.uk/2/hi/uk_news/magazine/7085003.stm (accessed December 9, 2009).

14   David Rose and Ed Douglas provide convincing evidence of the media disparagement in their biography of Hargreaves, *Regions of the Heart: The Triumph and Tragedy of Alison Hargreaves* (London: Penguin, 1999).

15   Susan Ware and Stacy Lorraine Braukman, *Notable American Women* (Cambridge, MA: Radcliffe Institute for Advanced Study, Harvard University Press, 2004), p. 425.

16   Retrieved from www.nasa.gov/centers/kennedy/about/information/astronaut_faq.html#5 on January 10, 2010.

17   According to the US Department of Labor Statistics (retrieved from www.dol.gov/wb/stats/main.htm on December 9, 2009), the top 10 most prevalent occupations for employed women in 2008 were: secretaries and administrative assistants, registered nurses, elementary and middle school teachers, cashiers, retail salespersons, home health aides, supervisors of retail sales workers, waitresses, receptionists, and bookkeepers.

18   As cited by Rose and Douglas, *Regions of the Heart*, p. 273.

19   Ibid., p. 275.

20   As reported by Athearn, "Jokers on the Mountain."

21   Five states have charge-for-rescue laws on the books. The laws allow recovery of rescue costs when people violate applicable laws (Oregon), knowingly enter an area closed to the public (California and Idaho), or show reckless or intentional disregard for personal safety (Hawaii and New Hampshire).

PART II

QUEST FOR THE SUMMIT

Cultivating the Climber

CHAPTER 5

HIGH ASPIRATIONS

Climbing and Self-Cultivation

You've climbed the highest mountain in the world. What's left? It's all downhill from there. You've got to set your sights on something higher than Everest.

Willi Unsoeld

*Now I see the secret of making the best persons,
It is to grow in the open air and to eat and sleep
with the earth.*

Walt Whitman, *Leaves of Grass*

Why Do We Climb?

Anyone who has climbed for any length of time has been confronted with the question why. This question crops up as predictably as the turning of the seasons just as soon as one progresses beyond the safest and most controlled sorts of climbing, like indoor climbing. Why place yourself in terrifying situations? Why endure the suffering of "screaming barfies" or the deprivation of spartan bivouacs? Why run the risk of injury, even death? Why climb? As my long-suffering wife puts it after more than two decades of watching me scrape up big walls, frozen waterfalls, and alpine peaks, "I love the outdoors, I just don't see why that needs to involve suffering and mortal fear." The question of why is put to climbers by their friends and loved ones, and debated by climbers themselves around a thousand camp fires. The difficulty of arriving at any easily communicable answer to this question is, perhaps, the point behind Mallory's famous retort, "Because it is there."[1]

The enduring mystery of this topic is the result, I think, of a question that has no answer, or perhaps a question with answers as varied as the climbers to which it is put. That doesn't mean we shouldn't ask it; it's an important question. But I think Christian Beckwith gave one of the more honest and eloquent answers to this question – one that certainly resonates with my own experience – when he wrote that "frequently, alpinists don't start in the mountains, but come to them from a distance, lured as often as not by something they'll spend the rest of their lives trying to understand."[2]

Why Should We Climb?

While I may well spend the rest of my life trying to understand why I *do* climb, I think there are many good reasons for why I, and others, *should* climb. This chapter attempts to describe one of those reasons. I will argue that climbing is, among other things, a crucible in which certain character traits, or *virtues*, can be forged. These virtues, in turn, make the climber who cultivates them a better person.

This is, of course, not to claim that virtue is the only reason we should climb. The question of why we should climb is easier to answer precisely because it admits of multiple simultaneously true answers: the challenge, both physical and mental; the beautiful areas to which it often takes you; the deep friendships it is capable of forming; and the sheer joy that climbers find in ascending snow, ice, and rock. However, given the constraints of time and space, virtue is what I will focus on here.

Building the Best Person

In order to get clear on just how climbing promotes virtues, we first have to get clear on the virtues themselves and why they are important. Today, many people will no doubt feel that talk of "virtue" smacks of a certain

Victorian prudishness or fastidious piety, but I will be using this term in its ancient, rather than modern, sense. Virtues are simply the dispositions that we praise in good people, the dispositions that help these good people to live good lives. Aristotle (384–322 BCE) is arguably the chief proponent in the Western tradition of what we have come to call "virtue ethics," and we'll use him as a guide, though not a final authority, in what follows.

"Virtue" is a translation of *arête*, which carries connotations of both virtue and excellence. So when Aristotle says that someone possesses the virtue of courage he means that that person has cultivated a certain human excellence, in this case courage, to a sufficient degree that it contributes to his flourishing. Flourishing, in turn, is the goal of all human activity; we all want to "live and fare well." *Eudaimonia* is the Greek word for flourishing, though it is often, and somewhat misleadingly, translated as "happiness." Thus, for Aristotle, the goal of life is to flourish (*eudaimonia*) and cultivating the virtues (excellences or *arête*) is, in large part, the path to such wellbeing.

Aristotle treats a variety of themes in his major ethical work, the *Nicomachean Ethics*, including topics as diverse as science (which is an intellectual virtue) and friendship (which either "is or implies" virtue). However, the most interesting subset of virtues for this inquiry is the "moral" virtues, which include courage, generosity, honesty, pride, temperance, and similar traits. Aristotle's account of virtue is exceedingly rich, and it would require a book-length treatment to do it justice. All we can do here is scratch the surface by focusing on a few aspects of his account in order to get a sense of how climbing can contribute to the cultivation of important virtues.

First, Aristotle points out that moral virtues are acquired through habituation (*hexis*); they are not innate and cannot be taught. A person becomes a good builder of homes by actually building; no one can do it naturally and no amount of reading about it will allow you to square the frame of a house. You need to practice. At first, no doubt, you will frequently fail. However, with diligence, a person can develop the ability to build houses very well. What is true for building, says Aristotle, is true for virtue. No one is born courageous and no amount of reading about courage will suffice to make a person courageous. Rather, a person becomes courageous through habituation. She practices courage by doing courageous acts until being courageous becomes part of who she is, that is, until it is an entrenched habit.

Well, which actions should we do in order to cultivate virtue?

Aristotle warns us that a discussion of virtue is "adequate if it has as much clearness as the subject matter admits of, for precision is not to be sought for alike in all discussions."[3] While philosophy can say a great deal about ethics, it cannot do so with mathematical precision, specifying exactly how to act in every conceivable situation. What we can say is that while the precise actions issuing from virtuous characters cannot be exactly prescribed, virtue is "destroyed by excess or defect, and preserved by the mean."[4] All moral virtues are a mean between two extremes (or vices).

Take, for example, courage, which is a crucial virtue for climbers. It is obviously possible to lack sufficient courage; however, it is also possible to be too courageous. Fools rush in where angels fear to tread. Moral virtue operates on a sort of "Goldilocks Principle." How does Goldilocks evaluate things? She avoids extremes. Too big; too small; just right. Too hot; too cold; just right. The Goldilocks Principle works well for illustrating some of Aristotle's other claims about virtue as well. Goldilocks not only avoids extremes, she looks for what "fits" her. A bed too big for Goldilocks might be just right for me, and porridge just right for Goldilocks might be too hot for me. This is why Aristotle says "the master of any art [including a given virtue] avoids excess and defect, but seeks the intermediate and chooses this – the intermediate *not in the object, but relative to us*."[5] Casting off on the infamous Bachar-Yerian might be a courageous act for a 5.11 leader well versed in Tuolumne knob climbing, but it would be ridiculously foolish for a fledgling 5.9 sport climber. Conversely, it might be courageous for that 5.9 leader to climb a runout 5.9 that, in turn, would not be courageous for the 5.11 leader, who would find it a relatively casual affair. The point here is not who climbs harder, but who is cultivating the relevant excellence of character.

Therefore, Aristotle's third pertinent point is that it is not enough to simply do the virtuous act. In order to actually be courageous, we have to do the courageous thing in the right way, that is, in the way that the courageous person would do it:

> It is no easy task to be good. For in everything it is no easy task to find the middle . . . anyone can get angry – that is easy – or give and spend money; but to do this to the right person, to the right extent, at the right time, with the right motive, and in the right way, that is not for everyone, nor is it easy; wherefore goodness is both rare and laudable and noble.[6]

  BRIAN TREANOR

There is a difference between a virtuous act committed by a virtuous person and a virtuous act committed by any other person. The 5.9 leader on the Bachar-Yerian is acting rashly (the name for the vice of an excess of courage), and this is true even if she somehow pulls off the ascent.

Part of the difference lies in how the agent *feels* during the commission of the act. In the cause of courage, it is not enough to do the action that is the mean between cowardice and rashness, one must feel the proper balance of fear and confidence; an excess of either would mean that the person in question is not yet courageous, although she may well be doing the courageous action. That virtuous actions are possible without yet being a virtuous person follows from the idea that moral virtue is the result of habituation. A person could, for example, do the properly courageous action – say, cast off on an R- or X-rated route near the limit of her onsight ability – but do so with too much, or too little, fear. She would be doing the virtuous thing, but she would not be doing it in the virtuous way.

Climbing and Self-Cultivation

Unlike modern ethical theories originating in the Enlightenment, virtue ethics helps us to appreciate all sorts of ethically significant behaviors that simply fly under the radar of theories like utilitarianism and deontology.[7] There is nothing particularly significant about one's first big wall solo for a deontologist; it's hard to see how such an action matters in terms of, for example, treating other persons as ends-in-themselves. However, as soon as we appreciate the importance of virtues for flourishing and the cultivation of good character, all sorts of activities, including climbing, become ethically charged in ways in which we are not accustomed to thinking.

Although people start and continue climbing for all sorts of reasons, most people who have climbed for any length of time understand that climbing has changed who they are. As Doug Robinson says, "you'll come down changed . . . from the mountaintop."[8] Realizing this, some people begin to consciously use climbing as a tool for self-cultivation. Like any other activity that encourages the cultivation of particular habits and dispositions, climbing tends to encourage the cultivation of certain virtues (and, it's true, certain vices).

The Only Rule Is There Are No Rules
(Except the Ones That Matter)

Climbers often claim that one of the attractions of climbing is that there are "no rules." In one sense this is certainly true. Climbing has no international governing bodies to speak of. No one will suspend you for the season for pulling on gear, placing an unnecessary bolt, or manufacturing a hold. However, in another equally important sense climbing is all about rules. Pretty much anyone can "climb" El Capitan if allowed to chop a staircase into the face or install metal rungs as part of the ascent.

As Lito Tejeda-Flores explained in his seminal piece "Games Climbers Play," climbing can be, and is, broken down into various subdisciplines or games, each with its own set of rules. You can pull on gear when aid climbing, but not when free climbing. You can use porters and fixed ropes on an expedition, but not if you are climbing in alpine style. Climbers *artificially* create challenges, and these challenges define climbers, climbing, and the virtues it cultivates. It is precisely these rules that make climbing such a remarkable arena for cultivating virtue, as I will argue below. As with any other informal group or tribe, these rules are imposed by consensus, a consensus that can, and does, change over time. When Todd Skinner and Paul Piana made the first free ascent of the Salathe Wall on El Cap, their chosen style mimicked the big wall ethic on which they were building: the leader free climbed the pitch and the second often jugged. However, today, climbers generally think that free climbing El Cap means that one climbs each pitch free, whether following or on lead – no jugging allowed. Why? Simply because the community of climbers says that this is what it means to free a big wall.

Different climbing games emphasize different virtues or classes of virtues. Aid climbing tends to cultivate problem solving and organization rather than physical fitness. Sport climbing emphasizes physical skill and persistence over bravery. Unsupported backcountry climbs (rock, ice, or mixed) tend to encourage humility, self-sufficiency, and appreciation of nature. And so on. Style matters as well. Think of the difference – in terms of the experience and therefore the dispositions, habits, or virtues it helps to cultivate – between headpointing and onsighting. However, despite the diversity of climbing games and styles, there are commonalities that suggest specific virtues associated with climbing "in general." Among the virtues that climbing generally, though not always, helps to foster are courage, humility, and reverence for the natural world.

Courage

Courage is perhaps the most obvious virtue cultivated by climbing. Non-climbers often remark, "I could never do that – I'd be too scared," and most climbers acknowledge that dealing with fear is part of the game when climbing. Aristotle says courage is a mean between cowardice or feeling too much fear and rashness or feeling too much confidence. The ubiquity of danger in climbing means that climbers are always negotiating the territory of courage (the virtue), cowardice (the deficient vice), and rashness (the excessive vice). The examples of connection between climbing and courage are simply too numerous to list.

Think, for instance, of climbing subdisciplines that purposely increase the uncertainty or the risk and therefore call for more courage: head-pointing, highball bouldering, free soloing, onsighting, new routing, and unsupported climbs in the greater mountain ranges, to name just a few. There are few endeavors in which people so regularly choose a more difficult and dangerous path by consciously rejecting technological means to overwhelm an objective. Climbers, however, often choose to forego technological advantage – eschewing beta, bolts, or supplemental oxygen – in the name of style or the pursuit of a particular experience.[9] Why? According to a claim often attributed to Steve House, "the simpler we make things, the richer the experience." Doug Robinson called this phenomenon "technological inversion," the process whereby climbers consciously choose simpler means for bolder and more difficult objectives, using experience, skill, and courage to adapt to challenges rather than using technology to eliminate them.

I had the good fortune to speak at length with Royal Robbins several years ago. He confessed to me that during his long climbing career he had often been tempted, during frightening moments, to grab a piece while pioneering new free climbing routes. What stopped him was the realization that he would never be able to undo that action, an action that might avoid a fall but which would forever taint the ascent. Once you blow the onsight, you can never get it back. You can climb a route many times; but you only get one chance to onsight it. I think many serious climbers – that is, people for whom climbing is important, not simply people who climb – realize the importance of such decisions.

John Sherman's account of his ascent of Gothic Nightmare in the Mystery Towers illustrates well the relationship between overcoming fear and cultivating courage. Wrestling with gear in the notoriously soft and insecure mud that passes for rock in the Fishers, Sherman found himself strung out above a half-pitch of dubious placements. After one of his pieces blew out, he retreated onto a lower piece and hung with the intent of descending so that his partner could finish the pitch. However, resting on the piece, he had time to reflect on his situation: "Then came the bigger fear. Not the threat of imminent injury, but the fear that if I didn't go back up, I would be a chickenshit forever."[10] Many climbers I know have faced similar moments. Though no single action could reasonably make you a chickenshit "forever," Sherman sensed intuitively that the decisions we make while climbing have a cumulative effect – each time you back down it becomes easier to back down again.

The point is not that an individual climber should always choose the more dangerous or risky approach; it is certainly possible to be overconfident and too rash. Sometimes retreat is the best option; and it is entirely possible to let one's desire or ambition overreach one's skill and experience. In these cases, continuing a climb is rash. This is why many top free soloists are at pains to point out how often they downclimb and retreat when a climb feels wrong. There is a right time to push past your fear and a right time to heed it. Steve House backed off K7 on five separate occasions over two years while attempting to solo a new route on the peak – including his fifth attempt, on which he confesses he "pushed too far" and acknowledges that his successful retreat and escape did not "justify taking so many chances."[11] However, those judicious retreats allowed House to return a sixth time to the mountain when, using the knowledge and experience gained in the earlier attempts, he successfully climbed K7 for its second ascent. Courage is about taking the right risk, not just any risk.

Humility

Climbing can cultivate many other virtues, not all of which are as obvious as courage. Among these less expected virtues is humility. True, climbing has its share of overblown egos, and the prevalence of such characters might suggest that climbing is better suited to cultivating the vice of arrogance than the virtue of humility. However, for every blustering spray-lord swaggering around base camp loudly boasting of his successes (real or imagined), there is, somewhere unnoticed, one of the "best climbers you've never heard of," a (literal) *amateur* who quietly pushes herself climbing and let's her accomplishments, and failures, speak for themselves.

The behavior of climbers with too little humility should not lead us to think that the virtue of humility lies in radical self-abnegation. Insofar as humility is a virtue it is possible to miss the mark by having either too much or too little of it. Humility is the characteristic of those who have an appropriately modest view of their own accomplishments and importance. In some sense it shares characteristics with what Aristotle calls "proper pride"; it acknowledges both the extent and the limits of one's powers. A humble person owns her successes and failures. She neither pretends that there is some cosmic significance to putting up her most recent route, nor engages in the self-denigration of insisting her accomplishments are without any significance.

Again, the "rules" of climbing can help to illuminate things. One of the benefits of the "rules" is that they allow us to compare different ascents. Most climbers have had the experience of realizing after, or even during, a particularly difficult ascent, that the first ascensionists pioneered the climb using radically inferior technology: weaker ropes that handled poorly; hip belays to catch falls; grossly inferior shoes and clothing; straight shafted bamboo ice axes; bongs (or nothing) for protection in wide cracks; and often an incredible restraint when placing fixed protection like bolts. The reality is that while climbing Birdbrain Boulevard or the Nose-in-a-Day is still a significant accomplishment, it is no longer the heroic feat it once was and this is generally not due to the superior skill and courage of today's climbers. Next time you smear your way up a runout Tuolumne slab, remind yourself that Bob Kamps was climbing these routes in Pivetta Cortinas, which were nothing more than stiff-soled hiking boots! Imagining the conditions in which many classic climbs were pioneered leads, in many climbers, to a real – that is to say *honest* – appreciation of their own skill. Maintaining this honest assessment of oneself is what led Yvon Chouinard to suggest that "the rules of the game[s] must be constantly updated to keep up with the expanding technology. Otherwise we overkill the classic climbs and delude ourselves into thinking we are better climbers than the pioneers."[12]

Using technology, rather than skill and courage, to overcome challenges leads to what Reinhold Messner famously called the "murder of the impossible," the prime example of which he believed to be bolting: "Today's climber . . . carries his courage in his rucksack, in the form of bolts and equipment."[13] "Faith in equipment has replaced faith in oneself."[14]

In his equally famous essay on clean climbing, Doug Robinson wrote that "pitons have been a great equalizer in American climbing. By liberally using them it was possible to get in over one's head, and by more liberally using them, to get out again. But every climb is not for every climber; the ultimate climbs are not democratic." Climbers, he continues, should have the "humility to back off rather than to continue in bad style – a thing well begun is not lost."[15]

Reverence for the Natural World

The honest assessment of one's abilities measured against both the challenges of a climb and the abilities of other climbers helps to cultivate humility. However, climbing often serves to cultivate another sort of modesty that we might call "reverence for the natural world."

The end result of all climbing is that the mountains "win," which is perhaps why many great climbers eventually move beyond martial metaphors for climbing, from "conquering" a mountain to "experiencing" a climb.[16] If we do more than casually repeat the same novice routes, eventually we come up against climbs that defeat us. Sometimes we will rise to the challenge, train, improve, and succeed where at first we failed; however, the eventual dominance of the mountains is assured. There will always be climbs that are too difficult and measured against the permanence of the mountains all of our victories are temporary. Such a situation cannot but help to solicit humility in those who experience it.

Climbers are fortunate in that their passion takes them to some of the world's most compelling natural landscapes. The Alps fascinated the Romantic poets for a reason, because they elicit the feelings of wonder and awe that the Romantics called the "sublime." Seen against the backdrop of the solidity and permanence of the mountain, our own fragility and transience are put in sharp relief. In regular, close contact with the magnificence of the natural world, climbers can appreciate, more than most, the awesome grandeur of the world's wild landscapes.

Intimate familiarity with the natural world – what Jack Turner calls "gross contact"[17] – is perhaps the single most common denominator among those who care for it. This should not be surprising. People only value what they know and love, and climbers are much more likely to know and love the natural world. The power of gross contact with the wild is no doubt why some of the USA's greatest environmentalists were climbers: Henry David

Thoreau, John Muir, David Brower. Each of these pioneers is explicit in linking his environmentalism to his time in the mountains:

> I wish everyone who seeks to lead the environmental cause could experience the peak moments of a climb. There is a lot to be learned from climbing mountains – more than you might think – about life, about saving the Earth, and not a little about how to go about both. Tough mountains build bold leaders, many of whom, in the early days, came down from the mountains to save them.[18]

Cultivating Virtue in a Domesticated World

In a longer essay it would be very easy to argue that climbing can help us to cultivate friendship, self-sacrifice, endurance, persistence, hardiness, judgment, and a host of other virtues. Of course, climbing is not the only way to cultivate virtue. People can cultivate many of these dispositions through other means of habituation. However, given the state of contemporary society, climbing is particularly well suited to cultivate certain virtues, and we should not lose sight of this.

Our world has changed a great deal in the last century. For many of us – that is, many of us who live in wealthy, industrialized nations – our world has become hyper-technological and controlled, and as a result overly safe and coddling. Today, we exert an astonishing degree of dominance and control over the natural world. Technology has developed to such a degree that it virtually eliminates danger, even discomfort. We believe that, or at least act as if, there is nothing we cannot do – think of genetic modification, nanotechnology, and geo-engineering. This degree of control has led to a situation in which danger and risk have been all but eliminated from our lives.

While these changes obviously have substantial benefits, they also come with some unintended and unwelcome consequences. Our control and dominance over the natural world leave us with few outlets for the cultivation of virtues like courage (because there is no risk), humility (because there is nothing we cannot or should not do), and reverence for the natural world (because we see it as nothing more than a bundle of resources for our technology). The loss of these virtues impoverishes us as human beings.

Kurt Hahn and Lawrence Holt founded Outward Bound in 1941 after noticing something surprising about the survivors of torpedo attacks on ships. Among the people who survived the initial impact and explosion, it was very often the case that the younger and fitter men died while the older men survived. What could explain this? Holt became convinced that the younger generation lacked essential characteristics that the older generation possessed. When faced with real adversity they lost hope and, ultimately, their lives. It was the purpose of Outward Bound to transform young people by exposing them to challenges.

Climbing can do something very similar by putting us back in touch with circumstances that we cannot fully control, circumstances with real risk (though, of course, different kinds of climbing do this to different degrees). This correlation between climbing, risk, and the domestication of society has not gone unnoticed:

> Risk, of course, has always been one of the abiding satisfactions of [climbing], however strenuously we all deny that to outsiders, pretending we do it for the view or the loneliness or the sense of physical well-being. "Life is impoverished," wrote Freud, "it loses its interest, when the highest stake in the game of living, life itself, may not be risked." . . . Perhaps this is one reason why climbing has become increasingly hard as society has become increasingly, disproportionately, coddling.[19]

Why Climb?

This argument does not claim that climbers are more virtuous than non-climbers, even with respect to the virtues that climbing can cultivate, like courage. People must be evaluated on a case-by-case basis. Nor does the argument imply that all climbers possess the virtues of courage, humility, and reverence for the natural world. Common sense, as well as myriad examples, suggests this is not the case. Rather, the point is that climbing offers us an uncommonly good tool for the cultivation of certain virtues, virtues that are, frankly, otherwise difficult to cultivate in contemporary society. Are there other ways to cultivate these virtues? Yes. Do climbers climb for reasons other than self-cultivation? Definitely. Nevertheless, climbing can be used, has been used, and is used as a tool for self-cultivation; and while climbing might be, in a sense, frivolous, it is clearly not useless. Courage, humility, and respect for the natural world remain virtues, both in the sense that they are conducive to flourishing and in the sense that we value and praise these

characteristics in others. And climbing offers us one of the best ways to mold these virtues in the context of the world in which we live.

NOTES

1   Though it should be noted that Mallory was much more eloquent in answering this question at other times. A couple of years before he famously quipped "Because it is there," Mallory offered the following: "What we get from this adventure is just sheer joy. And joy is, after all, the end of life. We do not live to eat and make money. We eat and make money to be able to enjoy life. That is what life means and what life is for." Cited in many places, but see, for example, Jonathan Waterman (ed.) *The Quotable Climber* (New York: Lyons Press, 1998), p. 235.

2   Christian Beckwith, "Editor's Note," *Alpinist* 12 (Autumn 2005): 8.

3   Aristotle, *The Nicomachean Ethics*, trans. David Ross (Oxford: Oxford University Press, 1980), pp. 2–3.

4   Ibid., p. 31.

5   Ibid., p. 37.

6   Ibid., p. 45.

7   Utilitarianism, associated with Jeremy Bentham (1748–1832) and John Stuart Mill (1806–73), argues that the moral action is the one that results in the greatest happiness for the greatest number. As such, it believes that the moral worth of an action is determined by the consequence of the action. Deontology is a word applied to theories stressing our duties or obligations, and it is most strongly associated with the philosophy of Immanuel Kant (1724–1804). Kant argued that a moral action was one that conformed to the "categorical imperative," one formulation of which states: "Act only according to that maxim whereby you can at the same time will that it should become a universal law." Therefore, for Kant, the morality of an action is determined by the maxim (the subjective rule by which an agent makes a decision), having nothing to do with the consequence of the action in question. One of the corollaries of Kant's philosophy, referred to in the passage above, is that all rational beings should be treated as "ends-in-themselves" rather than simply means to achieve my own ends.

8   Doug Robinson, "Moving Over Stone," in *A Night on the Ground, a Day in the Open* (La Cresenta: Mountain N' Air Books, 1996), p. 146.

9   A seminal essay on this topic is Lito Tejada-Flores' "Games Climbers Play," in Ken Wilson (ed.) *The Games Climbers Play* (London: Baton Wicks, 1996), pp. 19–27.

10 John Sherman, "Tales from the Gripped," in *Sherman Exposed* (Seattle: Mountaineers Books, 1999), p. 157.

11 Steve House, *Beyond the Mountain* (Ventura: Patagonia Books, 2009), p. 212.

12 Yvon Chouinard, *Climbing Ice* (San Francisco: Sierra Club Books, 1978), p.188.

13 Reinhold Messner, "The Murder of the Impossible," in Ken Wilson (ed.) *The Games Climbers Play* (London: Baton Wicks, 1996), p. 300.

14 Ibid., p. 301.

15 Doug Robinson, "The Whole Natural Art of Protection," in *A Night on the Ground, a Day in the Open* (La Crescenta: Mountain N' Air Books, 1996), p. 127.

16 Steve House, *Beyond the Mountain*, p. 260, sees climbing as a "struggle, which at the outset one knows can never be won, though much can be experienced."

17 Jack Turner, *The Abstract Wild* (Tuscon: University of Arizona Press, 1996), p. 26.

18 David Brower, *Let the Mountains Talk, Let the Rivers Run* (Gabriola Island: New Society Publishers, 2000), p. 23.

19 Al Alvarez, foreword to Ken Wilson (ed.) *The Games Climbers Play* (London: Baton Wicks, 1996), p. 16. A number of other people make similar claims. For example, "choosing to play [the game of "technological inversion"] in the vertical dimension of what is life of wild nature makes us climbers. Only from the extreme of comfort and leisure do we return willingly to adversity. Climbing is a symptom of post-industrial man" (Chouinard, *Climbing Ice*, p. 186).

CHAPTER 6

MORE THAN MEETS THE "I"

Values of Dangerous Sport

Some people go to immense expense and effort to engage in a sport that carries great risk to life and limb, eagerly climbing to such altitudes that the human body literally begins to die. Climbing a mountain, maybe especially one of the giant Himalayan peaks, has always captured the imagination of people, but "because it's there" doesn't really seem to explain why. Why endure the frostbite-inducing cold, white-out conditions, hurricane-force winds, potentially crushing avalanches, and arduous trekking simply for the possibility of standing for a few moments on the top of a mountain? Not only do some hardy souls have this desire, they're even willing to pay huge sums of money, with some commercial climbing expeditions charging up to US$65,000 per climber – not to mention they must be willing and able to leave their regular day-to-day lives behind for two months or more. What is it that climbers find valuable in risking life and limb? The answer, I suggest, depends on the kind of climber. Let me explain.

Philosopher J. S. Russell took on this question of dangerous sport – which he defined as "sport that involves activity that itself creates a significant risk of loss of, or serious impairment to, some basic capacity for human functioning" – and argued that its value lies in the opportunity it provides for enhanced self-knowledge and self-affirmation.[1] This seems right, but there's more to the story. I think that there are two kinds of value derived from dangerous sport: one is self-referential in the way suggested above, while the other is better characterized as self-transcendent or self-negating.

Jonathan Simon made a distinction that will be useful here between "summiteers" – who focus on the individual quest to reach the summit by whatever means necessary – and "mountaineers" – who draw value from relationships with each other and with the environment.[2] I will draw on narratives from mountain climbing to show examples of these two types. On the one hand, there are those individuals (summiteers) who engage in dangerous sport with eyes locked on the goal, focused on themselves as individuals locked into combat with their own limits. On the other hand, there are those individuals (mountaineers) who participate in dangerous sport for the less tangible values found in encounters through the process of engaging in the sports themselves. An account of the value of dangerous sport is incomplete without acknowledging both of these types.

Just to be clear about my starting points, this is the argument locating the value of dangerous sport in self-affirmation:

> Dangerous sport in its best exemplars, particularly those in which substantial bodily danger is an immediate and ever-present risk, represents an opportunity for confronting and pressing beyond certain apparent limits of personal, and indeed human, physical and psychological capacities in ways not afforded by normally available human activity. Thus, I say that the dominant, distinctive value of dangerous sport consists of an activity of self-affirmation because dangerous sport invites us to confront and push back the boundaries of the self by creating contexts in which some of the ordinary bounds of our lives can be challenged. Hence, we discover and affirm who we are and what we can be by confronting and attempting to extend these boundaries.[3]

And here is how the distinction between summiteering and mountaineering is filled in: "[Summiteering] portrays climbing as a powerfully redemptive symbol of personal triumph over adversity," which "often reduces to the goal of getting to the summit (preferably first, fastest, or with the greatest display of fitness by, for example, proceeding without oxygen in a high-altitude ascent)."[4] Mountaineering "valorizes the act of 'summiting' but also other aspects of life on the mountain, including confronting extremes of weather, self-reliance in extreme conditions, exposure (in climbing discourse, the immediate proximity to a fearsome drop-off), and especially the close work with partners sharing in the pleasures and dangers of the experience." Further, "participants have long assumed the force of norms and debated precisely what principles should govern risk takers in their interactions with each other and with nature."[5]

Taking ingredients from those starting points and mixing them with my own thoughts, I want to assign three characteristics to the summiteer and three to the mountaineer. The summiteer:

1. is goal oriented;
2. gains self-knowledge or self-affirmation (from attainment of the goal);
3. and may show self-concern to the point of neglect of others.

The characteristics are interrelated and mutually influence one another. The summiteer's pursuit of self-knowledge (characteristic 2) is valuable, but only if it is undertaken for the right reasons. If the pursuit is spurred solely by a goal-directed motivation (characteristic 1), it may lead to a narcissistic neglect of others (characteristic 3).

The mountaineer:

1. is process oriented;
2. achieves self-transcendence, or self-negation, and self-knowledge;
3. and may show moral responsibility for the welfare of others.

As above, these traits do not operate in isolation from one another. The mountaineer doesn't actively pursue self-transcendence, but attains it (characteristic 2) because the focus is on the process not just the goal (characteristic 1), resulting also in a concern for others on the mountain and even for the mountain itself (characteristic 3).

To help understand the distinction between the two types of climbers, I'll look at each of these six characteristics and offer passages from climbing accounts as examples. And, in the end, I hope to have shown that being a mountaineer is better than being a summiteer. But first we have to agree that mountain climbing is, in fact, a dangerous sport.

The Death Zone

Humans were not meant to live at high altitude. The evidence for this is that the body begins a process of deterioration at about 17,000 feet and the pace of the process quickens as the altitude increases. Climbers have trouble sleeping and eating. They lose weight due to this and to the wasting of their muscles. Anything over 26,000 feet (or 8,000 meters) is referred to as the Death Zone because the process of dying moves so rapidly. On their way to that altitude, climbers camp further and further up, teaching their bodies to adapt to the conditions. But, once there, all sorts of internal systems go haywire in response to a decline in barometric pressure which leads to a decline in oxygen intake, starving the lungs and brain of oxygen. In a condition known as pulmonary edema, the lungs fill with fluid, leaked from blood vessels. When the air sacs in the lungs fill, climbers struggle to breathe and cough up pink fluid. This makes it difficult to draw in a sufficient amount of the thin oxygen available at that altitude, and so they face cardiovascular arrest and death. Equally deadly is cerebral edema, where oxygen deficiency causes fluid to accumulate in the brain, increasing pressure inside the skull. A climber with this condition experiences a splitting headache, dizziness, drowsiness, hallucinations, and finally coma followed by death. As one writer remarked, life at that altitude is "a literally mind-blowing experience of having millions of brain cells die in minutes."[6] Put simply, it just isn't possible for the human body to acclimatize in the Death Zone.

Add to this the dangers of operating in an environment where the temperatures are bone-chilling and the winds so fierce they can rip tents from the side of the mountain, throw in unexpected avalanches and difficult pitches, and the numbers bear out the danger. Although Everest is the highest of the 14 mountains that are more than 26,000 feet above sea level, it is far from the deadliest. K2, the second highest peak, has a dismal success rate, allowing only about 10 percent the number of successful climbs as Everest, with a death rate nearly three times as great.[7] An analysis comparing the number of deaths to the number of successful summits (through 2003) found that it is actually the tenth highest peak, Annapurna, that claims the most lives: "For Everest, the ratio turns out to be seven to one. For K2, which has the reputation of being the hardest and most dangerous of the high peaks, the ratio is a little over three to one. But for Annapurna, it's exactly two to one. For every two climbers who get to the top, one climber dies trying."[8] These numbers are certainly grim enough to warrant calling mountain climbing a dangerous sport. So what sort of value do people find in such an activity? The answer depends on what type of climber a person is; first I'll look at those who are summiteers.

Summiteers

Summiteers have three characteristics. The first is that they are goal oriented. Never mind the journey, it's the outcome that drives summiteers, some of whom will pay almost anything and do almost anything to get to the top. This has brought the explosion of commercial expeditions, where a person pays a huge sum to have meals catered and gear carried, and finally to be led, sometimes literally by the hand, to the summit. For these people, failure to reach the summit constitutes breach of contract. As Jon Krakauer remarks, "having paid princely sums to be escorted up Everest, some climbers have then sued their guides when the summit eluded them."[9] Obviously, for these people, the value of climbing is less in the experience than in attaining the goal of reaching the summit.

Other climbers, while willing to do the work for themselves, still may be driven toward attaining some particular goal. It's no longer possible to attain the goal of being the first to summit any of the higher peaks, but it is possible to be the first of some narrowly defined group, for example, "first woman, first Japanese woman, first Japanese woman over fifty, first breast cancer survivor, and so on. . . . highly publicized expeditions frequently string together arbitrary if independently worthy goals to establish some credible claim to being first."[10] So, for summiteers, there must be a goal – be the first to summit, or the fastest to summit, or the first to summit without supplemental oxygen, or the first this that or the other to summit, or just summit no matter how much assistance that requires.

Attaining the goal of reaching the summit, especially when reaching it only after great adversity, results in the second characteristic of summiteering: the kind of self-discovery and affirmation noted by Russell. Through the process of overcoming the adversity that necessarily comes with summiting a mountain, a person experiences an enhanced sense of self-awareness and/or personal growth. Listen to climber Hannes Taugwalder as he speaks of using the mountain as a measure of character:

> You have the feeling, you see this huge mountain and then you want to use your strength, your courage, your power, you want to measure yourself against the mountain – it calls to you, "Come on, try, try to climb me" – it's like an exclamation, and you feel it in your soul and you have to go.[11]

A mountain may do more than measure one's character; it may applaud it. Sir Edmund Hillary describes such self-affirmation like this: "If you find something that's difficult and dangerous and perhaps a little frightening, but you persist and overcome it, that gives you a much greater sense of satisfaction."[12]

After interviewing many climbers, Nicholas O'Connell concluded that the value they find in this dangerous sport includes a revealing of character, but also an improving of it:

> Long, exhausting, nervy routes serve as the purgatories through which they must pass to test and perfect their character. For climbing is about more than the completion of a difficult route; it is also about the completion of oneself.[13]

Of course, it makes sense that climbing would be fertile ground for engagement with one's inner self simply because it is, at least to some degree, an individual activity, where some things must be undertaken alone. True, there are often others in a climbing group, but each member of the group still has to do some things for him or herself. Unlike team sports, the actions of other members of the climbing group do not influence to a great degree the accomplishments of any individual member. The group may provide support, but each member has to accomplish some tasks alone, and so is directly responsible for the consequences of those actions. In this way, "mountain climbing may be one example of an activity that combines group altruism with individual selfishness."[14]

As hinted above, the individualistic aspect of mountain climbing may lead from self-discovery to self-interest to selfishness, as witnessed by the fact that mountain climbing literature is rife with accounts of stolen oxygen canisters and gear from high camps. This is the third characteristic of summiteering – a disregard for basic moral obligations. This sort of ugly, single-minded pursuit of the summit was evidenced on Everest in the now-infamous 2006 season, when in mid-May David Sharp, a 34-year-old British climber, was left sitting under a rock overhang about 1,000 feet below the summit of Everest. Sharp was on his way down after summiting when he collapsed from oxygen deficiency. As he sat, dying, he was passed by *at least forty* climbers, none of whom stopped to attempt a rescue. Interestingly perhaps, in light of the point that people are continually searching for new firsts, one of those forty was Mark Inglis, a New Zealander, on his way to become the world's first double-amputee to summit.

When pushed by the media to explain how they could have neglected a fellow climber in distress, several of those who had passed Sharp by argued forcefully that, given the altitude and conditions, there was nothing that could have been done to save him. Ten days later, an American guide, Dan Mazur, gave the lie to their claims when he came across Lincoln Hall, a 50-year-old Australian climber, who had been left for dead. Instead of plodding past, Mazur gave up his own summit attempt to sit with Hall until rescuers arrived. Hall was successfully carried down the mountain, his only permanent injuries due to serious frostbite on his extremities.

Ten years earlier, in 1996, in explaining the choice of a Japanese climbing group to step over three climbers in trouble on Everest, one of the Japanese said: "We were too tired to help. Above 8,000 meters is not a place where people can afford morality."[15] Noted mountaineer David Roberts recognizes the high incidence of narcissism in achievers in many areas, but claims that in climbers "the narcissism all too often goes hand in hand with a disturbing coldness, an absence of compassion."[16] This tendency to lose morality has been acknowledged, but hasn't been pushed beyond the relatively harmless (like tripping in hockey). The arena of dangerous sport, it has been said, "is a place, indeed, where what would normally count as criminal behavior or plain and utter recklessness, or poor judgment is not judged or constrained by the normal conventions of ordinary life."[17] In a hockey rink, such a suspension of the ethical may be acceptable, but it has far more dire implications in the Death Zone. In such a place, one might prefer to be in the company of climbers who are different from summiteers. I'll take that route myself at this point, leaving the summiteers and moving on to examine the three characteristics of the mountaineers.

Mountaineers

The first characteristic of mountaineers is that they are process oriented, describing their time on the mountain as one of relationship with the mountain rather than a race to the top. Instead of an enemy challenge to be conquered, a mountain is often described as a being with whom the mountaineer shares an experience. Mountaineer Ed Webster says he often comes to a point in his time high on a mountain when "I would reach what I guess I would call a state of grace, where I felt that we were living amongst these great tremendous mountains and that somehow they were our friends – there wasn't this adversarial relationship."[18] Another climber,

Steven Venables, suggests that "it's that sense of complete, total engagement with a mountain that attracts people. Mountaineering takes you into situations which you would not achieve in any other way."[19] One of the most accomplished climbers in the world, Reinhold Messner, says: "I'm trying to live with the mountain. I'm not fighting with the mountain. But it's a relationship between the mountain and me and not between me and someone else."[20] Notice that none of these descriptions makes any reference at all to reaching the summit. Rather than focusing on what lies above, these mountaineers are completely in the moment, focused on themselves and the mountain in relation.

This openness to experiencing the mountain as another being rather than an object to be conquered leads often to the second characteristic of mountaineers – a kind of self-transcendence. Where the summiteer is engrossed in an examination of self or an affirmation of self, the mountaineer seems to escape self altogether. Many climbers describe an opening of the self to the vastness of the world in the particular moment. For example, Reinhold Messner describes it this way:

> There are many ways to pray. And praying is a meditation. For Buddhists, praying is nothing but to forget everything, to be empty, and to be open for new experiences.
>
> But meditation is not our Western way. We are not able to do it. We have an active approach to life. But I think through climbing I reach the same goal. And in this way climbing is for me praying, because if I climb, I am so concentrated that I become empty and open for new experiences.[21]

Marshall Ulrich points to something similar in his account of climbing Everest, explicitly devaluing summiting as the point of the climb. According to Ulrich:

> So what do you accomplish if you summit Mount Everest? I say, "Not much, unless you learn something along the way." I truly was overwhelmed with gratitude at the summit of Mount Everest. Gratitude for where I came from, who I am, and where I am going. Gratitude to all those people in the world who demonstrate that being an island unto myself is simply living a hollow life. Gratitude that I was blessed to be able to be in that one place, in that one moment, and open my heart to the world and heaven above.[22]

It is the isolation of self-focus that Ulrich denounces as being a hollow life. Instead, value comes with moving beyond one's goals and accomplishments to turn one's focus outward, away from the self and toward the enveloping world.

Putting the first and second characteristics together, mountaineers feel themselves in relation with the mountain, concentrating on the process, or the moment, rather than on the outcome, or the summit. This allows them to move beyond self and be open to the mountain, the world, and their fellow climbers. It is this last relationship that forms the basis for the next aspect.

The third characteristic of mountaineers is that they exhibit a sense of moral responsibility for their comrades on the mountain. In response to the 2006 events on Everest, Sir Edmund Hillary issued some of the harshest criticism, saying that leaving a fellow climber to die would have been unthinkable when he was climbing, that one would never just trudge on by, and that those who did just that should forever be ashamed. Dan Mazur didn't choose to come across Lincoln Hall, freezing to death on Everest, but he didn't hesitate, once he did, to give up his chance to summit – and to get his clients to the summit – no matter how easily the odds against a successful rescue might have allowed him to rationalize a decision to look the other way and walk past. Michael Kodas tells the story of a climber who fell and broke his ankle 7,850 meters up on his way to the summit of K2: "At that altitude, many climbers consider a busted leg synonymous with death, but immediately after the accident, ten climbers from various countries formed a rescue team that would spend three days bringing [the climber] down."[23] It appears that what a climber takes to be possible, or even obligatory, depends upon what kind of climber one is – summiteer or mountaineer.

Heinrich Harrer, one of the first climbers to make a successful ascent of the Eiger, also stresses the responsibilities climbers have to one another:

> Let us grant courage and the love of pure adventure their own justification, even if we cannot produce any material support for them. Mankind has developed an ugly habit of only allowing true courage to the killers. Great credit accrues to the one who bests another; little is given to the man who recognizes in his comrade on the rope a part of himself, who for long hours of extreme peril faces no opponent to be shot or struck down, but whose battle is solely against his own weakness and insufficiency. Is the man who, at moments when his own life is in the balance, has not only to safeguard it but, at the same time, his friend's – even to the extent of mutual self-sacrifice – to receive less recognition than a boxer in the ring, simply because the nature of what he is doing is not properly understood?[24]

For Harrer, the prospect of leaving a fellow climber behind simply does not arise. A good climber moves past a narrow focus on self and summit to look out for others engaged in the same experience. An individual accomplishment that comes with the loss of another climber is no accomplishment at all, but rather a failure of courage.

Conclusion

In the way of a brief conclusion, I agree that dangerous sport is valuable because it provides the opportunity for enhanced self-knowledge and self-affirmation. I hope I have shown, however, that this is not the whole story. There is another type of value found in dangerous sport that is self-transcendent or self-negating. The first type I located as belonging to the class of summiteering; the second belongs to the class of mountaineering. A full account of the value of dangerous sport should include acknowledgment of both classes. Further, my own view is that mountaineers, while not necessarily better climbers than summiteers, are morally better people, having found motivation internally in the experience of the climb instead of only externally in the goal of reaching the summit. The character traits exhibited by mountaineers – courage, compassion, and care for others – would appear on most any list of the virtues. The traits exhibited by summiteers – selfishness, single-mindedness, and a deficiency of sympathy – are generally found on a list of vices. Which traits one exhibits depends largely on one's motivation, which determines what kind of climber one turns out to be in the end.

Ed Viesturs, one of the few men in the world to summit all 14 of the peaks rising above 26,000 feet, points out that Himalayan Sherpas have long recognized that there are two very different kinds of climbers. Not needing to label them as summiteers or mountaineers, the Sherpas clearly distinguish between the two types and clearly value only the latter:

> On my expeditions, I've always noticed that as early as the first days at base camp, the Sherpas can tell which Westerners are there for the right reasons. Climbers who simply love being in beautiful places and relish the joy of climbing for its own sake win their approbation; those who just want to get it over with and go home boasting of reaching the top, don't.
>
> The Sherpas have taught me to tread lightly and gently while climbing these magnificent peaks. To climb with humility and respect. And that mountains are not conquered: they simply do or do not allow us to climb them.[25]

  PAM R. SAILORS

Without labeling them as summiteers or mountaineers, the Sherpas clearly distinguish between the two types and value only the latter. And no one knows climbing better than the Sherpas.

NOTES

1   J. S. Russell, "The Value of Dangerous Sport," *Journal of the Philosophy of Sport* 32 (2005): 1–19.
2   Jonathan Simon, "Taking Risks: Extreme Sports and the Embrace of Risk in Advanced Liberal Societies," in Tom Baker and Jonathan Simon (eds.) *Embracing Risk: The Changing Culture of Insurance and Responsibility* (Chicago: University of Chicago Press, 2002), pp. 177–208.
3   Russell, "The Value of Dangerous Sport," p. 2.
4   Simon, "Taking Risks," p. 181.
5   Ibid., pp. 181–2.
6   Jennifer Jordan, *Savage Summit: The True Stories of the First Five Women Who Climbed K2, the World's Most Feared Mountain* (New York: Harper Collins, 2005), p. ix.
7   Ibid.
8   Ed Viesturs, *No Shortcuts to the Top: Climbing the World's 14 Highest Peaks* (New York: Broadway Books, 2006), p. 219.
9   Jon Krakauer, *Into Thin Air: A Personal Account of the Mount Everest Disaster* (New York: Random House, 1997), p. 23.
10 Simon, "Taking Risks," p. 190.
11 Quoted in Mick Conefrey and Tim Jordan, *Mountain Men: A History of the Remarkable Climbers and Determined Eccentrics Who First Scaled the World's Most Famous Peaks* (Cambridge, MA: Da Capo Press, 2001), p. 259.
12 Quoted in Nicholas O'Connell, *Beyond Risk: Conversations with Climbers* (Seattle: Mountaineers Books, 1993), p. 61.
13 O'Connell, *Beyond Risk*, p. 11.
14 Adam Ewert, *Outdoor Adventure Pursuits: Foundations, Models, and Theories* (Columbus: Publishing Horizons, 1989), p. 57.
15 Krakauer, *Into Thin Air*, p. 241.
16 David Roberts, *On the Ridge Between Life and Death: A Climbing Life Reexamined* (New York: Simon and Schuster, 2005), p. 347.
17 Russell, "The Value of Dangerous Sport," p. 13.
18 Quoted in Conefrey and Jordan, *Mountain Men*, p. 257.
19 Quoted in Conefrey and Jordan, *Mountain Men*, p. 258.
20 Quoted in O'Connell, *Beyond Risk*, p. 31.
21 Quoted in O'Connell, *Beyond Risk*, p. 32.
22 Marshall Ulrich, "Transformation of an Adventure Runner," *Marathon and Beyond* 10 (2006): 36.

23 Michael Kodas, *High Crimes: The Fate of Everest in an Age of Greed* (New York: Hyperion, 2008), p. 157.
24 Heinrich Harrer, *The White Spider: The Classic Account of the Ascent of the Eiger*, trans. Hugh Merrick (New York: Jeremy P. Tarcher/Putnam, 1998), p. 21.
25 Viesturs, *No Shortcuts*, p. 322.

PHILIP A. EBERT AND SIMON ROBERTSON[1]

CHAPTER 7

MOUNTAINEERING AND THE VALUE OF SELF-SUFFICIENCY

Exceptional human achievement is not just one of the things we value most – it *is* valuable. The history of mountaineering is filled with great achievements – achievements that mark the triumph of the human spirit, the overcoming of challenges few are capable of meeting, the telling of incredible courage and skill. In short, mountaineering gives expression to deep human values – it *is* valuable. Nonetheless, some mountaineering achievements are more valuable – more impressive and admirable – than others. Consider, for example, the following three cases:

(a) In 1953, Hermann Buhl made the first ascent of Nanga Parbat (8,125 meters), the ninth highest mountain in the world and at the time only the third 8,000er to be ascended. Buhl set off from his expedition's high camp, expecting his companion to follow. Realizing he was not, Buhl continued alone with minimal equipment, hardly any food or water, and no supplementary oxygen. He reached the summit after 18 hours, having ascended 1,300 meters (in vertical height) of hitherto unexplored ground, soloing free with technical difficulties later confirmed to be around UIAA 6 – an exceptionally high standard at the time, even for those climbing at sea level with ropes and protection. On his descent, he endured a standing bivouac on a small exposed ledge at around 8,000 meters, eventually returning to high camp after a 41-hour *tour de force*.[2]

(b) Suppose, instead, that Buhl's companion, Otto Kempter, did join him and that together they climbed the same route Buhl climbed in (a): they ascend the same terrain, overcome the same technical difficulties, and so on.

(c) Imagine that Sherman, a rich ethics professor, buys into a large expedition to climb Everest by the standard South Col route. The expedition, led by well-qualified guides and supported by a team of porters, follows a preestablished course, making extensive use of fixed ropes, pre-stocked camps, and supplementary oxygen. Our aspiring ascensionist relies on his guides and porters not just to pave and climb the route but to ensure his safety on it. He eventually stands on Everest's summit (for a happy ending, let's assume he safely returns home).

Most of us would agree that (a) represents a more impressive and admirable mountaineering achievement than (b), and that both (a) and (b) are markedly superior to (c). Why do we think this – and why should we?

There are likely to be several factors relevant to our evaluations. Here it will be useful to distinguish two dimensions along which the value of a mountaineering achievement can be assessed. One concerns the nature of the route itself – its overall seriousness, as determined by its technical difficulties, boldness, length, remoteness, altitude, objective dangers, and so on. We could call these the "objective" features of the route.[3] Generally speaking, the more objectively serious a climb is, the greater the mountaineering achievement by those who succeed on it. The second dimension concerns not so much *what* is climbed but the *style* in which it is climbed – or *how* it is climbed. And here, we believe, a central feature that makes some climbs better than others is *self-sufficiency*. In fact, we think that self-sufficiency is a fundamental value of mountaineering itself – something that is both valuable in its own right and adds to the value of any given mountaineering endeavor.

In this essay we are going to explore and defend the following claim: *other things being equal, the more self-sufficiently a mountaineering objective is achieved, the better that achievement.* But what is self-sufficiency? Is it

  PHILIP A. EBERT AND SIMON ROBERTSON

always good? Is it a mark of every great mountaineering achievement? Is it something to which every mountaineer should aspire?

What is Self-Sufficiency?

We often speak of *people* – mountaineers, say – as being self-sufficient. But since self-sufficiency is something that is exhibited in people's *activities*, when we talk about self-sufficiency here we focus on what mountaineers do and how they do it.

It is common to distinguish different types of mountaineering, or different ways in which mountaineers pursue their objectives. We will take the following to represent three main contrasting styles:

- Alpine style vs. deploying siege tactics
- Climbing solo vs. climbing in a team
- Free climbing vs. aid climbing[4]

These are of course broad categories that admit more fine-grained distinctions. For example, a mountaineering team could comprise hundreds of members (climbers, doctors, Sherpas, porters) or just two people. Furthermore, a single mountaineering expedition might combine elements of each contrasting pair. Although Hermann Buhl climbed the final 1,300 meters of Nanga Parbat in alpine style, solo and free, the expedition up to then deployed siege tactics involving a team of mountaineers climbing both free and with aid. Likewise, a single mountaineer might deploy a mixture of free climbing and aid climbing on a single pitch. So there are various ways in which these different styles might be combined. Nonetheless, the first option in each contrast pair – alpine, solo, and free – represents what we commonly regard as the "purist" form of mountaineering. Purity and self-sufficiency are closely connected. Indeed, it is by pursuing one's mountaineering objectives self-sufficiently that one achieves purity of style; and the more self-sufficiently the objective is achieved, the purer the style of mountaineering. What, though, is it to climb self-sufficiently?

Our very rough answer is this: the self-sufficient mountaineer relies primarily on his own ability to move over the climbing medium (be it rock, snow, or ice – or, in Scotland, frozen turf); the clothing and equipment he uses is the bare minimum that anyone would need in order to make progress and to survive in the conditions he finds himself. Significantly, then, the more self-sufficiently a mountaineer pursues his mountaineering objectives, the more he relies only on himself – and, by implication, the less he uses, or relies on, additional resources. Inevitably, there are complications – depending on, for instance, what these "additional resources" include. For present purposes, though, some examples should suffice to clarify the basic idea: a team deploying siege tactics uses significantly more resources – fixed ropes and people, for instance – than climbing alpine style; an aided ascent uses pitons, ladders, and the like, that a free ascent does not; and, obviously, when climbing solo one neither involves nor relies upon people besides oneself. The more an ascent approximates the ideals of climbing alpine style, solo and free, the more self-sufficient and pure it is.

As a final part of our preliminary exposition of what self-sufficiency is, it is worth emphasizing a point already implicit – namely, that self-sufficiency comes in degrees: a climber can pursue and achieve his mountaineering objectives *more* or *less* self-sufficiently. Rarely is a significant mountaineering achievement maximally self-sufficient. (Indeed, there is an unsurprising correlation here: the objectively harder the mountaineering route, the less self-sufficiently it tends to be climbed.) Many mountaineering achievements combine a mixture of the above contrast pairs. It's therefore possible that a single mountaineer exhibits a high degree of self-sufficiency in one respect (by climbing solo, say) but a low degree of self-sufficiency in another respect (if he deploys extensive aid, say). Or an expedition might comprise many members supporting each other but rely on few fixed ropes or no aid. As a result, any assessment of how self-sufficiently a mountaineering objective is achieved can be a complex matter.

The Value of Self-Sufficiency

So our main claim is that, other things being equal, the more self-sufficiently a mountaineering objective is achieved, the better that achievement. For ease of presentation, let's call this self-sufficiency thesis (S). We are going to argue for (S) shortly. But we need to first make some preliminary points about (S) itself.

  PHILIP A. EBERT AND SIMON ROBERTSON

Note firstly that (S) makes an *evaluative* claim, since *better* is an evaluative notion. We can here understand "better" to imply any or all of the following: that one mountaineering achievement can be more impressive, or merit greater admiration, or represent a more worthwhile achievement, than another. Second, to say that one mountaineering achievement is better than another indicates that the better achievement is *good* in some sense, since "better" just means "more good" or "has more value." We claimed at the beginning of the essay that mountaineering is itself a valuable human activity. But there are also values "internal to" mountaineering – values by which we can compare the value of different mountaineering achievements and assess whether some achievements are better, *qua mountaineering* achievements, than others. (S) claims that self-sufficiency is one of these internal values.[5] Third, (S) implies not just that some mountaineering achievements are better than others, but that some are better than others *because* they are achieved more self-sufficiently.

The second and third points together imply that there is something good about achieving mountaineering objectives self-sufficiently. It adds to, or enhances, the overall quality of a mountaineering achievement because there is something good about climbing in a self-sufficient way. Let's mark this by saying that self-sufficiency is a *good-making* or *value-enhancing* feature of mountaineering. We now need to explain this.

It is important to emphasize that self-sufficiency is just one good among others. Many other things can contribute to the overall value of a mountaineering achievement, including what we earlier called those "objective features" of a route that determine its overall seriousness: technical difficulty, boldness, length, remoteness, altitude, and so on. Thus, even if self-sufficiency is a value-enhancing feature of mountaineering, it is only *one* feature that contributes to a mountaineering achievement's overall quality. Nonetheless, we shall see shortly that self-sufficiency is in fact a rather fundamental value. What, though, is it about self-sufficiency that is good? Why is it good?

The answer cannot be that climbing self-sufficiently is more likely to contribute to successfully meeting one's mountaineering objective. For climbing self-sufficiently generally makes the objective features of the route more difficult to overcome and so makes the outcome less certain. In addition, it often makes the route more dangerous for the climber. For the more self-sufficient a climber is, the less he can rely on the sorts of resources that would make his climb safer – others to belay him, fixed ropes to descend, aid to pull on, and so on. We might summarize this by saying that climbing in a self-sufficient style is more *committing*: there is typically less guarantee of success or indeed survival, with no easy way back to safety (sometimes the only way off the mountain, and hence the only means of survival, is a successful ascent of the mountain itself).

We think there are two things about self-sufficiency that make it good, both of which concern the *style* in which a mountaineering objective is achieved. One emerges from the previous point: the committing nature of climbing self-sufficiently makes it more impressive. For by minimizing the resources one uses to achieve one's mountaineering objective – thereby increasing the difficulties and dangers, while making success less certain – the greater the achievement when one succeeds. This is closely connected to another core value of mountaineering itself – *adventure*. Mountaineering is, by its very nature, an adventurous activity; this is part of its attraction and value. And since climbing in a self-sufficient style makes one's mountaineering activity more committing and adventurous, it expresses a purer and more valuable example of mountaineering itself.

The second respect in which self-sufficiency is good is this: let's assume that mountaineering is a valuable activity. It is partially constitutive of the very activity of mountaineering that you achieve your mountaineering objectives exercising your own abilities. For example, you would not be mountaineering (in any meaningful sense) if you are quite literally being hauled up an entire mountain by other people. Achieving your objectives by means of your own mountaineering abilities is exhibiting some degree of self-sufficiency. So it is partially constitutive of the very activity of mountaineering that a mountaineer achieves his objectives with some degree of self-sufficiency.[6] Therefore, if mountaineering is a valuable activity, and if part of its value comes from being done in good style (that is, self-sufficiently), self-sufficiency must be a good-making feature of mountaineering.

With this argument for the value of self-sufficiency in place, let's return to (S). In the previous section, we claimed that self-sufficiency comes in degrees: a mountaineering objective can be achieved more or less self-sufficiently. Central to (S) is the idea that the value of a mountaineering achievement can vary in proportion to the degree of self-sufficiency it exhibits. Indeed, if self-sufficiency is a good-making feature, it is also plausible to suppose that its presence adds to or enhances (that is, increases) the overall quality of a mountaineering achievement. For if it is (partially) constitutive of mountaineering that a mountaineer achieves

  PHILIP A. EBERT AND SIMON ROBERTSON

his objectives self-sufficiently, then (other things being equal) the more self-sufficiently a mountaineer achieves his objectives the better that achievement.

Note, though, that (S) claims: *other things being equal*, the more self-sufficiently a mountaineering objective is achieved, the better that achievement. What do we mean by "other things being equal"? We can explain it as follows. Recall from our opening example (a) that Hermann Buhl climbs Nanga Parbat alpine style, free and solo. In example (b) Kempter joins Buhl and they together climb the same route. So in both scenarios the climbers overcome the same objective features of the mountain. That is, they overcome the same technical difficulties, ascend the same terrain in comparable time, encounter similar dangers, and so on. We can thereby hold all these variables constant and say that, in scenarios (a) and (b), other things are indeed equal. The "other things being equal" clause in (S) thus implies that, when comparing the value of different mountaineering achievements, *were all factors pertaining to the route's objective seriousness the same*, then the more self-sufficiently the mountaineering objective is achieved, the better that achievement.

We now have the resources by which to explain why, in our opening examples, (a) marks a better ascent than (b), and why (a) and (b) are both better than (c). Part of the explanation for why Hermann's ascent of Nanga Parbat (example (a)) is better than Sherman's ascent of Everest (example (c)) lies in the fact that Hermann climbed in a far more self-sufficient way, since he climbed alpine style, solo and free. And since the more self-sufficiently a climber achieves his mountaineering objectives the better the achievement, Hermann's ascent marks a better mountaineering achievement. (This might be only part of the explanation, of course. Indeed, Hermann also surmounted an objectively more serious route than Sherman.)

Similarly, (a) represents a superior ascent to (b). We could suppose, for instance, that in scenario (b) the two climbers belay each other, pull on some pitons and fix ropes for the descent. Hence, Buhl's climb in scenario (a) displays a greater degree of self-sufficiency than he and Kempter display in (b). In that case, Buhl's more self-sufficient climb marks the greater mountaineering achievement. That is *not* to imply that climb (b) would not have been a great achievement – indeed, it could well have been. The point is simply that because (a) represents a more self-sufficient style of ascent, it marks an even better achievement.

That is our basic account. However, there are complications. We shall preempt a number of likely objections. Responding to them will serve to further clarify – and strengthen the case for – the self-sufficiency thesis itself.

Objections

First objection

Our argument for (S) implies not just that self-sufficiency *can be good* but that it is *always* good. Surely though, one might argue, a mountaineer can be *too* self-sufficient – whereby it is implausible to suppose that self-sufficiency is always good. For example, in December 2005 the extremely talented mountaineer Jean-Christophe Lafaille made a solo attempt to climb Makalu (8,462 meters) – hitherto unclimbed in winter. He established a number of camps, carrying all equipment alone above his advance base at 5,300 meters, without supplementary oxygen and with no other climbers around for support or rescue. On January 27, 2006, he set off 1,000 meters below the summit for the final push. He was never heard of again. Some have suggested that Lafaille's attempt was *foolhardy*.[7] More generally, it is easy to imagine all sorts of foolhardy mountaineering endeavors, where people choose to climb as self-sufficiently as possible but whose chosen climb outstrips their abilities, and who die as a result. So, the objection goes, self-sufficiency is not always good.

An initial point to note in response is that (S) concerns the value of mountaineering *achievements*. So if the foolhardy climber does not achieve his objective to any significant degree, the objection loses force. The more interesting objection therefore concerns someone who, like Lafaille, does fulfill his objective to some relevant degree – after all, Lafaille got very close to the top – but who dies partly because of pursuing it self-sufficiently.

There are various replies we could make here. Our preferred response is to say that self-sufficiency is always good – and to add that, although the self-sufficiency displayed by a foolhardy climber is *good to some degree in virtue of being self-sufficient*, it may also be *bad to some degree by being foolhardy*. Thus, even if a mountaineer pursues his objective self-sufficiently, the value of his doing so may be *outweighed* by the disvalue of his foolhardiness. Nonetheless, self-sufficiency remains a good. Thus, in Lafaille's case, even if (as some have urged) what he did was foolhardy,

   PHILIP A. EBERT AND SIMON ROBERTSON

what he achieved self-sufficiently was indeed impressive and admirable. (We here leave open whether he was foolhardy or just unlucky.)

Second objection

(S) involves an "other things being equal" clause. When comparing cases like examples (a) and (b), that may be fine. However, how might we compare the respective value of ascents like (a) with the following?

(d) In 1990, a twenty-strong Soviet team made the first (verified) ascent of the "last great Himalayan problem," Lhotse's South Face. It deployed siege tactics with six camps. Nonetheless, it was the objectively hardest route then climbed in the Himalayas.

It may seem that our account faces an undesirable dilemma. On the one hand, (S) might appear to imply that, because Buhl's ascent in (a) was achieved more self-sufficiently than the Soviets' ascent in (d), it must be better than the hardest Himalayan climb ever achieved. But that seems highly questionable. On the other hand, and to avoid that worry, we seem forced to concede that (S) gives us no way to compare the values of climbs like (a) and (d) – or indeed the value of *any* climbs in which other things are *not* equal. If that's the case, self-sufficiency cannot be as fundamental a value as we are claiming.

However, this objection rests on a misunderstanding of (S) – in particular, the "other things being equal" clause. (S) is not intended to provide a *comprehensive* model by which to establish the *overall* value of a mountaineering achievement (since there are many values besides self-sufficiency relevant to an overall assessment); it claims only that self-sufficiency adds to the overall value of any mountaineering achievement. Thus (S) implies that, were Lhotse's South Face climbed more self-sufficiently, that would have marked an even better achievement. Hence, although we accept the second horn of the supposed dilemma, we do not regard this as an objection to (S). For given that self-sufficiency is only one mountaineering value, (S) was never intended to supply a comprehensive model by which to tally up all good-making features of mountaineering achievements and to thereby deliver some conclusion about their overall value. In that respect, (S) is quite a modest thesis. This raises a further issue, though: if self-sufficiency is just one mountaineering value, in what sense is it fundamental? Our answer: by climbing self-sufficiently, one actually makes the mountaineering objective more serious and the objective features of a route more difficult to overcome. For by climbing more self-sufficiently a climber increases the "subjective difficulty" of the objective features. And since the overall value of a mountaineering achievement depends on the difficulties overcome, by overcoming those difficulties self-sufficiently the resulting achievement is even better. Self-sufficiency thereby functions like a catalyst for other mountaineering values: it enables them to have the value they do and thereby increases the overall value of the achievement.

Third objection

When asked who reached the summit of Everest first, Hillary and Tenzing have always insisted that they climbed it together and that there is therefore little point to that question – after all, *they* did. Our account, however, seems to imply that a team cannot climb self-sufficiently. Even worse, we are leaving out an especially significant aspect of the mountaineering experience – the valuable experiences that come from being part of a team.

Again, though, this misconstrues our main claim. All we are committed to is that, if Hillary or Tenzing had instead climbed Mount Everest alone, that would have been an even better mountaineering achievement. But we are not denying that teamwork can be an important part of a valuable mountaineering experience – indeed, it can be a very rewarding part of it. Nor have we ruled out that a team can climb with a high degree of self-sufficiency. For one thing, as mentioned earlier, it is not strictly the individual mountaineer who is self-sufficient; rather, self-sufficiency is a feature of the way the mountaineer engages in his mountaineering activities. Thus, if a team engages in the activity of mountaineering in a self-sufficient manner (by climbing alpine style or free, say) one can speak of a self-sufficient team. It might be less self-sufficient than a solo (alpine style and free) ascent. But self-sufficiency comes in degrees; and mountaineering teams can exhibit it to some (often quite a high) degree.

Fourth objection

It might be claimed that our account implies the following counterintuitive conclusion: that when the competent yet blind climber Erik Weihenmayer summited Mount Everest in 2001, because he relied more heavily on guides than fully sighted guided clients might, his achievement was *less* impressive than their's.

  PHILIP A. EBERT AND SIMON ROBERTSON

Here it is again important to see the force of our "other things being equal" clause. (S) does not provide a model by which to compare the value of Weihenmayer's ascent against that of a full-sighted person – since then other things are *not* equal. But if another blind climber summits Mount Everest in better (or worse) style, then that achievement would count as better (or worse) in virtue of being more (or less) self-sufficient. Moreover, our thesis is compatible with valuing Weihenmayer's achievement along dimensions other than self-sufficiency. Indeed, the subjective difficulties facing a blind climber in surmounting the route's objective features are significantly higher than those facing a fully sighted climber. Thus, Weihenmayer's ascent marks a rather impressive and significant achievement.

Fifth objection

Our account seems to suggest that *every* mountaineer *should* climb *maximally* self-sufficiently. But surely that's implausible – or worse: a dogmatic, even irresponsible, imperative encouraging grave foolhardiness.

Our response is a resounding *no*. First, (S) makes an *evaluative* claim; that is, a claim about the *value* of mountaineering achievements. It is not a *normative* claim about what people *should* do. Second, even if self-sufficiency (as a valuable feature of mountaineering) is *relevant* to how one should try to mountaineer, it doesn't follow from this that every mountaineer should climb maximally self-sufficiently in all circumstances. How self-sufficiently a mountaineer *should* climb depends on many factors, including his abilities and the seriousness of the obstacles facing him. If, when on a climb, a mountaineer is faced with either using aid or dying from a fall, nothing in our account requires him to refrain from using aid. There are, after all, many factors relevant to how one should act in any given circumstance; even if self-sufficiency is one of them, it is not necessarily decisive or overriding.

Sixth objection

Given the response to the last objection, it might seem that our thesis provides little or no basis for assessing how people should go about mountaineering. So what's the point in drawing attention to all these claims about the supposed value of self-sufficiency?

It is true that (S), as stated, is an evaluative thesis which does not by itself tell us what mountaineers should do or supply a decision procedure for how to go about mountaineering. Nonetheless, we have argued that self-sufficiency represents an *ideal* constitutive of the very activity of mountaineering. This gives our account some normative traction. For given that mountaineering objectives achieved self-sufficiently generally mark better mountaineering achievements, and given that the ideals constitutive of an activity (like mountaineering) are things to which those who engage in the activity should aspire, it follows that mountaineers should at least aspire to climb self-sufficiently. Or to put things another way, in order to make the best style of ascent you can, you need to (and in that sense should) climb as self-sufficiently as you can.[8]

Concluding Remarks

We have argued that self-sufficiency is a valuable feature of mountaineering and that it always adds to the value of a mountaineering achievement. We have also suggested that self-sufficiency underwrites the value of many other aspects of mountaineering; in that respect, it is a rather fundamental value. More provocatively, we have even suggested that self-sufficiency is (partially) constitutive of the very activity (not just the value) of mountaineering. This has the following implication. Consider someone who calls himself a "mountaineer" but who relies on others, perhaps guides, to short-rope him up significant stretches of a mountain, thereby exhibiting no real mountaineering ability. According to the view we've presented, this "mountaineer" does not actually engage in the activity of *mountaineering* – he is not, after all, even minimally self-sufficient. Hence, whatever he achieves in the mountains does not count as a *mountaineering* achievement. It might well be a valuable human achievement in some other respect. But this way of summiting a mountain is no more a *mountaineering* achievement – and hence of no more value *as* a mountaineering achievement – than taking the gondola (or helicopter) to the summit.[9]

NOTES

1 This essay is dedicated to the memory of Alan Matheson (1959–2002), climber and friend. We miss you Al.
2 See Buhl's über-classic *Nanga Parbat Pilgrimage* (London: Baton Wicks, 1998). Buhl actually used the drug Pervitin – a.k.a. crystal meth – in his

ascent (it was given to him by the expedition doctor – such drug use was common in mountaineering then). Whether it is easier to onsight-solo grade 6 at 8,000 meters high on meth or sober is not something we are in a position to evaluate.

3   This is not to deny that subjective differences between people can affect how they experience such features. For example, one climber might find a technical section harder than another climber. Even so, what they experience differently are objective features of the route itself.

4   Ascents undertaken with "siege tactics" deploy (a more or less continuous series of) fixed ropes linking a number of camps where food and equipment are stocked. They typically rely on large teams, working in a pyramid system with climbing partnerships leapfrogging one another and returning to lower camps once each successively higher camp is established. Alpine style climbing, in contrast, involves the ascentionists (usually a small team) carrying all their own gear, ascending (and hopefully descending) the route in a single push. Himalayan ascents have traditionally deployed extensive sieging, though alpine techniques are now increasingly applied to the Greater Ranges. We note the following assessment of siege mountaineering: "This is the dinosaur of the climbing game: big and old fashioned, it has long been rumoured to be dying out. . . . However, it is still around and probably will remain so while national interest and media coverage are required to sponsor expeditions." Allen Fyffe and Iain Peter, *The Handbook of Climbing* (London: Pelham Books, 1997), p.294. See the glossary for descriptions of the other styles.

5   The claim is of course restricted to mountaineering contexts. We are not saying that self-sufficiency is desirable in all non-mountaineering contexts. One author thinks that "solo, non-aided" sexual relationships provide good evidence to the contrary; the other author isn't so sure.

6   This may be quite a provocative thesis. Most of what we say is compatible with a more modest claim: that it is partially constitutive of mountaineering *well* that a mountaineer achieves his objectives self-sufficiently. But we'll stick to the provocative thesis – see the final section for some further implications.

7   See Andy Kirkpatrick's online assessment at www.andy-kirkpatrick.com/stories/view/lafaille/.

8   If self-sufficiency represents a mountaineering ideal, this is something that funding bodies should take into account when deciding which expeditions to fund – or at least something that those funding bodies that value the highest forms of mountaineering achievement should take into account. In practice, though, many bodies simply sponsor those expeditions they believe will give them the most media coverage.

9   We would like to thank the audience of a research lunch seminar in the Department of Philosophy in Stirling for their comments on an earlier version of this essay.

CHAPTER 8

IT AIN'T FAST FOOD

An Authentic Climbing Experience

I'll never forget the first real climbing fall that I witnessed. I was 13, it was a crisp, sunny day in North Yorkshire, and the fall seemed endless in my mind. In reality it was probably about 7 meters – still no small fall – and what was most unnerving was the matter-of-fact acceptance of it by the surrounding climbers. There were pats on the back, laughing, and animated discussion of what had gone wrong, even though Martin – the climber and a supervisor of our group – was still shaking so much he couldn't roll his own cigarette.

Replaying the fall in my head, it was obvious that Martin had simply bitten off more than he could chew and had found himself in a situation where the difficulty of the climb outstripped his abilities. It was also obvious that Martin could have chosen to climb this particular rock face in such a way as to avoid any possibility of a serious fall. A rope could have been set up from the top of the climb, so that Martin's fall would have simply resulted in him resting his weight on the rope. Surely, this would have been a safer way of climbing the route! Instead, Martin had risked life and limb by placing protection into the natural features of the wall as he went, only to see most of it rip out as he fell until the final tiny piece, twisting under the strain, held his weight as his feet skimmed the ground.

While all of this was exciting to witness, it made little sense. I was unaware of the unwritten codes and rules of climbing that directed Martin's decision to attempt the climb in the manner that he did. It certainly wouldn't have mattered to me back then just how I got to the top of a climb, as long as I got there. After all, what else is climbing if not going from the bottom of a rock face to the top?

I came to learn that just as there are many different routes on a single rock face (the route that Martin was trying to climb was rather aptly named Resurrection), there are many different ways to climb them: from the bottom up placing protection as you go; from the bottom clipping the rope into pre-placed bolts on the wall; with or without extensive top-rope practice beforehand; with or without advice on the individual moves of a climb from someone who has climbed it before; with or without a rope at all; and so forth. I also came to learn that just how a climb is done is incredibly important to climbers.

Martin would not have attempted Resurrection any other way. And I'm sure that if I'd suggested that, for the sake of his own safety, he just top-rope the route, he would have referred to his particular brand of climbing rules as explanation. Most probably, he would have said some-thing along the lines of "why don't you just tell me to go get a ladder and use that! There's no challenge in top roping, lad. It's cheating, just like using a ladder." While this may seem a strange thing to say, it's clear that by adhering to certain rules or standards in his climbing Martin was hoping to preserve a certain challenge, and thereby an accompanying sense of personal achievement in facing that challenge. He was, in essence, playing a kind of game with clearly codified rules. Breaking the rules or cheating – climbing *unethically* – would rob the game of any value for Martin.

Now, while many climbers may find the rules of Martin's particular game unpalatable or selfish – after all, they involve a very large potential for serious bodily harm to occur – they would accept that Martin was involved in the same sort of game as them. No matter how different their standards, they would assume that there is enough shared ground to make the difference between their style of climbing and Martin's one of degree and not one of kind.

This is really the great advantage of looking at the various styles of climbing as a species of related climbing games: their underlying unity as a sport, which otherwise might have been missed, becomes more obvi-ous. For example, if we compare bouldering with traditional climbing, on the face of it they might look like discrete activities. In bouldering, very short sections of rock, not very high from the ground, are climbed, and the use of ropes, harnesses, and belayers are not permitted. In trad climbing, the opposite is true. The terrain, equipment, required skills, and rules are all different, and both activities appear quite distinct. However, when we realize that the rules of bouldering are in place in order to preserve the same kind of challenge and satisfaction in climbing small-scale, accessible pieces of rock as is found in climbing the larger crags and cliffs of trad climbing, then we can appreciate the similarity bouldering has with trad climbing. According to this view, then, the various rules and standards of the different styles of climbing, from big-wall and expedition climbing through to sport climbing and deep-water soloing, have evolved to equalize or at least provide a minimum level to the challenge and sense of personal satisfaction involved in each style.[1]

So what does this have to do with philosophy? Well, one philosopher who had a great interest in our relation to the natural world and who, I'm sure, would have been fascinated by the decision of many climbers like Martin to risk injury or death in the pursuit of scaling a piece of rock ethically is G. W. F. Hegel (1770–1831). Hegel was one of the main figures in the flourishing of German Romanticism in the nineteenth century that so influenced the famous poet Samuel Taylor Coleridge, who, incidentally, was responsible for one of the earliest recorded mountain routes on UK rock – Broad Stand (1802) in the Lake District. Like many of his contemporaries, Hegel was concerned with the different fundamental ways we conceive of the world and our relation to it (what in philosophical terminology would be called our underlying metaphysical commitments). In his most famous work, *Phenomenology of Spirit*,[2] Hegel argues that our interactions with and experience of the world are always based on preconceptions about the fundamental nature of ourselves as subjects and the world we inhabit. These preconceptions are basic ways of thinking about the world and our role in it that we take as certainties; they are unquestioned and are employed instinctively without an explicit awareness of their role in providing our experience. For example, the notion that I apprehend the world directly via my senses without applying concepts to it is one such way of thinking. If this were true, then gaining knowledge of the world would be wholly passive. I would be like a sponge – simply soaking up information from the world through my senses of vision, hearing, etc. Of course, there have been (and, I'm sure, still are) people who hold to this view. One of Hegel's aims in the *Phenomenology* is to show that such unquestioned preconceptions lead to difficulties and problems in our experience of the world. And, if we don't question and modify those preconceptions accordingly, then we will be unable to solve these problems. Where Hegel can be of help to us here is in bringing out some of the underlying preconceptions that may be involved in our experience of different climbing games.

It is these underlying preconceptions and their relation to our experience of different climbing games, along with their different rules and standards, that form the basis for this essay. I intend to suggest that the challenge and satisfaction involved in the various climbing games is *not always of the same kind.* That is to say, I think that some climbing games preserve and offer a more authentic experience than others. Hegel's philosophy can help illuminate what I mean by saying this, and we'll turn to him in the final section of this essay. First, by way of preparation, I'll briefly compare the rules and standards of two common but broad styles of climbing: traditional (trad) and sport climbing.

It Ain't Fast Food!

The relation between sport and trad climbing is often presented by using a well-worn analogy with food.[3] In a recent, very popular climbing film that focuses on onsighting – the attempt to climb routes without any prior information, knowledge, or practice on the route – a famously forthright and influential UK trad climber makes the following comment:

> I've never seen climbing as a sport – it's anathema to me, that. Climbing isn't a sport, it's a way of life . . . it ain't fast food! (John Redhead)

While John is here, for the most part, referring to climbing in general, his comment that "it ain't fast food" is made in reference to trad climbing and trad onsight attempts. It's obvious that John sees a lot more being involved in this kind of climbing than the simple playing and practicing of a game, and that it is this style of climbing that, for him, truly represents what climbing is. This opinion may appear to be quite hard line, but it nicely illustrates a common use of the food analogy, which is to suggest that trad climbing is not akin to fast food, unlike sport climbing, and that it in some way offers a more profound, worthwhile, and authentic experience. Surprisingly, perhaps, this view doesn't frequently meet with much resistance from climbers who practice sport climbing.

After all, the rules and standards of sport climbing do ensure that it embodies the virtues of fast food: speed and affordability. The drilling of bolts into the rock for protection is permitted and so sport climbing involves less equipment and has low requirements for knowing how to place pro or build anchors. This generally allows a lot more climbing to be done in less time. Instant gratification – just like a ready meal! Also, like fast food, sport climbing is relatively cheap and within most everyone's budget: it doesn't involve buying the expensive and specialized protection used in trad climbing, which may only be useful for a handful of routes. Sport climbing also permits the repeated practice of moves on top rope, which combined with the fact that more climbing can be done in the same amount of time, results in sport climbing affording more opportunity for improvement in aspects such as strength and flexibility. In these respects it is quite satisfying to many climbers.

The obvious flip side of this analogy is that trad climbing is akin to slow-cooked haute cuisine. Here the rules and standards ensure that trad climbing takes time and involves the equivalent of expensive, arcane ingredients. These rules usually prohibit the use of any protective aid other than removable devices that can be carried and placed by hand by the climber while climbing (for example, nuts and cams). Trad rules also usually involve a climb being established from the ground up, without prior practice and with limited or no prior inspection. This can involve a climber spending hours or days on a single route, climbing up and down trying to unlock the sequence of moves and protection without the safety of a top rope. Obviously, then, trad climbing may prove to be an acquired taste. But that said, to its supporters it tastes amazing!

Of course, most people eat both kinds of food, just as most climbers indulge in both styles of climbing, and the analogy seems to work quite well – ironically, the French tend to champion fast-food climbing while climbers in the UK and US are slow-food connoisseurs. What's most useful about this analogy, though, is that it raises questions about the satisfaction or sense of personal achievement involved in both styles of climbing. Admittedly, I am often just as satisfied with a greasy burger as I am with a 3-star Michelin carpaccio (particularly after a hard day of climbing!). But there is a potential for a deeper level of satisfaction with the carpaccio that is arguably not present with the burger. This is reflected in the comparison of the two climbing games. In sport climbing, the satisfaction comes from the simple act of climbing to the top of a technically challenging route while adhering to the rules. The rock itself is here somewhat secondary in the experience – a means to an end. In trad climbing the satisfaction initially seems to be of the same kind, namely, that of succeeding in climbing to the top of a technically challenging route within the rules. But on closer inspection the focus of the experience in playing the trad game appears to be radically different from that in the sport game. The preparation, tailored to a particular climb and to a particular rock type, is of key importance in trad climbing. And the danger that one encounters is more directly correlated to the natural features of that piece of rock. In trad climbing, the whole process in relation to a specific section of rock adds a further, deeper layer to the satisfaction – the rock becomes an end in itself.

So does this extra layer imply that the trad game is fundamentally different from the sport game? Isn't eating just eating (or climbing just climbing)? And does this make the trad game somehow richer or more authentic? I think that it does, but to understand why we need to leave the food analogy behind and see precisely what this extra layer cashes out to in terms of our experience. This is where Hegel can help.

We Are What We Eat

If we recall, one of Hegel's basic aims in the *Phenomenology* is to expose and attack the frequently unquestioned preconceptions that we possess regarding the fundamental nature of the world and our relation to it. One such preconception is that what is fundamentally real and enduring is the self. According to this preconception, the world is essentially secondary – it is just what the self makes of it with its different powers (mental and physical). Encountering the world, then, will not be dissimilar, in a certain sense, to looking in a mirror. When I look in a mirror my presence produces an image which I recognize as an image of myself. The image is temporary and secondary; it relies on my existence in order to persist and I have power over it. If I wave my hand, the image does the same. If I jump up and down the image also jumps up and down. Similarly, when I experience the world, it appears to me according to the way I categorize it, and I can physically manipulate the objects and things I encounter.

But this alone won't secure the truth of the preconception – that I am what is fundamentally real. In a mirror, the image still has an existence independent from myself in the mirrored surface. I could only truly demonstrate my power and primacy over the image by completely overcoming its independence. I might easily do this by destroying the mirror, but then I destroy the image as well and along with it any sense of the power and primacy of the self. Similarly, to truly demonstrate my power and primacy over the world I would need to completely remove any independence from myself that a given object may posses, and by using the world in this way – by physically consuming, exhausting, or destroying an object – I would destroy any sense of power or primacy over the world.

The problem this leads to is essentially a feeling and sense of alienation. If I attempt to demonstrate my power and primacy by effectively destroying the objects I encounter in the world, then I equally destroy that by which I was securing and demonstrating this power and primacy. Once one object is done away with, I'll have to find another one to destroy, and I am quickly led into an empty regress. The certainty and reality of the self that is to be gained in this way is always conditioned by the object to be destroyed, and the world in its independence will always seem separate and alien.

The solution to this regress, says Hegel, comes in the form of a specific type of recognition. If I can learn to see *myself* in the world while *leaving the independence of the world intact*, then my self-certainty will be objectively present in the world, and the world will no longer seem alien. Hegel famously shows how such recognition comes about, and just what it involves, through a rudimentary social relation in which one person is subordinated to another – that of a master and slave. This "master and slave" passage of the *Phenomenology* is justly famous and has had a massive influence on several intellectual movements of the nineteenth and twentieth centuries, including both Marxism and existentialism in their conception of selfhood.[4]

What we see is that the experience of the slave provides the solution to the regress, for it's this experience and not that of the master that allows the preconceived self-certainty to be redressed, and a more balanced view of the self in relation to the world to be realized. But before we look at the slave's experience, I should note that while Hegel talks about a social relation between individuals in the master and slave passage,[5] many of the aspects of this relation, along with the lessons to be learned, apply themselves quite straightforwardly to the different experiences involved in the trad and sport climbing games.

When he looks at the experience of the slave, Hegel identifies three key elements that are required for the solution and new outlook. The first is an acute sense and feeling of fear in which the transitory nature of life is reinforced. In submitting to the master and in working for him, the slave is no longer wholly in control of his natural existence. (This feeling is obviously not available to the master who has submitted to no one.) The second element is the setting aside or subordination of desires and will. The slave is forced to modify and set aside his own will and desires in the

  BEN LEVEY

service of the master; the fear he experiences compels him to do so. He must simply do the master's bidding for fear of death, and, consequently, he is freed from enslavement by his own will and desires, and he is able to put them aside. The third element is that of working on the world while accepting and respecting its independence. The slave does not just consume or destroy things, rather he must work on things according to the will of the master, and he must leave those things as independent existences. After all, those things are for the master's enjoyment only. In working on things in this way, the slave comes to identify with these things. He *too* is an independent existence, subject to the will of another, *just like the very objects he works on*. In this way, the slave comes to recognize "in the independent being [of the object] its *own* independence" and "becomes conscious of what he truly is."[6]

So, through his fear, work, and relinquishing of desires, the slave learns that he's not essentially primary or independent from the world, but instead is essentially *the same as it*. Most importantly, this sense of identity with the world has come about while leaving the things of the world in tact – the independence of the world no longer needs to be overcome in order to secure the slave's certainty and reality of self. If we return to the earlier analogy of looking in a mirror, we'll recall that the problem was that the reflected image had its own independent existence in the mirror, and the mirror needed to be destroyed in order for the person looking into the mirror to secure his sense of certainty and primacy over the image. We can now see that, in terms of this analogy, the slave has identified with the mirror that's casting the reflection – both the reflected image and mirror are the slave, and so the mirror no longer needs to be destroyed to ensure the slave's self-certainty. The poor master, on the other hand, is simply left staring at his reflection, the independence of which is still to be overcome. That is, the master may gain some self-certainty by using the slave as an extension of his will, but he still cannot identify with the world or with the slave as part of the world.

If we compare the three elements of the master and slave relationship to the trad and sport climbing games, we can see that in choosing to climb in the way that he did that day – in following his trad rules – Martin was choosing an experience akin to that of Hegel's slave! Obviously, Martin's experience on Resurrection involved a fair amount of danger – in terms of the earlier food analogy we might say that puffer fish was on the menu! To be more precise, this experience involved Martin knowingly risking his very existence. And I'm sure that while he was quivering above the marginal protection on the route, pleading with the rock to reveal a place to put more pro, Martin felt the same kind of fear as the slave. Martin also experienced the frustration of his desires that day. He obviously had to set aside his desire to climb Resurrection cleanly, and more immediately his desire to place more protection was frustrated by the lack of natural features such as cracks and pockets on that stretch of rock. Generally, in trad climbing, the desire to safely climb any particular line is usually frustrated or dictated to by the naturally occurring features of the rock and the objective danger that they present. This is precisely where the work came in for Martin. In accordance with the rules of the climbing game he chose to play, Martin couldn't work on the route by rehearsing the moves on the safety of a top rope, and the rock itself has to be left in its original, independent, and unaltered state. To climb Resurrection, Martin could only get on the route above the marginal protection, in the grip of fear, and work there to find a way to reach the top.

It appears, then, that strict trad standards like Martin's will ensure an experience akin to that of Hegel's slave and, equally, involve the kind of self-realization and identification with the world inherent in that experience. It is this that makes trad climbing authentic – it provides this kind of personal growth and self-realization, as well as personal satisfaction. From this perspective, John Redhead's assertion that trad climbing is a way of life and not a sport no longer appears as hardheaded and dramatic as it may have done so earlier. But if the kind of challenge trad rules are aimed at preserving involves this experience of self-realization, what about sport climbing?

Well, sport climbing certainly involves fear – finding yourself 30 meters off the ground and about to fall onto a small metal bolt glued into the rock by persons unknown is never a worry-free experience. However, this fear is rarely as visceral and consuming as it is in trad climbing. By bolting a route much of the objective danger can be lessened – bolts are in general safer than the forms of protection used in trad climbing – and, more importantly, as the rock is altered from its natural state, the natural features of the rock no longer dictate the possible lines for climbing. Working on such a route can occur relatively free of fear; we can rehearse the moves on top rope as much as we like before attempting the climb in one push. In sport climbing it seems that the independence of the rock is subordinated to the desire to climb it safely by a line of our choosing, and our experience in this case seems fundamentally closer to that of Hegel's master – where the independence is to be overcome – rather than that of the slave – where it is identified with. Accordingly, we make do with the limited satisfaction of simply having played the game ethically.

For Hegel, we may experience both roles, master and slave, just as we might eat all kinds of cuisine. But both roles are *not*, at base, the same. We'll recall that one of Hegel's aims in the *Phenomenology* is to highlight the difficulties and problems that arise from deeply held, unquestioned presuppositions regarding the nature of the world and our relation to it. In the case of the certainty and primacy of our own selves, it's the key elements involved in the experience of the slave that allow and lead to a solution to the difficulty that arises by providing a more accurate view of the nature of the self and its relation to the world. These elements are also present in trad climbing, and we might say that the trad climbing game involves an instinctive questioning and redressing of a deeply held presupposition as part and parcel of its rules, while the sport climbing game does not.

Of course, I have here limited my discussion to only two climbing games, but this is more for reasons of brevity than for any concern that the master/slave distinction couldn't be applied to other climbing games. It may well be the case that other climbing games (say, alpine and expedition climbing) also offer the authentic experience of the slave, while others still are limited to that of the master. I will leave this for you, the reader, to consider.

In reality, it is the case that most climbers play many kinds of climbing games, and we may all enjoy the limited satisfaction of exerting our will on the world and playing the role of master from time to time, though it may well lead us to crave the insight and self-realization involved in the experience of the slave. But whatever climbing games we play, we should be wary of the assumption that these games are fundamentally of the same nature, and that our activity in climbing ethically (that is, in accordance with the rules) provides the same kind of challenge and satisfaction. If there's one thing that Hegel can teach us here, it's that this is not the case.

NOTES

1 The classical statement of this view is Lito Tejada-Flores' "Games Climbers Play" which was first published in *Ascent* in 1967 and can be found in *The Games Climbers Play*, ed. K. Wilson (London: Diadem Books, 1978), pp. 19–27. Tejada-Flores later revised his view slightly in "Beyond Climbing Games: Alpinism as Humanism" in *Summit* (Fall, 1990).
2 G. W. F. Hegel, *Phenomenology of Spirit*, trans. A. V. Miller (Oxford: Oxford University Press, 1977). All quotations from this text will be cited using the abbreviation PS followed by the relevant page and paragraph number.

3 For a good example of how this kind of analogy is typically employed in the climbing press, see Sarah Flint, "How Do You Like It? Fast or Slow?" available online at www.ukclimbing.com/articles/page.php?id=2177.

4 For useful introductions to Hegel's thought in the *Phenomenology* and the influence that the master/slave section had on later thought, see R. Stern, *Hegel and the Phenomenology of Spirit* (London: Routledge, 2002) and Frederick C. Beiser, *Hegel* (New York: Routledge, 2005).

5 This is an aspect of the standard interpretation of the master/slave section. However, there are a number of interpretations by famous thinkers that eschew this standard approach for a more metaphorical reading. For example, see J. McDowell, "The Apperceptive I and the Empirical Self: Towards a Heterodox Reading of 'Lordship & Bondage' in Hegel's Phenomenology," *Bulletin of the Hegel Society of Great Britain* 47 (2003): 1–16.

6 PS 118, para. 195.

CHAPTER 9

ZEN AND THE ART OF CLIMBING

The only Zen you can find on the tops of mountains is the Zen you bring up there.

Robert M. Pirsig

Illustration: Ordinary Mind in Eldorado Canyon

Every few minutes, when you feel secure enough to shift your concentration away from the crack you've been ascending for the last hour or so, you turn to face the vast expanse before and below you. From this height the robust creek you traversed earlier is only faintly visible, emerging periodically between the gaps in tree cover. The canyon walls give way to gentle hills then plains – intermittent patches of vegetation and signs of civilization. It's a perfect day. There is no place you'd rather be than right here, right now – climbing. Discrete thoughts fade away, leaving you with a pervasive feeling of spaciousness and wonder. Ah! everything comes into perspective.

At some point a breeze comes along and gently reminds you that you are several hundred feet off the ground. You are not at the summit and yet you feel so *alive*. With a heightened sense of focus, you lock in on the next hold and continue your climb.

Introduction

Within this introductory illustration of a rather typical rock climbing experience is a glimpse at the essence of Zen – the experience of living fully, freely, and naturally in the world. This way of being – with a deep awareness of existence – is often what lures people to climb in the first place. Zen, like a summit view, is inherently pleasing, for it reminds us of the splendor of nature beyond – as well as within – ourselves. It can be argued that both climbing and Zen awaken us to the wonders of life by helping us find the extraordinary in the ordinary. If nothing else, both disciplines allow us to discover, manifest, and even lose ourselves in the process of *living* as we seek the summit.

More a "way of liberation" than an intellectual construction, to borrow Alan Watt's phrase, Zen emphasizes above all else experiential wisdom, or *prajna*. Curiously, Zen is both one of the most compelling concepts in Eastern philosophy and one of the most confounding for Western philosophers. The fact that Zen is often referred to as "ordinary mind" but is portrayed as extraordinary, only adds to the confusion and frustration many Westerners feel as they seek to understand Zen. Still, one thing is clear: Zen permeates climbing. From the trail to the summit, from bouldering to free soloing, and from the beginner to the expert, Zen is a palpable reality for climbers and as such deserves thorough philosophical inquiry.

The Route Itself

This essay will make the case that climbing embodies the principles and spirit of Zen. Just as others have written about Zen in the art of motorcycle maintenance, archery, and even playing guitar, I will articulate how Zen manifests in the art of climbing. I am quick to point out that I believe Zen experienced through climbing is not wholly different from – much less superior to – Zen experienced through, say, surfing. There is more than one way to access Zen and climbing is but one path towards that "summit." The following pages will seek to demystify Zen and illuminate some of its most poignant philosophical truths and insights. Special attention will be given to the parallels between Zen training and climbing. The reader will see that one does not have to be a Buddhist, philosopher, or professional climber in order to understand, appreciate, and

ultimately experience Zen through climbing. In the *zendo*, or meditation hall, of the great outdoors, where the beginner and expert climber practice in the same space, Zen is open to and attainable by all.

But First, the Origin of Zen

Zen has its roots in a discourse generally called the "Flower Sermon" given by the Buddha Shakyamuni atop Vulture Peak somewhere in modern-day India. During a gathering of his disciples – in which the Buddha was silent for a long time – he simply held a single lotus flower for all to see in order to make a point. No one understood except for Mahakashyapa, who smiled, *realizing* the Buddha's silent teaching. The Buddha acknowledged his disciple's natural reaction and proclaimed to the group that Mahakashyapa alone had received his transmission. While it is difficult to define exactly *what* was transmitted between teacher and student, it is viewed that Mahakashyapa's authentic response – his smile – showed that he experienced *satori*, or sudden enlightenment. Perhaps he saw in that one moment the eternal beauty and mystery of existence.

What is Zen?

Bodhidharma, who is considered to be the founder of Zen and brought Zen to China from India, told us that "Zen is: a special transmission separate from the scriptures; direct pointing at one's mind, seeing one's nature, becoming a Buddha."[1] This definition is helpful in light of the elusiveness of the Flower Sermon, but more articulation is needed. The word *Zen* is a Japanese translation of the Chinese word *ch'an*, which in turn is a Chinese translation of the Sanskrit *dhyana*, referring to "a state of meditative absorption in which all dualistic distinctions disappear leaving the realization of the fundamental unity of all things."[2] This should resonate with climbers who speak of "being in the zone" and "being in the flow," both of which are synonymous with Zen or "meditative absorption" in my view. When one is in this frame of mind – fully aware, deeply in tune with oneself and one's surroundings – one can see the essence of things, which in turn is liberating. It can be difficult to put realizations into words. Sometimes all one can do is smile, like Mahakashyapa.

Zen and the limits of language

Like a great climb, Zen can be described but words fall short of the actual experience. The inadequacy of words for articulating the reality of direct experience – and Zen itself – is wonderfully conveyed by the Zen patriarch Huineng (638–713), who said: "The truth and words are unrelated. The truth can be compared to the moon and words can be compared to a finger. I can use my finger to point out the moon, but my finger is not the moon, and you don't need my finger to see the moon."[3] In this way, climbers and Zen practitioners can relate to one another, for both would agree that above all, words are secondary to experience – *what it feels like*. To truly know something, such as what it's like to climb the Bastille in Eldorado Canyon, you have to experience it yourself.

Climbers have much to say about their intimate experiences on the rock. Common phrases overheard at crags and post-climb breweries include "Being in the zone," "Getting into the flow," "Finding the groove," "Not thinking about it," and "Just doing it." Each of these sentiments expresses the essence of Zen, which arises so effortlessly when we are simply and naturally *ourselves*. Each suggests "meditative absorption" and "the realization of fundamental unity." Even route names tend to have a Zen-like quality, inviting us to understand the meaning of Between Nothingness and Eternity and Sweet Catastrophe. These climbing expressions, like so much in Zen, may appear confusing but are made clear – or *realized* – through direct contact. Similarly, when Zen masters are asked for answers, they are known to give irrational and sometimes shocking replies, such as "Scoop clear water from the heart of the fire."[4] This expression might not make sense on an analytic level, but if it shatters a student's reliance on words, invokes action, and elicits an authentic response, then it's no less valid as a vehicle for insight and liberation. Ultimately, in both climbing and Zen, action and direct experience trump *conventions* such as language.

The purpose of Zen

In the seminal book *Zen Mind, Beginner's Mind*, Shunryu Suzuki states that the purpose of Zen is "to see things as they are." This sounds simple. Perhaps Zen is not as mysterious or mystical as we imagined. Suzuki is writing about penetrating barriers, both mental and physical, and the experience of liberation. Practice, such as through meditation

  ERIC SWAN

(or climbing), helps us achieve this goal through the cultivation of discipline, concentration, and self-awareness; together, they help us break through habitual patterns and experience the world anew. Ironically, when the mind is "tamed" it is also set free, which in turn increases our ability to discover the extraordinary (such as a new line) in the ordinary (a familiar crag). Shunryu Suzuki is best known for the notion of "Beginner's Mind," which we will turn towards next in order to further understand the power of simplicity in both Zen and climbing.

The Beginner's Mind

Suzuki famously said, "In the beginner's mind there are many possibilities, but in the expert's there are few."[5] Just as a child looks to the world with wonder, we can look towards the world with similar eyes – if we are willing to be free, free of the filters that cloud our direct experience of "what is." When we suspend our preconceptions and truly open ourselves up to experience, we demonstrate Beginner's Mind. This is not to be confused with playing dumb and being careless, because after all, climbing can be a dangerous sport; but rather, being open minded as if every moment is new. In Zen and in reality, no one instant in time is like the next. All phenomena exist in a constant state of change – arising and passing away – as if they are constantly being born and dying. This gives rise to freedom. In this view, you create your experience in the world moment by moment, day after day. *You* determine your reality through the choices, if not through the preconceptions – or lack thereof – to which you bind yourself. This perspective on "the way things are" can be liberating, as it inspires one to overcome mental and physical barriers and live fully.

Examples of Beginner's Mind are numerous as we look at the field of climbing. It is present in the climber who onsights a new route, finding her way to the top through intuition and fluidity of movement. It is present in the boulderer who is able to send a route after learning from the rock and discovering its natural line. It is present in the climber who surfaces *refreshed* after a plunge while deep-water soloing off the coast of Spain. And it is even present in the minds of today's masters, such as Chris Sharma, who after traveling the world and sending its most difficult climbs, still manages to approach his craft with a fresh perspective – even when he's climbing that V8 in Santa Cruz for the hundredth time.

Parallels Between Zen Training and Climbing

We have learned that the aim of Zen is "to see things as they are." To achieve this perspective one must suspend the influence of a self-absorbed and wandering mind. This is generally done through four main pathways: ordinary physical work; *zazen* (or sitting meditation); *koans* (problems beyond logic); and *sanzen* (interviews with the master). We can use this system of training in order to understand how climbers might further experience and cultivate Zen. The following sections will examine the physical work of climbing; describe climbing's meditative properties; argue that each route is like a *koan*; and discover wisdom through interviews with climbing masters.

Physical work and the experience of Zen

Climbing and Zen have long traditions of venerating physical work, which is manifested through their mutual emphasis on discipline and attention to form. In Zen this stems from the conviction that enlightenment can occur at any time as long as one is totally immersed in the moment's activity. This includes mundane physical work, such as sweeping the floor – or, say, climbing a 5.8. Consider this famous Zen Buddhist proverb: "Before enlightenment: chop wood, carry water. After enlightenment: chop wood, carry water." In Zen everything is a means towards realization. In this way and others, Zen practice is non-dualistic. As the Heart Sutra – a teaching chanted in Zen temples – tells us, there is no separation between *this* and *that*, form and formlessness, even *nirvana* (translated as "liberation") and suffering. Your perspective determines your reality. Zen and climbing foster new ways of looking at the world in part through the "cleansing power" of simple physical work.

As much as climbers are known for living freely, the physical act of climbing requires tremendous physical and mental discipline. From planning how to safely send a single-pitch to planning for an expedition, climbing demands attention to detail. You don't wing any route unless you've attained a level of discipline and confidence in your climbing that you can "forget" instructions and simply enjoy the climb. So, too, Zen stresses the importance of mastering form before realizing the formless. Sometimes people make the mistake of conflating Zen's tolerance and spontaneity with a lackadaisical approach to life, but in truth, anyone who has ever set foot in a Zen center would attest otherwise. It may

    ERIC SWAN

appear paradoxical but Zen and climbing emphasize discipline and yet encourage the transcendence of such structure. This is true as long as the aim is realization, such as of your full potential or inner nature. In reality, climbers are always expanding the boundaries of possibility. There was a time when climbing a 5.15 route seemed impossible; climbers like Chris Sharma have shown otherwise on routes such as Realization (an interesting choice of titles) and Jumbo Love. And let me not fail to mention Dean Potter's ascent of the Eiger in August of 2009, in which he finished his free-soloing climb by base-jumping and soaring for a record time (nearly three minutes), combining the art of climbing with . . . well, flying.

The meditative aspects of climbing

In a fundamental and natural way, climbing requires as well as induces some degree of meditation. As soon as we start ascending, we leave unnecessary things behind and concentrate on the task before us; we enter "the zone." Just as climbing is a highly dynamic process, so too do we flow in and out of thinking and "not thinking." Climbing is very much an art as well as a discipline, and the meditative absorption we experience when climbing results in the clear-but-sharp mind we need to *respond to* and *act fully in* the situations we encounter on the rock. Plans for New Year's Eve and the items on the grocery list have no place here. They are only distractions, and when you're climbing with a distracted, future-oriented mind, you fall. If you were meditating in a Zen temple and you found yourself distracted, you might find yourself struck on the shoulders by a master's stick, a *keisaku*, as it's more properly called. If only you were to be so lucky to receive a gentle reminder to concentrate while climbing a thousand feet above the valley floor!

It might appear counterintuitive given the danger, but climbing can lead to a tremendous sense of tranquility and relaxation. This is part of its allure, especially for those whose lives are fast paced and stressful. There are moments, and even extended periods of time, when everything seems to slip away and you are left with a palpable sensation of peace – a *lightness of being*. Preoccupations of mind, such as what happened at work yesterday, seem to yield to more immediate objects of awareness, like the texture of the stone or the slow flight of a bird overhead. Sometimes the sensation of lightness can be so acute and so relieving you might feel as if you – whatever the "self" might mean to you – disappear or are somehow transformed through the act of climbing. No longer weighed down by insecurities, accomplishments, desires, or attachments, your perspective towards yourself and the world is lightened. You might feel more alive, more awake – more *free*. In the midst of this calmness and centeredness, you might discover in yourself a heightened awareness of your body, your mind, and your surroundings. This state of awareness bears much resemblance to meditation, or what is known as *zazen* in Zen Buddhism.

In the meditation hall, *zazen* is practiced while seated on cushions, but in the world of climbing, *zazen* is practiced through active physical movement. At the heart of both is regulation and awareness of the breath. Healthy and conscious breathing is integral for climbers, especially during the crux of a route. Naturally, stress and anxiety cause breathing to become constricted, which in turns affects the mind and its ability to problem-solve. As a technique, climbers check in with their breath in order to find their center, regain their control of the situation, and navigate through problems. In short, climbing is interwoven with meditation. Whether the intent is to cultivate awareness and relaxation, integrate mind and body, or suspend the overactive mind, a climber can be informed by and benefit from Zen meditation.

But Wait, What about the Thrill?

It seems incomplete to tout the meditative and peaceful aspects of climbing without acknowledging its other half – the thrill. There is no doubt that climbing is often accompanied or characterized by discrete sensations of excitement, arousal, and euphoria. Anyone who has taken the "sharp end of the rope" and held onto the rock for dear life is acutely aware of the feeling of adrenaline pulsing through the body. Even bouldering is thrilling; it tends to elicit a primal, animalistic response as you launch yourself upwards – dynoing in search of the next hold as if your life depended on it. Such exhilaration seems to be the opposite of relaxation, yet experience informs us that we don't have to be in a state of rest in order to feel liberation. Even if we're exhausted, it is elating – even purifying – to reach a summit after hours, days, even weeks of grueling climbing.

Problem-Solving Through Insight and Action

Zen and climbing emphasize action over intellect. This is what is known as *prajna*, or wisdom arising from direct experience. In our lives – and in the splendor of the natural world – there are limitless opportunities for discovery and liberation. Ever mindful of life and growth, climbers and Zen students alike go to great lengths in order to solve a problem, obsessing on a single problem for great lengths of time until they get it. In a sense, routes are like *koans*, problems that require something other than analysis and logic alone to solve. *Koans* are traditionally used by Zen teachers to induce insight, and a classic example is, "What is the sound of one hand clapping?" "Answers" in climbing and in Zen arise through insight and action, not pure intellect. They involve adaptability, learning from the environment, engaging fully in the present moment – and often considerable trial and error. Problems, whether they're routes or *koans*, are opportunities for *satori*, or realization. When climbers and Zen students break through a problem, it's as if an "enlightenment" has occurred.

Solving a climbing problem requires an understanding of nature and the immediate environment. There is a wonderful poem by Basho that will resonate with climbers: "From the pine tree, learn of the pine tree, and from the bamboo, learn of the bamboo." This might appear overly simplistic, but in Zen and in climbing the answers are always right in front of you; insights and progress come from "seeing things as they are." In climbing, an "answer" may mean bending the body in a different way in order to adjust to the contours of the rock, or unlocking a new sequence through non-conceptual thinking and simply going for it – whatever it takes to solve the problem.

Encounters with the Masters

Climbing and Zen share in common a high regard for the Masters. The honorees might eschew this title – and labels altogether – but we still look to them as if they were "enlightened" or "liberated." In a way, they are Buddhas – the Sanskrit term for "Awakened Ones." We marvel at their way of Being in the World. They are ordinary and yet *extraordinary*. They are deeply free. There is no separation between their life and their art. They walk among us, they climb the same stone that we do, but something about them is different. Sometimes they look like mystics or cavemen, and other times they look totally normal. We don't care about appearances, we care about their insights – their skills. What might we learn from interviews with the Masters? What might they say? What might they show us?

Derek Hersey: The Zen Master of free soloing
Derek Hersey was a Free Soloing Master. Originally from Manchester, England, Hersey was known for his free soloing marvels in Yosemite Valley and throughout Colorado, namely, Eldorado Canyon, Black

Canyon of the Gunnison, and Long's Peak. Any one of his climbs was an incredible feat, worthy of mention in the annals of climbing and human achievement. But Hersey's legend is largely unknown. Known by his friends as "Dirty Bird," Derek Hersey exemplified so much of the spirit of Zen, and in my view, he honorably illustrated what is meant by Zen in the art of climbing.

Derek Hersey was an atypical "monk," more in line with a vivacious hermit or "fool on the hill" than the shaved-head, austere variety. With his wild hair, gigantic smile, and contagious laugh, this man knew how to have fun – and how to climb some of the toughest routes of his time. In the film *Front Range Freaks*, there is classic footage of Hersey climbing in Eldorado Canyon, a state park outside Boulder, Colorado. Watching, you will see a man perfectly comfortable hundreds of feet above the deck, bending his body as he ascends notoriously challenging routes. Hersey's free soloing is a sight to behold, in no small part because he is grinning like the world's happiest child throughout the climbs.

In my view, these smiles – much like Mahakashyapa's smile – are clear and authentic manifestations of Zen, of Hersey's Buddha nature. You get a glimpse of his wonder and pleasure when he says, "You can look down . . . you know, take in the exposure, and you go, 'Oh, this is cool'."[6] When friends are interviewed by the filmmakers, they talk about how Hersey would yell across the canyon to them, usually from alarming heights, a further indication of how comfortable he felt and how much unbounded joy he experienced while climbing. The fact that Hersey was so unabashedly himself is enviable and indicative of Zen.

In 1993, at age 39, Hersey died doing what he loved: free soloing. Perhaps it's not surprising, but it would be a mistake to say Hersey had a death wish or was suicidal. In response to the question about whether his free soloing represented an intention to die, Hersey said, "But there's nothing else that makes me feel so alive." To which he added about the experience of climbing, "You're thinking, but not in words. You're thinking in movement and rhythm."[7]

Chris Sharma and Zen

Chris Sharma is unquestionably one of the best climbers in the world. He has won innumerable competitions, including the Bouldering Nationals when he was just 14. He has shattered the boundaries of rock climbing, traveled the world, and in my view, represents another example

  ERIC SWAN

of Zen in the art of climbing. Sharma's affinity for Buddhism, and Zen in particular, is well documented in film and in print. He exemplifies the spirit of Zen, appearing to be humble (but potent), ordinary (but extraordinary), self-aware, and most of all, authentic. In order to have a conversation with this Modern Master, we will take a closer look at this inspiring talent through his own words. The quotations below are drawn from Chris's own journal, which was published in the article "The Beginner's Mind: Chris Sharma's Revealing Journal." Here are some Zen-like excerpts:

> I need to learn to move on the rock like water. The more I can flow on the rock like water, the more I understand and the less separation there will be between us. Climbing hard will come naturally from that point, like a flooded river wiping out a bridge without even having to think about it.

> It's nice to be so focused when trying a hard route. These moments are so pure; there is no separation and there is nothing to think about or understand because it's all right there. The here, the present, the moment. Everything!

> Having no agenda or expectations is giving me a lot of flexibility and openness to be in the moment, climb what is appealing, and just flow.[8]

For further insights from the man himself, the reader is strongly encouraged to peruse the full article/journal. Chris writes candidly about his own process of finding balance and meaning, and cultivating Zen through climbing. His writings bring to mind a quote: "Zen begins at the point where there is nothing further to seek, nothing to be gained."[9] If this is true, Chris Sharma is a Modern Master.

Other Masters: Finding the extraordinary in the ordinary
In the Zen tradition it is dualistic and counterproductive to both separate and deify people. The reader will remember that Zen is about glimpsing the fundamental unity behind all things, not further masking it through our own beliefs and judgments. With this in mind, the author wishes to recognize Chris Sharma and Derek Hersey for their extraordinary climbing achievements and character, but also acknowledge that there are thousands of other masters around the world, including some at our local crags and gyms. Perhaps there is someone you are thinking of. As far as climbing magazines and films are concerned, his or her name is totally unknown. Is this person any less a Zen master in your estimation?

Probably not, because in your view this person quietly and consistently flows on the rock, time after time, year after year. Not only is this person reliable and effective – so much so that you entrust your life with him or her – but this person is simply fun to climb with. He or she may be remarkably insightful on matters on and off the rock. To you, this person is extraordinary *and* ordinary – a master you can learn from as you travel your own path towards the summit of your potential.

Conclusion

Clearly, there is much in common between Zen and climbing. Through discipline of mind and body, both phenomena can result in a profound – and sometimes ineffable – experience of joy and communion with nature. Both require total engagement of one's full being, which in turn allows for the realization of one's full potential – the *expression* of one's inner nature. Now that we understand Zen, nothing stops us from *experiencing* Zen. We merely have to engage fully in all that we do, moment by moment, without rigid attachment to outcomes and hope for personal gain; in so doing, we will experience Zen. In a sense, we can "forget" our training and enjoy the climb. It's time to chalk-up and commit ourselves to the stone. Nirvana awaits.

Epilogue: Finding Nirvana

You are no one special. You have simply come to Mallorca, Spain, after reading a magazine article about the ecstasy of deep-water soloing. Wearing only a bathing suit, rock shoes, and chalk bag, you are ascending the face of a wide cliff band that rises steeply out of the Mediterranean Sea. Thirty feet below, the water gently swirls in a fusion of green and blue illuminated by the summer sun. In a dihedral you splay your legs apart and smear your feet against the orange and white limestone. Your footing is totally secure and your forearms are pumped from the crux you just cranked through, so you drop your arms to the side and shake them out. Resting for a moment, you let out several deep exhales. Looking up from this position, you notice features in the rock that would allow you to top-out to the left, to the right. Heck, you could even pencil-dive from

this height. You have many options before you, many paths towards the same goal. Right now, that goal is to push the limits of your climbing skills and to have fun in the process. It suddenly strikes you that on the one hand you are totally locked into the rock, and on the other, you are totally free. This freedom of movement and of choice is your definition of nirvana.

NOTES

1   Tsai Chih Chung, *Zen Speaks: Shouts of Nothingness*, trans. Brian Bruya (New York: Doubleday, 1994).
2   D. Fontana, *Discover Zen: A Practical Guide to Personal Serenity* (San Francisco: Chronicle Books, 2001).
3   Tsai Chih Chung, *Zen Speaks*.
4   A. Watts, *The Way of Zen* (New York: Pantheon, 1957).
5   S. Suzuki, *Zen Mind, Beginner's Mind* (New York: Weatherhill, 1970).
6   P. Mortimer, *Front Range Freaks*. DVD. Axolotal Productions (2003).
7   Mortimer, *Front Range Freaks*.
8   C. Sharma, "Chris Sharma's Revealing Journal: The Beginner's Mind," *Climbing* (2003): 221.
9   Ibid.

PART III

CUTTING THE ROPE

Climbing Ethics

CHAPTER 10

FREEDOM AND INDIVIDUALISM ON THE ROCKS

 From bouldering to big-wall climbing, the sport of rock climbing consists of an arbitrary set of games that are constantly evolving in many branching directions.[1] One thing these games have in common is they have no formal rules. Climbing attracts people who like the freedom of this unorganized sport. Ian McNaught-Davis writes: "Most climbers regard our activity as a freedom sport, in other words it is free of rules and regulations, we are free to do it where we like, when we like and with anyone we choose. But this is not quite correct."[2] While there are no formal rules, climbers are constantly debating ethics that restrict their freedom, hopefully with the goal of maintaining the integrity of the sport. Most importantly, ethics debates are a sign that climbers are exercising their freedom and expressing their individualism.

Ethics debates expose a tension between the freedom of individual climbers to be self-defining and the climbing community's need to define meaningful accomplishments. The goal of this essay is to examine this tension. This will be done by analyzing three great climbs as exemplars of how climbers express their individuality within the context of a climbing community, that is, the people, traditions, and culture of climbing. To aid this analysis I will enlist the help of three philosophers who offer different views on the tension between the individual and the community.

Before discussing the three climbs, I would like to explain my understanding of ethics in climbing culture. The term "ethics" can be used in many ways. One way refers to identifying standards of behaviors and practices that are commendable and those that are unacceptable. For example, many professions have ethics codes. At least one ethics code has emerged for climbers: the International Mountaineering and Climbing Federation's document "To Bolt or Not to Be." This document articulates a code of ethics for developing and redeveloping climbing areas. For example, one ethical standard listed in the document is "runouts may not be neutralized [on existing routes] by additional bolts (don't take the edge off a runout)."[3] This standard is not an innovation; it represents the common judgment of the climbing community, which emerged through informal discussions, often heated, that arose at local climbing areas due to conflicts. For example, several years ago I was climbing a route on North Carolina's Looking Glass Wall, which I had done several times before, and noticed a bolt had suddenly appeared on this classic traditional route. The route had been climbed hundreds of times without the bolt. Some climber took the edge off the runout between cracks by adding a bolt. The offending bolt was promptly removed. Anyone who has climbed in North Carolina quickly learns that the local climbing community is fiercely protective of its historic, traditional climbing ethic.

More significantly, rock climbing ethics is about characterizing self-imposed restraints to create challenges that define worthy accomplishments. In doing this, climbers identify traits or excellences required to achieve worthwhile accomplishments. Through ethics debates climbers are exercising their freedom to shape the standards that in turn shape their character as climbers. Climbers are not completely free to be self-creative based on personal preferences. The games they play shape the excellences they must acquire to play those games. For example, because climbing games have no formal rules or judges, they all require climbers to have personal integrity and honesty. Often, there is no one who can see if a climber briefly grabs a piece of protection (cheated) during an ascent. Climbers must have integrity in reporting their accomplishments. Also, different climbing games require different types of excellences. For example, as will be discussed below, ground-up face climbing requires a particular kind of self-mastery analogous, but different, to the moral virtue of courage. The ethics of the ground-up game requires climbers to overcome the fear of taking long falls. It is individual climbers who value this kind of self-mastery and it is through dialogue with each other, the community, and tradition that they create the ethics that promotes this value. It is by thoughtfully participating in ethics debates that climbers shape the values that shape their characters. There is a mutual influence of individual values, community values, and the ethics of the climbing game, all influencing and shaping each other.

Nietzsche and the Bachar-Yerian

In the early 1990s I met some friends in Tuolumne Meadows to climb. One crisp morning we were climbing on a cliff below the enormous vertical wall of Medlicott Dome. Far above us we could hear two German climbers yelling back and forth; they were attempting the famous Bachar-Yerian route. We stopped to watch.

The Bachar-Yerian is considered one of the world's great rock climbs. It is a beautiful line that follows a black streak in the middle of a 500-foot vertical wall of perfect golden granite. The face would be impossible to climb except it is studded with crystals ranging from the size of billiard balls to marbles. Its world-class reputation is due to the route's spectacular situation, technical challenge, and, most importantly, a test of will. The Bachar-Yerian has all the factors that make a great climb, with a heavy emphasis on psychological mastery. This challenge comes from the distances the climber must go between pieces of protection on difficult climbing, which exposes the climber to long falls and possible injury.

The climb's reputation is an expression of its principle author, John Bachar. Bachar was one of the great climbers of the 1970s and 1980s. Sadly, he recently died in a climbing accident. Bachar's reputation was built on his free-solo ascents of difficult routes and his championing of a strict "ground-up" ethics. Ground-up, as the name indicates, means that the climber starts at the bottom of the route and finishes at the top. This style is in opposition to the now common practice of rehearsing the climb and placing bolts while hanging from ropes anchored above the climb. Bachar vehemently opposed this style of climbing as chickening out.[4]

Returning to that morning in Tuolumne Meadows, as my friends and I watched the climber cautiously move up the wall, we could see the distance between him and his last piece of protection grow. Finally, he stopped below a difficult move. A fall from there would send him hurtling down the face for 80 feet. I had a sick, nervous feeling in my stomach as I watched him hesitantly move up and down several times. He was trying to figure out the sequence of difficult moves and calm his mind.

The climber finally committed to the move and confidently moved up and clipped his rope into a bolt. He immediately let out a yell of triumph.

Bachar was playing a serious game when he created this climb. It was designed for the elite climber seeking a challenge. The ethics of the Bachar-Yerian reflects the values of commitment and self-mastery. To a limited extent, Bachar's climbing ethics embodies aspects of the philosophy of the nineteenth-century German thinker, Frederick Nietzsche. Nietzsche's philosophy is unapologetically elitist. His ethical ideal requires uniquely powerful individuals to break free of conventional morality and to create their own set of values. Nietzsche termed this ideal the *Übermench*, often translated as "Overman."[5] The *Übermench* is a free spirit and becomes an authentic individual by creating subjective values and acquiring the commitment to live by them. The purpose of life for Nietzsche is using one's freedom to realize a self-created purpose. It is a difficult and dangerous task. In his quest for freedom and power, the *Übermench* accepts risks and sacrifices self-preservation. For the *Übermench*, happiness is the feeling that power is growing; "It is the will to perfection, the striving for distinction."[6]

The existential philosophy of Nietzsche was in the air during the creation of the Yosemite climbing subculture in the 1970s. This counter-culture ethos no doubt influenced Bachar and his friends. Bachar was part of a group of young California climbers who called themselves the Stonemasters. The Stonemasters were free sprits; they rejected the conventional values of society and lived to climb. However, Bachar's climbing ethic was perhaps more extreme than most of the Stonemasters. John Long writes:

> John Bachar, through passion and heroic effort transformed himself into one of the greatest figures in twentieth-century adventure sports. . . . We all had the edgy rapture of watching John go where no climber had gone before. If ever a Stonemaster carried the name on his sleeve (and he scribbled it on his boots as well), it was John Bachar.[7]

Bachar was willing to take greater risks on a more frequent basis to achieve his climbing goals. Yet these risks were highly calculated and he lived a life of extreme discipline and commitment to self-mastery. In this regard, he realized the Nietzschean ideal of an individual.

For Nietzsche, the free individual values self-mastery over self-preservation. In terms of Bachar's climbing ethics, this ordering of values was necessary "to create something that [was] truly [his] own, a monument to [his] uniqueness."[8] For example, the German climber we watched that day in the Tuolumne Meadows faced an 80-foot fall. If he failed to overcome his fear, the consequence was a long fall resulting in probable injury. Mostly likely he felt a sickening wave of panic welling up within him that would overwhelm his ability to concentrate. Everything depended on him being able to suppress this wave of panic and execute the moves. If I might speculate, when the climber let out the triumphant yell it was an expression of happiness derived from a rush of power.[9] One can imagine that he selected this route just because he valued the feeling of power that came through self-mastery.

However, the values inherent in this great route follow Nietzsche's ethics only to a limited extent. Nietzsche sees the tension between the individual and the community as negative. The values of the community restrain the freedom of the great individual to be self-defining. However, in Bachar's case the community played a largely positive role by providing a context for the meaningfulness of his accomplishments. So, on the one hand, the ethics of the Bachar-Yerian reflects the individualistic values of self-overcoming and the will to power. On the other hand, the significance of the Bachar-Yerian is arguably the ultimate expression of the ethics of the Tuolumne Meadows climbing community. Bachar was in dialogue with the many ground-up climbers who had put up difficult, sparsely protected routes before him. Anyone who has climbed the glacial polished faces of the Tuolumne domes knows the feeling of power and self-mastery required to climb the 20–30-foot runouts that characterize the area.

So while the Bachar-Yerian is the expression of the free spirit of its author, it is equally an expression of the values of the local climbing community. Bachar was a unique individual who pushed the standards of commitment and self-mastery. However, the Tuolumne climbing community defined the significance of his great route and shaped his character as a climber. Bold run-outs are the tradition in Tuolumne; Bachar took the tradition to a new dimension, the sheer vertical faces.

To Bolt or Not to Be and John Stuart Mill

Just a couple years after Bachar created his great route a revolution in climbing styles began. This new style of climbing – "sport climbing" – was in direct opposition to the ground-up style. In sport climbing, the process of creating routes starts from the top of the cliff. Climbers safely attach themselves to anchors then descend to clean, practice, and bolt the climb. When they were first introduced, these tactics were condemned as unethical and a long debate ensued.[10]

The spark that ignited the sport climbing revolution was the development of Smith Rock in eastern Oregon. One event that brought attention to Smith Rock was a photo of Alan Watts climbing Chain Reaction on the cover of *Mountain* magazine. The spectacular photo showed Watts clutching the jagged edge of an overhanging arête as he moved toward a dramatic roof. The tan volcanic rock stood out against a perfect blue sky. Ambitious climbers who saw the photograph wanted to do that route. Once top climbers started traveling to Smith Rock, the news quickly spread about this new style of challenging climbing. With their eyes opened to new possibilities climbers introduced sport climbing at their home crags, which led to heated debates at local crags around the country. In locales, angry traditional climbers chopped the bolts placed by sport climbers. This aggressive act created acrimonious, adversarial debate.

The route that is widely considered to have marked the acceptance of sport climbing in North America is To Bolt or Not to Be. To Bolt or Not to Be was of such high quality that it has attracted the world's most accomplished climbers to test their skills for over two decades. The creation of this beautiful and difficult climb legitimized sport climbing.[11] In effect, the route was the argument for sport climbing that persuaded a skeptical and in some cases hostile US climbing community.

A French climber, Jean-Baptiste Tribout, did the first ascent of this great route in 1986. It was by far the hardest route at the time and the first 5.14 in North America. The route was the vision of Alan Watts, who cleaned, bolted, and named it, but did not climb it until three years after the first ascent.[12] To Bolt or Not to Be climbs the middle of a steep, blank face on perfect, volcanic tuff. The route is as psychologically challenging as it is physically challenging.[13] Every move on this climb is technically demanding; right to the end of its 135 feet the climber must muster the will to concentrate and execute demanding moves. However, this route requires a different kind of self-mastery than the Bachar-Yerian. For example, To Bolt or Not to Be is rated 5.14a compared to 5.11c for the Bachar-Yerian, but that comparison is close to meaningless. Both climbs are test pieces for elite climbers today. The closely spaced bolts of the sport climb allow the climber to forget about falling and focus on executing the intricate, technical, and physically demanding moves. The psychological mastery required is found in summoning the will to execute complex sequences of precise moves while becoming increasingly exhausted, mentally and physically. The greatness of To Bolt or Not to Be is qualitatively different from the Bachar-Yerian; it is a different climbing game born out of a different ethic, and it requires some distinct qualities of excellence.

The philosophy of John Stuart Mill will be more helpful than Nietzsche's for considering the tension between the individual and the community in the debate over sport climbing. There are similarities between Mill and Nietzsche; both thinkers place the highest priority on the freedom of the individual to be self-creating in opposition to the repressive meddling of the community. But while the emphasis in Nietzsche's philosophy is on the will to power, the focus of Mill's philosophy is on originality and diversity. While Mill pits the individual against the community, arguing for maximum liberty for the individual to be self-creating, the liberty of the individual can have indirect benefits for the community.

Mill's liberal philosophy is individualistic, but it also has social goods in mind. According to Mill, society declines when individualism is suppressed and people are required to conform to a precast social mold. If an individual is not given room to exercise originality, "human life becomes a stagnant pool" and society degenerates.[14] When a person is given the autonomy to choose the course of their life and the kind of person they will become, it challenges their intellect, imagination, and creativity. By being challenged their native capacities grow and develop. This benefits not only the individual, but also indirectly enhances the community. Mill writes: "In proportion to the development of individuality, each person becomes more valuable to himself; and therefore capable of being more valuable to others."[15] For this reason, the community should not impose any collective standard of the good life. The person who follows tradition is not free and never grows. Individuals are free when they pursue the good life as they see it. Further, in this pursuit they do not need the affirmation of the community for justification or legitimacy. Self-creation is self-justifying because it leads to personal growth.

The no-rules character of climbing games and culture is attractive to many people because it creates an opportunity for the development of individuality. It is a highly creative and demanding activity that can foster the kind of well-being of which Mill speaks. Humans are constructed to exercise practical reason, to set goals or life-plans for themselves, and to figure out how to realize these goals. Climbing can be a way for people to do this, to challenge and develop their native capacities. The creation of great routes like the Bachar-Yerian or To Bolt or Not to Be are expressions of creativity, originality, and individuality. Moreover, the differences between these climbs demonstrate that there can be many kinds of great routes that attract different kinds of climbers. We are not all built the same way; we have different native strengths and abilities. The liberty of climbing should, and does, give free scope to the varieties of character. The International Mountaineering and Climbing Federation's ethics document states: "A pluralism of the various climbing games is desirable and is welcomed as an expression of the legitimate individual preferences of climbers." Some climbers thrive on risk, while others relish technical challenges, while still others are attracted to both. The ground-up game favors climbers who enjoy the self-mastery associated with risk. The sport-climbing game favors those who relish the self-mastery emphasized by technical challenges.

Mill's philosophy of individualism and freedom would encourage Watts' innovations because they increase the diversity of climbing experiences. He would be critical of the climbing communities' interference. It is worth noting that the Yosemite climbing community of the 1980s would never have let sport climbing develop in California. In fact, Watts quit climbing in the Valley due to the hostility he felt from the locals. Because Watts climbed in the relative obscurity of Smith Rock, he was given the freedom to experiment. Watts and his circle of friends *were* the local climbing community in eastern Oregon and more or less only answered to each other. Watts was given the freedom to exercise originality and in so doing he expanded the diversity of climbing games in ways that benefited the climbing community as a whole. The physical and technical abilities of North American climbers grew tremendously with the invention of sport climbing, as did the number of climbers.

However, Mill's ethics on the relationship between the individual and community is limited. Like Nietzsche, Mill sees the tension between the individual and the community as negative. For Mill, the interference of the community restricts the freedom and personal growth of the individual by blocking possible experiments in living. While this certainly happens and Mill is right to oppose it, the community also plays a positive role in legitimizing individual experiments. If new ways of living are to transcend personal expression, they need to be validated by others. For example, it was not enough that Watts found sport climbing a satisfying expression of his originality to make that style of climbing significant. Ultimately, the larger, skeptical climbing community had to be convinced that this new style of climbing was worthwhile.

To Bolt or Not to Be was a convincing argument for sport climbing because it fulfilled the criteria of a great climb while pushing the requirements for mastery and excellence in new directions. But to be considered a great climb and worthwhile accomplishment it needed to earn the respect of the climbing community. Further, the legitimization of sport climbing changed the character of climbing, which in turn changed the character of climbers. Anyone who has spent months trying to master a difficult sport climbing project knows the fortitude and discipline, the sustained mental and physical effort, required to redpoint a climb at the outer edge of one's abilities. Sport climbing pushed physical and technical mastery to standards that were unattainable in the ground-up game.[16]

The ethics of Nietzsche and Mill offer insights on freedom and individualism that can be applied to climbing. Climbing has a flavor of Nietzschean self-overcoming and will to power and shares Mill's emphasis on originality, diversity, and pluralism. However, both philosophers are limited by the negative account of the role of the community and its tradition. For example, it was seen in the cases of the Bachar-Yerian and To Bolt or Not to Be that the community and its traditions played positive roles by providing a meaningful context for the climbs and in legitimizing these individual climbing achievements.

Coda: Taylor and The Path

In the summer of 2007, a friend and I took a climbing trip to Lake Louise in Banff National Park. Next to where we were climbing we noticed a rope hanging down a huge overhanging face. The rock was a grayish-white quartzite with vertical black and gold streaks running down the face; we could see widely spaced pieces of protection in the few cracks that ran horizontally across on the wall. We both marveled at the climb some ambitious climber was attempting. We later found out that the route was named The Path and the climber was Sonnie Trotter. Trotter is one of the most accomplished young climbers in the world today. Later that same day, he climbed the route.

Trotter is a talented individual who, along with a few other climbers, is advancing a style of climbing that combines aspects of traditional climbing with sport climbing. Like sport climbers, they start from the top by initially rehearsing the climb, but they refuse to use bolts and only place cams and stoppers in cracks for protection. The Path is the result of a dialogue between two climbing games or traditions. It combines the distinct types of mastery inherent in the Bachar-Yerian and To Bolt or Not to Be. The climber must overcome the fear of taking long falls while executing extended sequences of technically and physically demanding moves of the kind found on sport routes. However, there were tensions in this dialogue.[17]

The Path violates the ethical demands of ground-up style by starting the process with a top rope and the extensive rehearsing of moves by hanging on protection. In addition, there was an unclimbed sport route where Trotter placed his route and he removed the bolts. While he received permission from the climber who equipped the line, his actions gave rise to a controversy. However, overall these tensions were largely creative and positive. The Path is likely to become a great route and some of the best climbers in North America have already traveled to Lake Louise to test themselves on it. Further, Trotter was able to create The Path because his character as a climber has been shaped by both the sport and traditional climbing games.

In looking at the issues raised by The Path, the Canadian philosopher Charles Taylor will be helpful in providing a more complete account of the tension between the individual and the community by including a positive role for the community.[18] Taylor argues that the isolated individualism of Nietzsche and Mill can lead to trivial forms of life and self-absorbed individuals. The community, for better and sometimes for worse, plays an essential role in the process of individual "self-creation." Taylor affirms the ideal that we should be free to decide for ourselves the course of our lives. However, these decisions should be made in dialogue with others. The meaningfulness of who we become is the result of a conversation with others. The others in this conversation include significant people in our lives as well as the community, culture, and traditions in which our lives are embedded. Taylor calls this a horizon of significance. If every subjective, personal choice is as significant as every other choice then we are lost, directionless on a flat plane. How can we know what is worth pursing with our freedom without any landmarks? The horizon of significance consists of landmarks that are identified as meaningful through dialogue. Further, others are not morally required to accept our choices of significance simply because they are *our* personal choices. Rather, they can and should ask us to justify our choices and explain why they are significant.

The Path, again, is likely to become a great route: it is a strikingly beautiful line, it is an extreme athletic challenge, and it requires multiple types of mastery, all of these at the highest level. However, climbers are not obliged to accept Trotter's creation as significant simply because it is a free expression of *his* individuality. The route is an argument put before the community, which must justify the worthiness of the accomplishment for it to be meaningful. Further, the significance of Trotter's achievement in The Path can be made by comparing it to climbs that have already risen to greatness, like the boldness of the Bachar-Yerian and technical difficulty of To Bolt of Not to Be. Further, in a certain remote sense, Trotter was in dialogue with Bachar and Watts in the creation of The Path. These great climbs and climbers constitute the horizon of significance by which we can find a meaningful location for The Path and our personal achievements as climbers.

The Bachar-Yerian, To Bolt or Not to Be, and (likely) The Path are landmarks, among many, by which climbers find direction. Significant climbs and the climbers that create them provide orientation for what achievements are "worthwhile, and others that are less so, and still others that are not at all."[19] Great climbs and great climbers are peaks on the horizon for climbers by which climbers can locate excellence. These landmarks are given significance over time as a result of dialogue among climbers. Further, this dialogue takes place within the context of a culture and tradition. In essence, climbers are discussing what kinds of self-imposed restrictions create great climbs, which grounds the rules or ethics of climbing games, which in turn defines the qualities of character, excellences climbers should acquire. By participating in ethics debates, climbers are free to determine the kinds of climbers they should become.

In his blog about the controversy over The Path, Trotter writes: "Climbing to me is freedom, freedom to move, freedom to think, freedom to travel, freedom to explore."[20] Recalling the quote from Ian McNaught-Davis, "Most climbers regard our activity as a freedom sport, in other words it is free of rules and regulations. . . . But this is not quite correct." In climbing, freedom is exercised within the context of the climbing community and its traditions; its horizon of significance. One way climbers exercise their freedom is by participating in dialogue about the significance of great and near-great climbs and what excellence and mastery mean to climbers. Ethics debates are a sign that climbers are exercising their freedom and expressing their individualism. But it must now be added, freedom and individualism are exercised within the horizon of significance provided by the climbing community, its people, traditions, and culture.

NOTES

1 Lito Tejada-Flores, "Alpinism as Humanism, Second Thoughts on Climbing Games," available online at www.alpenglow.org/themes/alpinism-as–humanism/index.html (accessed November 30, 2009).

2 International Mountaineering and Climbing Federation, "To Bolt or Not to Be," online at www.theuiaa.org/commissions_mountaineering.html (accessed January 7, 2010).

3 Ian McNaught-Davis, "Foreword," "To Bolt or Not to Be."

4 Duane Raleigh, "Being John Bachar," *Rock and Ice* 166 (March 2008).

5 Frederick Nietzsche, *Thus Spoke Zarathustra*, in *The Portable Nietzsche*, ed. and trans. Walter Kaufman (New York: Viking Penguin, 1982).

6 L. Nathan Oaklander, *Existential Philosophy* (Englewood Cliffs: Prentice-Hall, 1992).

7 John Long, "A Short History of the Stonemasters," onolne at www.stone mastergear.com (accessed December 23, 2009).

8 Oaklander, *Existential Philosophy*, p. 99.

9 Frederick Nietzsche, *The Will to Power*, trans. Walter Kaufman and R. J. Hollingdale (New York: Random House, 1966).

10 Matt Perkins, "Rock Climbing Ethics: A Historical Perspecitve," *Northwest Mountaineering Journal* 2 (2005); online at www.mountaineers.org/nwmj/05/051_Ethics.html (accessed December 23, 2009).

11 Alan Watts, *Climbers Guide to Smith Rock* (Evergreen: Chockstone Press, 1992).

12 Nicholas Hobley, "Alan Watts Climbing Interview," online at www.planet mountain.com (accessed December 23, 2009).

13 Route description, "To Bolt or Not to Be," online at www.mountainproject. com (accessed December 30, 2009).

14 John Stuart Mill, *On Liberty and Utilitarianism* (New York: Bantam, 1993), p. 74.

15 Ibid., p. 72.

16 For example, Bachar noted that he could not find a climb harder than 5.12 that could be put up adhering to strict ground-up style, even though he had free soled 5.13. See Henry Barber, "Widsom," *Rock and Ice* 181 (October 2009): 61.

17 For a nice discussion of these tensions, see Andrew Bisharat, "To Boldly Go 'Sprad' Climbing," *Rock and Ice* 178 (June 2009): 36.

18 Charles Taylor, *The Ethics of Authenticity* (Cambridge, MA: Harvard University Press, 1991).

19 Ibid., p. 38.

20 Sonnie Trotter, blog entry, "It's Right to be Wrong," September 25, 2009, at www.sonnietrotter.com (accessed December 27, 2009).

WILLIAM RAMSEY[1]

CHAPTER 11

HOLD MANUFACTURING

Why You May Be Wrong About What's Right

One obvious area where climbing and philosophy intersect is with regard to the normative dimension of climbing – the ethical or unethical behavior of climbers. Some of the ethical issues in climbing involve a straightforward extension of more general moral principles. For example, it is wrong to lie about your climbing accomplishments because it is generally wrong to lie about accomplishments; it is wrong to needlessly endanger others at the cliff because, more generally, it is always wrong to needlessly endanger others. However, other ethical issues involve factors that are unique to climbing and thus cannot be resolved by invoking broader moral rules. Is it wrong to place bolts on rappel? Is it cheating to use pre-placed gear on a traditional pitch? For these sorts of questions, broader moral rules do not apply in any straightforward way, and climbers must work out for themselves what is right or wrong within the context of climbing.

Still, even when the normative question is unique to climbing, broader and basic philosophical considerations have a role to play in figuring out appropriate answers. For activities like climbing, it is possible to tailor a form of *practical* or *applied* ethics. Practical ethics is the search for rational and morally defensible solutions to specific moral dilemmas. Traditionally, these dilemmas have involved important matters like developing biomedical research, new technologies, or areas of concern like global warming. However, a kind of practical ethics can be applied to far less weighty matters, including recreational activities like rock climbing. While climbers need to decide for themselves many of the rules they ought to abide by, it doesn't follow that anything goes or that a simple majority opinion is decisive. It is certainly possible for climbers, just like anyone else, to embrace rules that are ill-conceived or that, all things considered, don't really make sense. Thus, it is perfectly reasonable to ask if certain long-standing rules or attitudes should be revised or even abandoned; one of the best ways to do so is by adopting the sort of approach used by practical ethicists.

In this essay I am going to try to do something like this with regard to the topic of hold manufacturing or "chipping." In various discussions of this issue we almost exclusively hear (or see) expressions of open hostility toward manufacturing. Yet, despite this widespread criticism, hold manufacturing often occurs during the preparation of new routes, many of which are subsequently described as "classics," even by staunch manufacturing opponents. It would be an understatement to say that climbers are a bit schizophrenic on this issue. By applying some of the same strategies that are common to applied ethics, I'll show how popular attitudes about hold manufacturing are unreasonable and out of sync with other common attitudes and practices in rock climbing. In other words, I'll do what many consider anathema; namely, present a limited defense of hold manufacturing.

Practical Ethics

In practical ethics, as with most of philosophy, the sort of reasoning strategies employed are in one sense mundane but in another sense somewhat unique. The sense in which they are mundane is that good philosophy does not involve any sort of esoteric reasoning principles or bizarre formula. Good philosophy is just thinking very carefully and clearly about some topic in a coherent and critical manner. If there is a calculus for philosophy, it is just good old-fashioned deductive and non-deductive logic, combined with a willingness to follow the argument where it leads. The sense in which this is unique is that, as it turns out, people don't do this sort of thing very often. Instead, people regularly reason in a manner that is driven by biases, embrace beliefs incompatible with other things they believe, fail to think through their positions and what they entail, and often endorse arguments that are fallacious. While practical ethics simply involves careful, coherent reasoning, careful, coherent reasoning is not something we do very well.

It is for this reason that practical ethics can be both helpful and yet often disturbing and iconoclastic. It often reveals how our ordinary views on a topic that we thought we understood are mistaken and indefensible. Thus, practical ethicists often play the role of social critics, challenging conventional assumptions and attitudes. A classic example of this is Peter Singer's now-famous argument about our moral obligations to people in dire circumstances. Singer asks us to judge the morality of a man who stands and watches a small child drown in a shallow pond, simply because wading out to save the child would ruin his expensive suit. Nearly everyone agrees the man's inaction is deeply immoral, even monstrous. This and a host of other cases reveal that people are deeply committed to the following moral principle: If it is within a person's ability to prevent something very bad from happening without sacrificing something of great significance, the person is morally obligated to do so. Given this, Singer argues that our own inaction toward those suffering in developing countries – say, the staggering 20,000 children who die daily from easily treatable ailments – is morally indefensible because it is incompatible with this moral principle. In short, when you choose to buy an iPod rather than giving the same money to Oxfam, your behavior is on a par with the man who watches the child drown.

Over the past forty years, Singer's argument has received considerable attention and there have been a variety of attempted rebuttals (some of which you may be considering right now). It is beyond the scope of this essay to survey this debate, except to note that it seems that none of the proposed rebuttals actually work, or at least work very well.[2] For our purposes, what *is* worth noting is the set of intellectual commitments on display in Singer's argument. One such commitment is to overall consistency and rationality in one's reasoning. If a person is committed to principle X, and if that person also believes or does something that is incompatible with principle X, then that person is irrational because her beliefs or actions do not form a coherent set. If someone holds an attitude that appears inconsistent with other things believed, then that person should offer a compelling justification for the attitude that removes the appearance of incoherency.

A second commitment in practical ethics is to follow the argument to where it logically leads, even if it takes one down a path that challenges longstanding views. What makes a good philosophical argument *interesting* is that, besides clearing away confusion, it also sometimes upsets the apple-cart of consensus. Good philosophy in general, and good practical ethics in particular, is often distressing and even maddening because it demands we rethink strongly held beliefs. When confronted by cogent arguments that challenge their beliefs, people often fall back on various anti-intellectualisms: "You are being too philosophical!" or even "You are thinking about this too much!" If one is committed to intellectual responsibility, as one should be, this attitude won't do. Here's a tidbit of philosophy beta: if while arguing you find yourself digging in and attacking the process of reasoning itself, then you have just lost the argument.

Practical Ethics and Hold Manufacturing

Keeping these general points in mind, we can turn to rock climbing and ask if there are any controversial matters that lend themselves to this sort of critical analysis. I think there are, and that one such topic is hold manufacturing. What follows is what happens when someone who once had an anti-manufacturing attitude examines that attitude from the standpoint of a practical ethics for climbing.

To begin, it will help to reflect a bit on the nature of the hold manufacturing controversy. Unlike most controversies, the debate here is not fueled by two equally outspoken camps who publically disagree. With very few exceptions, virtually no one openly defends hold manufacturing. In the climbing literature there appears to be almost universal consensus that any form of manufacturing is very bad. Indeed, even in one of the very few defenses of manufacturing, a notorious 1990 essay by Duane Raleigh, the practice is described as "fundamentally terrible" and "degrading."[3] So given the apparent consensus that manufacturing is bad, in what sense is there a controversy? The controversy exists because despite the open expression of anti-manufacturing sentiments, hold manufacturing is nevertheless practiced in the development of many new routes. In other words, common *statements* are in conflict with common *actions*, resulting in a deep incongruity about the way some rock climbs are developed. This odd double standard is often reflected in popular descriptions of various routes. Take, for example, The Nose as a free climb. It is generally known that, besides the various pin scars that make certain cracks free-climbable, there is a section of the free variation – what is often described as the "Jardine Traverse" – where the holds used by all free climbers have been chiseled into the granite. So, on the one

hand, it is widely claimed that routes with manufactured holds are tainted and that manufacturing should never be done. And yet, at the same time, a route that is made possible with manufactured holds is widely regarded as one of the greatest free climbs in the world. And this is true of many routes throughout the globe, in many popular destinations. Routes like Le Rose et le Vampire at Buoux, Bronx at Orgon, or The Crew at Rifle, to name just a few, are generally viewed as classics or groundbreaking achievements, even though their existence depends, at least in part, on a style of route preparation that is openly deplored.

What should we make of this? Well, one possibility is that the manufacturing of holds is indeed always profoundly wrong, and yet we just choose to ignore this much of the time. But I think a more plausible diagnosis is that, despite the overt furor and indignation over manufacturing, we really aren't very clear about what, exactly, is wrong with it. Upon deeper reflection, the popular arguments against manufacturing are unconvincing and don't hold up to close scrutiny. In other words, the reason manufacturing still occurs in the preparation of many routes despite its widespread condemnation is because the condemnation itself is not properly justified. Indeed, if we pursue a practical ethics with regard to hold manufacturing – that is, if we commit ourselves to careful and consistent reasoning – we wind up with an analysis that suggests, at least in certain circumstances, manufacturing should be regarded as acceptable.

How would such an analysis go? Replicating a common strategy in practical ethics, we can develop an argument that has the following form: the first premise would express a general normative principle that most climbers believe about acceptable practices in route development. The second premise would claim that hold manufacturing is a legitimate application of this principle (and thus an anti-manufacturing attitude is in conflict with the accepted principle). The conclusion would be that manufacturing in some circumstances is an acceptable practice. Here is such an argument:

(a) There are circumstances such that, in the preparation of a route, modifying the rock in order to make it climbable is acceptable.
(b) The set of circumstances in which rock modification is acceptable sometimes includes the manufacturing of holds.
(c) Therefore, the manufacturing of holds is sometimes acceptable.

While (a) might initially strike some as implausible, I think it is easy to show that it is a principle that most climbers embrace. The more controversial premise is (b), so I will need to spend some time defending it. Of course, (c) follows directly from (a) and (b), so if you accept those two premises, you need to accept (c).

Before we evaluate premises (a) and (b) we need to clarify a couple of things. First, we should get a little clearer on what is meant by "hold manufacturing." There is obviously a continuum of different rock alterations that have been described as hold manufacturing, including the unintended creation of holds with pitons, the reinforcing of existing holds with glue, the "comfortizing" of holds or aggressive cleaning, and of course the flat-out drilling of a hold in blank rock. Not much rides on how broad we make this continuum, so let's stipulate that manufacturing includes deliberately drilling pockets with the intention of creating climbing holds.

Second, we also need to specify the sort of circumstances I have in mind when I claim that manufacturing is acceptable, as I certainly don't believe it is defensible in every situation. Because so many climbers appear to have a zero-tolerance attitude against any sort of manufacturing, we can be fairly conservative while remaining revisionist. It is impossible to give a detailed description of all acceptable manufacturing scenarios, but fortunately we don't need to. Instead, we can describe the prototypical scenario and later worry about how far it is acceptable to stray from that. Let's say the archetype of acceptable manufacturing involves the preparation of an unclimbed sport route in a sport climbing area that has mostly high-quality climbable sections but also segments of blank rock with no climbable features. To link the climbable sections a limited number of holds are manufactured in the blank sections. That is the paradigmatic sort of practice the following argument is intended to defend. Now, let's consider the premises.

The truth of (a) is easy to see once we consider general attitudes about the removal of loose rock by the person who prepares the route. When bolting a route it is almost universally agreed that it is acceptable to remove any loose blocks, crumbly or muddy rock, hollow flakes, fragile knobs, and so on. Indeed, the removal of loose rock is not only seen as ethically acceptable, but it is generally treated as obligatory. Route equippers who do not remove loose rock, especially on sport climbs, are often chastised for doing a poor job in preparing the route for others. Since the removal of loose rock is clearly an instance of modifying the rock in order to make it climbable, then modifying the rock in order to make it climbable is something that practically everyone finds acceptable.[4]

Premise (b), by contrast, is something that, as noted, most climbers explicitly and even vehemently reject. Why should anyone accept this premise? Why should anyone think that hold manufacturing is an acceptable form of rock modification?

We know that there is a climbing-specific normative principle embraced by most climbers and that principle says it is okay to modify the rock for the purpose of creating a climbable route. The removal of loose rock is one such type of modification, and (b) claims that the manufacturing of holds is another. Insofar as she wants to be intellectually responsible, someone who rejects (b) has the burden of presenting a compelling reason for thinking that hold manufacturing should *not* be treated as on a par with removing loose rock. In other words, the burden of proof is with those who embrace (a) but reject (b). Simply claiming it is wrong, and leaving it at that, won't do. Below are four popular reasons that are commonly given for rejecting (b). As we'll see, none of them are any good, despite their initial plausibility and despite the fact that they all stem from very reasonable concerns.

Reason 1: Rock Modification is Acceptable Only for Safety Reasons

Attitudes about the removal of loose rock stem in part from the potential danger loose rock presents, and from a broader moral principle that one should not place others in unnecessary risk. The route preparer has some obligation to prepare the route in a way that does not expose subsequent climbers to unexpected hazards, and that's why removing loose rock is acceptable. But this justification does not apply to the manufacturing of holds, and thus (it is claimed) (b) is false.

This initially seems like a good reason to treat hold manufacturing as different from removing loose rock. However, there are two points that undermine the relevance of safety. First, not all forms of acceptable removal involve material that is potentially dangerous. Included in (a) is a general attitude that route preparers can and even should remove poor quality, flaky or dirty rock that may not pose any real hazard but that can nevertheless make the climbing extremely unpleasant. A similar attitude applies to dirt, vegetation, lichen, and weeds that might be found on holds or in cracks. Route preparers are described as having done a bad job if they leave obviously loose material on the route, even if the loose material can't really hurt anyone. Consequently, it is widely acknowledged that acceptable modification of the climbing terrain extends beyond safety concerns.

Second, it is important to remember the main choice confronting the route preparer is *not* between ignoring a potential hazard to others and removing that hazard. After all, if no route is established, the loose rock will pose no real danger to anyone. The real choice is between establishing a route (and doing whatever that requires) or simply walking away and establishing no such route. The upshot is that it really can't be claimed that modifying the rock in this way is *necessitated* by safety concerns, since there are always other options available (like only establishing routes on solid rock).

Reason 2: Hold Manufacturing Violates Important Environmental Commitments

Most climbers have a perfectly legitimate concern for preserving the natural environment, at least as much as possible. Manufacturing is often described as environmentally unsound because it alters and "disrespects" the rock. Thus, it should not be treated the same as removing loose rock.

To be sure, respect for the environment is a good thing. But we already accept that our use of the outdoors involves changing the environment in various ways. Trails to the cliffs, bolts in the rock, permanent anchors for rappelling, and the removal of loose rock and flora all involve a widely accepted modification of nature so that we can go climbing. It is hard to see why an environmentally driven concern for the rock would distinguish between the removal of loose rock and removal of solid rock to make something climbable. Moreover, it is hard to see why the removal of lichen, weeds, and grass, isn't *more* environmentally dubious than manufacturing, given that it involves the killing of a living part of nature (notice that, from an environmental perspective, the killing of a tree is considered far more serious than simply smashing a rock on the ground). Look at it this way. Geologists occasionally walk up to a cliff face with a hammer and knock off a few small samples for analysis. But no one seriously thinks that this kind of geological sampling is dubious on environmental grounds. Or think about just sitting at the cliff and picking up a rock and giving it a toss. Such an act certainly alters the natural landscape, but even the most committed environmentalists would hardly bat an eye.

There are some who agree that we sometimes need to alter nature for our purposes, but they insist that there is a continuum and that hold manufacturing is at the extreme end of that continuum, beyond an acceptable level of environmental impact. I have no problem with the idea that there is a continuum of environmental impact, and that there is a line on this continuum that we should not cross. What I reject is the proposed ordering that places manufacturing further down the continuum than other things we find acceptable. In comparison to trails, bolts, chain anchors, chalk, and the excavation of loose material, hold manufacturing on blank sections of rock is probably one of the *least* environmentally impactful aspects of rock climbing. You might be tempted to say that hold manufacturing *permanently* alters the rock, whereas things like chalk are only temporary. This is unrealistic thinking. Take a hike through Smith Rock, Eldorado Canyon, the Motherlode at the Red, or virtually any other popular cliff with darker rock, and from the trail you will see the very obvious chalk on the wall that has been there for the last twenty years, and will continue to be there for several generations to come. In truth, it is far easier to fill in a few drilled pockets than it is to wash all of this "temporary" chalk off the walls.

Reason 3: Hold Manufacturing Harms Future Generations of Good Climbers

Another argument that initially seems plausible is a forward-looking argument about the future of the sport. Here, it is claimed that by manufacturing holds to make a route possible today, preparers are robbing future generations of currently inconceivable natural lines that are in fact climbable. Had today's 5.15bs been "chipped down" to mere 5.14s, the Sharmas and Ondras of the world would now have nothing to project.

A number of considerations undermine this reasoning. First, in our description of acceptable manufacturing, we stipulated that proper modification only applies to truly unclimbable rock, such that no future climber could ever climb it. In discussions of this topic, there is a lot of fretting about discerning what is and isn't unclimbable rock. Statements like "Who's to say what is unclimbable?!" and "No one really knows what will be possible in the future!" are commonplace. Nonsense. While it is indeed true that people are climbing things today that were once described by some as unclimbable, it doesn't follow that unclimbable rock is impossible to detect. Unless you are completely ignorant of physics and human physiology, it is fairly easy to recognize sections of rock where you can know with certainty that it will never be climbed in its current form. If you think it *is* impossible to recognize truly unclimbable rock, let's make a deal. I'll go pick out a 20-foot section of rock on a cliff somewhere and declare it unclimbable. If, in the next 15 years, it is actually climbed in its current form, then I will pay you $10,000. If it is not climbed in that form, then you must pay me $10,000. Any takers?

A stronger response to this concern is to recognize that a general acceptance of hold manufacturing will significantly help, rather than hinder, future generations of climbers. The reason is this: at any given point in time, including future points in time, there is a lot more unclimbable rock in the world than just barely climbable rock. Pick whatever grade you think might be the cutting edge for some future generation. 5.17d? Okay, there is a great, great deal more rock out there in the harder-than-5.17d range that could be converted into a 5.17d than there is rock that is naturally 5.17d. So, if your concern is that the future 5.17d climber won't have enough routes to do, then you should endorse a pro-manufacturing attitude. Note, this point applies to *any* future grade and *any* future generation. While I'm not suggesting that this is an especially good argument *for* manufacturing (though some may come to see it that way), I am suggesting that the concern-for-future-climbers argument is a uniquely bad argument for opposing all hold manufacturing.

Finally, this criticism of rock modification is partly grounded in the assumption that it is always done to make the climbing easier – to bring the rock "down" to a lesser climber's ability. In truth, there are lots of climbs where holds have been chipped *off* the route to make it harder. Here again, rock modification beyond the removal of loose material actually benefits, rather than hinders, the very top climbers.

Reason 4: This is a Slippery Slope; Any Acceptance of Manufacturing Will Lead to Abuses

A final argument against manufacturing (and that is also grounded in legitimate concerns) stems from the idea that any sort of tolerance of manufacturing can lead to all sorts of abuse: the destruction of great natural but really hard lines, or the modification of existing routes.

  WILLIAM RAMSEY

The problem with this argument is that it has nothing to do with the point at issue. Of course, most things done badly are bad. But that has nothing to do with the propriety of the practice done responsibly. Note that few people think the existence of bad bolting entails the need to abolish all bolting. Route preparers who engage in irresponsible and gratuitous manufacturing await the same condemnation as those who engage in irresponsible and gratuitous bolting. Because my argument is a defense of the limited sort of manufacturing described above, the possibility of other kinds of manufacturing is largely irrelevant. Notice, by the way, that irresponsible manufacturing sometimes occurs *now*; our current condemnation of manufacturing hasn't prevented it from happening.

Conclusion

The upshot of this analysis should be fairly clear. The standard arguments (at least those I'm familiar with) for rejecting (b) are, upon reflection, not very compelling and fail to support a case against manufacturing. The anti-manufacturing attitude does not accord with other things most rock climbers believe, like the acceptability of modifying the rock to make it climbable. Given that those latter beliefs are deeply entrenched, the former attitude should be abandoned. Our conclusion (c), the claim that the manufacturing of holds is sometimes acceptable, is the sensible view to hold. Let me wrap up by considering a couple of other points.

First, isn't there *some* sense in which a non-natural route (with manufactured holds) is inferior to a completely natural route? Yes, I think that, all else being equal, a purely natural climb is usually better and more appealing than one with manufactured holds. In fact, in most outdoor pursuits, the more that is provided by nature, the better. As with snowboard jumps, kayak runs, mountain-bike paths, and so on, a naturally occurring medium in rock climbing is superior to one that is contrived and human made. But it is important to understand the sense in which it is superior. A route with manufactured holds is on a par with one that has, say, poorly positioned bolts or awkward moves or wildly inconsistent difficulties. In all such cases, we do not think the route preparer was being *unethical* to establish such a route. We just think that, all things considered, the route has some features that detract from its overall quality. This is the attitude that should be applied to routes with reasonably manufactured holds.

My second and final point is this. There are no doubt many of you who are reading this and getting increasingly angry about my defense of manufacturing. You may be thinking to yourself "some yahoo is going to use this as a license for chipping holds on something he is developing." But if you reflexively think that manufacturing is always a bad thing, then you haven't been paying attention. Given the deficiencies of the anti-manufacturing outlook, you should instead be considering the possibility that your outlook is more of a bias without proper support. Indeed, given how often an anti-manufacturing attitude is defended by appeals to nothing other than tradition, or that "it just *is* wrong" (with heavy foot stomping), it resembles other forms of dogmatic thinking. To help shift your perspective, consider this: if you are a serious climber who climbs relatively hard sport routes, then there is a very good chance that at some point you have done a route with at least a few manufactured holds. Moreover, there is also a good chance that despite the manufacturing, climbing the route proved to be a gratifying and rewarding experience. Now what should the appropriate attitude be toward the route preparer, who, after all, sacrificed considerable time, money, and energy so that you could have that experience? Does it really make sense to view the preparer with condemnation and scorn? That seems unappreciative at best, and at worst downright incoherent. Or is it instead more sensible to recognize that it is sometimes acceptable for preparers to modify the rock and create holds so that people can have the sort of experience you had? The latter position, I have come to appreciate, seems far more reasonable and philosophically defensible.

NOTES

1   I am grateful to various people for comments on earlier drafts. In particular, I'm thankful to Mike Doyle, Alex Honnold, Cynthia Levinthal, Matt Samet, Stephen Schmid, Alan Watts, Chris Weidner, and especially Andrew Bisharat for their helpful comments. Their assistance should in no way be viewed as an endorsement of the views expressed here.

2   Singer's original essay is "Famine, Affluence and Morality," *Philosophy and Public Affairs* 1, 1 (1972): 229–43. A more recent discussion of this issue can be found in his *The Life You Can Save* (New York: Random House, 2009). For criticism of Singer's views, see D. Jamieson (ed.) *Singer and His Critics* (Oxford: Wiley-Blackwell, 1999).

3   D. Raleigh, "Start Making Sense," *Climbing* 122 (1990): 136. The letters that appeared in subsequent issues of *Climbing* in response to this essay nicely

capture the extreme animus climbers have, not just for manufacturing itself, but even for mild endorsements of manufacturing.

4   There may be a few purists who do not even think this sort of modification is acceptable, who think all loose rock should be kept in place. Because I'm basing my argument on what is *normally* accepted, this rare outlook has little bearing on my argument.

CHAPTER 12

THE ETHICS OF FREE SOLOING

 Free soloing is a rather peculiar activity. If you tell your friends or parents what you are up to, they will tell you that you've lost it for sure. Still, almost every dedicated climber will at some point find themselves strangely drawn to do the deed.

Perhaps due to its peculiar character, the ethics of free soloing is not the usual topic for debate in the magazines. Ethics within the climbing community tend to be identified with *style* rather than the *morally right or wrong* – whether to have pre-placed quickdraws when redpointing that oh-my-God-so-hard 5.14, or whether to suck oxygen while sprinting up the Hillary Step. In contrast, climbing ethics – in the more appropriate sense of moral rights and wrongs – is concerned with the permissibility or impermissibility of one's behavior in the mountains and on rock faces, regardless of whether one's behavior is considered "good style." It's that kind of ethics which will concern us here. With that in mind, is it morally permissible to free solo?

The first time I seriously pondered the moral rights and wrongs of free soloing was on a day of ice climbing near my hometown. Then merely young, top-roping wannabes, I and my friends had just sat down below the ice in order to consume our (we felt) well-deserved coffee. Sipping the hot brew, I was surprised to see little splashes in my cup as small chunks of ice found their way into the coffee. As I looked up behind me, there were two guys free soloing ten meters above our heads, chopping at ice as they picked their way across the ice wall. While I must confess that philosophical reflection was not my initial response, it struck me that free soloing certainly isn't such a private activity as it's usually portrayed to be. Even if they wouldn't have hit me on the way down, I certainly didn't want to shoulder the responsibility of calling the helicopter, giving CPR, or anything like that. No way. In fact, I got rather angry, as the whole situation made me feel slightly taken advantage of. What right to free solo had they in the first place?

Answering such a question isn't easy, however, and simplifying the ethical discussion in order to come up with a clear-cut answer is not really helpful to anyone. What I will do below is discuss some of the common ways to argue about the moral permissibility of free soloing. While I make no claim to provide an exhaustive discussion on the topic, I hope to sketch some of the central perspectives and considerations involved. After giving a tentative definition of free soloing, I proceed by showing what a complex activity free soloing really is and what functions it can fill in the climber's life. Next, I turn to the ethical discussion. While starting with the idea of moral rights establishing a freedom for us to act as we see fit, I argue that the ethical dilemma is not solved by an appeal to rights. Instead, there are a number of considerations that must be carefully weighed before a reasonable assessment can be made.

What is Free Soloing?

Free soloing usually refers to climbing without a rope or safety equipment, on routes for which protection is typically required to guarantee one's safety, and high enough off the deck that a fall would result in serious injury or death. Such a description captures the kind of activity most climbers would describe as free soloing.

However, this definition excludes certain forms of climbing. For instance, in high-altitude mountaineering, taking a long plunge is not necessarily much of a risk when climbing; instead, the danger comes from *not* coming off the mountain. The dangers inherent in mountaineering – for example, avalanches – aren't lessened by tying into a rope. The exclusion of high-altitude mountaineering solos from the definition of free soloing might be acceptable. However, the inclusion of bouldering might not be. Bouldering without a crash pad ten feet above back-breaking rocks might get you a six month hospital stay and a wheelchair, but we wouldn't call it free soloing. Hence, we need to make a slight revision in the initial definition. Free soloing must include the possibility of a vertical or near-vertical fall *from a certain distance*. Admittedly, there is some gray area here. Nevertheless, I suggest that bouldering routes are those that are shorter than 6 meters (20 feet). This convention is the height some insurance companies use to define bouldering, and it seems quite reasonable.

So, let me propose a more fine-tuned definition. Free soloing involves the following components: (1) the climber is ascending a vertical or near-vertical route (2) without using any climbing safety equipment meant to prevent or shorten a fall, (3) which, if the climber were to fall, would likely result in death or serious injury because (4) the fall would be 6 meters or longer. All of (1) to (4) are necessary; if a climb fails to fulfill any of the criteria, the climb isn't a free solo. This definition is intended to reflect, to a fair degree, common usage. Note that the definition doesn't include a concept of *danger*: this is a deliberate omission on my part, as what is perceived as dangerous is difficult to determine objectively. For instance, if you're a 5.13 climber doing a 90-foot-long 5.4 route without a rope, it can be argued that the risk of you getting yourself killed is slight or insignificant. But we would still say that the climbing is free solo. Instead, what is crucial is the *possibility* of death or serious injury in case of a fall: it is that risk which gives the ethical questions surrounding free soloing their urgency.

Now, obviously you don't need to toss your rope away for a climb to be potentially lethal, so the ethics of free soloing applies, in various degrees, to all forms of climbing, which generally involve the possibility of death or serious harm resulting from making a mistake. However, as free soloing arguably is the paradigmatic instance of climbing with a potential for serious harm, it's an appropriate area for chiseling out some of the common arguments involved in the ethical discussion.

Before embarking on the actual discussion, we need to add the qualification that the free soloing must be freely chosen. Free soloing can clearly be *involuntary*. For instance, if your rope is accidently cut by a falling rock while climbing high above ground, you will find yourself cussing and swearing and free soloing. However, involuntary free soloing isn't the sort of climbing I will discuss below, since moral judgments usually require (some kind and degree of) voluntariness for the agent to be held morally responsible.

Why Do People Free Solo?

Understanding why people free solo is important for the ethical assessment of free soloing: just as we would judge the stealing of bread differently depending on if the theft is prompted by starvation or by a lust for mischief, we would arguably judge a free solo differently depending on what causes it. Ueli Steck's solo of Eiger's North Face (made in a stunning two hours and 47 minutes) or Dave MacLeod's solo of Darwin Dixit (F8c) might not have the same rationale as the climber who soloes a 5.8 once in a while at the local crag, and as a consequence our ethical evaluations might differ.

Despite what mom, dad, or one's loved one might think, free soloing is not due to mental instability. Climbers who free solo, or happen to be friends with someone who does, know that free soloing is, in most cases, a rational and serious undertaking: most soloists solo in good conditions; they are mentally prepared; they have often practiced the route while on rope; they often solo routes below their abilities; and they are ready to back off as soon as something doesn't feel right. In short, they don't exhibit any of the usual signs of mental instability and a death wish.

There are also those who think free soloists take risks because they must. One version of this view claims that our behaviors are genetically determined; some individuals (usually males) are simply born hardwired to take risks. Others might argue that some people have been socialized into being risk takers. As an example of the latter view, take the Russian village Stolby. In Stolby free soloing isn't regarded as something spectacular, but something you just do, like playing chess or picnicking with friends, with the small difference that one of you might not come home to dinner. On this view, we get socialized into patterns of behavior which determine what is or isn't "normal" – and acceptable – behavior. However, on both views the moral responsibility of the free soloist is lessened, as the voluntariness of the free solo can be questioned.

From a more philosophical point of view it can be argued that risk taking is actually needed for our well-being as humans. The French philosopher Simone Weil (1909–43) once argued that the experiencing of risk is a human need and not just a craving for some genetically blessed (cursed?) few.[2] We need, following Weil, a bit of danger now and then, just as we need food and shelter. Her assumption seems intuitively sound: as societies increasingly institutionalize safety, the popularity of risky activities tends to go up. On this view, free soloing might be a way to fulfill a basic human need.

However, many free soloists don't free solo because they feel that they have a *need* to do it. Commonly, the justification is that the experience somehow enhances their well-being. The free solo is sometimes described as an experience of absolute harmony, either with oneself or with nature. Sometimes it's regarded as an aesthetic experience, like listening to good music or watching a beautiful sunset. Others view free soloing as a way to boost their self-confidence: knowing that they had it in them to manage a climb with potentially lethal consequences, they walk through life convinced that they can handle whatever life will hand them. Yet others free solo because they think the experience will teach them something about life or themselves. And there are also the climbers who free solo as mental training. Alpinists, who are bound to encounter rough climbing with little or no protection, will certainly benefit from a bit of free soloing now and then. Finally, there are those who think it's nothing but plain fun. Get rid of all the things which tend to take the fun out of climbing – all the annoying fiddling with the rope, nuts that get stuck, complicated belay stations, etc. – and you have free solo climbing!

Not Anyone Else's Business!

Having said something about what free soloing is, or what it can be, it's time to look at some common ethical perspectives on free soloing. Let me begin with the moral standard which is widely referred to in the Western world as *individual rights*. Perhaps the most prominent philosopher in this tradition is John Locke (1632–1704), who argued we have – regardless of what the laws, treaties, or public opinion tell us – natural rights to *life* and *liberty*.[3] Over time, and with the help of a few philosophers, this idea has evolved into a claim that we have rights which entitle us to do whatever we want, as long as we don't harm others in the process. My rights give me the freedom to do as I wish and no one is allowed to interfere. This is a powerful idea to invoke since questioning the value and importance of our individual rights is generally taboo. It can be argued that free soloing falls (no pun intended) within such rights: if I slip and shatter on impact, that's my problem, not yours.

Nonetheless, the claim that I have a moral right to free solo is problematic. The value of individual rights, no matter how one prefers to justify them, is that they enable us to pursue our own personal idea of the good life – to become rich, to have eight kids, to worship God, to collect stamps, to free solo, or to do something really bizarre, like play golf. However, such rights often assume that we are capable of making rational decisions when pursuing our happiness. The problem is that we aren't always rational. We often make decisions although we lack solid information, we commonly draw the wrong conclusions when reasoning, and – as modern economists and psychologists have shown – we are even hardwired to make mistakes when evaluating consequences. Add to that individual differences in hormones and psyche, and we have a recipe for some really bad decision-making.

Let me give an example. Geoff gets his kicks driving 200 km/h on the Autobahn without wearing his seatbelt. Ending up as a paraplegic after having lost control of the car, Geoff makes a completely different evaluation of his decision. According to some psychologists, Geoff suffered from the "optimistic bias" – our natural inclination to think that while bad things certainly happen to others, they won't happen to us.[4] What the psychological evidence shows is that we aren't very good at objectively assessing risks, and hence we aren't well equipped to handle the liberty our rights protect.

Still, there is a more serious problem which we must address. Since we are all supposed to have rights, it's important that me exercising my right-protected liberty doesn't violate someone else's rights. That leaves us with the precarious problem of deciding where to draw the line for what is morally permissible behavior: Which actions are within my moral rights and which are not?

Some cases seem obvious violations – free soloing above an innocent ice climber enjoying his coffee, that's a no-brainer: if you risk killing someone by falling on him, then you have surely stepped outside your legitimate rights and intruded upon someone else's. And if you have promised your spouse that you won't free solo, then you have simply given up your right to free solo. Other cases aren't so clear-cut. Let's say that you are soloing an easy classic in the French Alps, say, Aiguille de l'Index. As usual, the Aiguille is crowded by hoards of climbers and stressed-out guides with clients huffing and puffing to keep up. Halfway up, you slip and end up with a broken leg on an exposed ledge. With no partner to assist you, you find yourself at the mercy of the other climbers on the route. No doubt, they will help you and make sure a chopper takes you to the cozy hospital down in the valley. Now, have you acted within your rights or have you violated someone else's? Consider the following. First, your unhappy decision to solo the route probably destroyed the experience of the paying customers venturing into the mountains for their first time. Frightened, they had to watch their guides leave them to attend to you. Second, every extra element in a climb is an additional risk, and the guides – compelled by human sympathy, if nothing else – had to help out in the rescue, thereby risking harm to themselves and possibly even their clients. Third, while you are happy not having to pay the rescue bill, the French tax payers are less happy, as your little adventure became a rather expensive one. Fourth, your family and friends, while relieved to hear that you survived, are nonetheless terrified when learning about the accident.

So there is no such thing as a private sphere where we are allowed to do whatever we want, since everything we do affects others. We have no absolute moral right to do things that may harm others. Free soloing seems only to be permissible if you climb on a deserted island, where society doesn't have to share the costs of your actions.

What Free Soloing Will Do to You

But maybe free soloing is *not* permitted even if you climb in isolation. Some philosophers would argue that the free soloist must not only consider the effects on others, but also the consequences the free soloing will have upon his character. Regardless of whether or not we live on a deserted island, most of us aspire to have a certain character: we want to be generous, not the Ebenezer Scrooge type; we want to be friendly, not mean; and, so on.

According to Aristotle (384–322 BCE), we should strive to develop a virtuous character which will help us to live a good life.[5] On such an approach, the primary question is who you are, not what you do. While Aristotle's ethical theory is an intriguing topic, it has one aspect which is of particular interest to us here. Aristotle argued that the way to become a virtuous person doesn't result from thinking long and hard about how to act ethically, but through training. You will develop a virtuous disposition by imitating those who you (and the community in general) already recognize as virtuous, even though you don't necessarily understand why they act as they do. Aristotle understood a crucial aspect of human

   MARCUS AGNAFORS

psychology – that what we do forms our character. We all know that external factors influence our actions (peer pressure, stress, economic rewards, and so on), but it's often forgotten that our actions influence our character. If you do certain things, even though you didn't have the disposition for them to begin with, you will develop a character reflecting your actions. The question, then, is whether free soloing will develop a desirable character in you.

It can be argued – rather plausibly – that risky behavior will form a risk-taking personality. And that's presumably not a good thing: having a risk-taking personality doesn't mean that you only do dangerous stuff on your spare time, it also means that you are more likely to take chances when driving, in your sex life (if you get off the deserted island, that is), and other activities. Also, having developed a risk-taking personality, you not only begin to routinely accept risks for yourself, but you will increasingly put the people you meet in jeopardy as well. So, free soloing can turn you into a reckless person.

However, the consequence might also be the opposite. Engaging in risky activities such as free soloing could be helpful for the constantly anxious individual as it enables him to confront (some of) his fears, building a character less dominated by fear. Moreover, carefully assessing the risks of free soloing on a regular basis could turn you into an awesome risk assessor. Or, then again, sadly, you might just slip to your death and never develop any character traits at all.

A Matter of Consequences?

In normal circumstances, however, we don't live (and climb) in isolation. Still, even if every action affects someone else, we are nevertheless regarded as having rights establishing a sphere where we can do as we please. For instance, you might feel slightly nauseous seeing me wearing pink (I wouldn't blame you), but most people would say that you feeling nauseous isn't enough to take away my right to wear pink. Hence, we need a way to tell which actions intrude upon others' lives in an acceptable way, and those that don't. A common means of determining what are permissible actions comes from the family of ethical theories called *consequentialism*; its most famous member being utilitarianism, originally advocated by Jeremy Bentham (1748–1832) and John Stuart Mill (1806–73).[6] The core idea of consequentialism is that the only thing that matters when assessing the moral status of an action is its consequences: if the result is good, so is the action. However, what makes for "good" consequences varies: common suggestions include happiness, well-being, or satisfaction of preferences.

Translated into the discussion on free soloing, it means that free soloing can be permissible, even obligatory, if it produces good consequences. Take the unhappy climber, Bill. Bill has low self-esteem and feels that there is no adventure in his life – he is a really depressing guy to be around. So Bill takes off to Yosemite and free solos Nutcracker and Royal Arches. To the joy of his friends and family, Bill comes home happy and full of an I-can-walk-on-water mentality. From a consequentialistic perspective, Bill's solo spree seems to be a morally good thing.

But the consequentialistic doctrine isn't easily applied. The critics would point out that Bill didn't know that he was going to succeed: he could just as well have been the victim of bad luck and died after a hold breaking loose. Beforehand, Bill's decision could just as easily have been described as morally wrong. In defense of Bill, it might be argued that, as is the case for any rational climber, Bill takes such things into account before soloing a route. While the unprepared climber might be committing a moral wrong when deciding to free solo, Bill isn't, since he meticulously prepared for the climbs. Bill obviously can't know for sure that he will succeed, but he can make a reasonable estimation, and as it comes out on the positive side, his free solo spree is (at least) morally permissible.

So the evidence said that Bill would make it, and he did. Fine. But accidents happen. Derek Hersey died falling off a route that would have presented him with few problems had only the conditions been perfect. Instead, he was surprised by rain and it cost him his life. Having the odds on one's side is sufficient to confer moral legitimacy to a potentially harmful action, it can be argued, if the potential harm is only minor. But in free soloing the potential harm is violent death and intense emotional trauma to friends and family. So given the very severe consequences, you shouldn't do it *at all*, just to be on the safe side.

Such an argument generates some unwanted consequences, however. The morality of playing it (entirely) "safe" will prevent us from doing things which are part of our daily routines. Forget driving a vehicle in traffic and faster than walking speed. Forget walking up a steep flight of stairs unless you are tied into a belay system. And forget the innocent little hobbies people tend to value so much, like spending a day at the golf course, since one of those little golf balls to the skull can leave one in a permanent vegetative state.

When looking at consequences the most persuasive argument against free soloing won't be too concerned with the potentially lethal consequences for you, but rather the devastating consequences for *others*. What is morally problematic with Bill's adventure is the fact that he is likely to leave a number of friends and family members behind if he dies. As any psychologist will tell you, if anything will have an impact on your well-being, it's the premature death of a family member or a good friend. And even if Bill escapes harm, his free soloing may have negative consequences for others. Rumors of free solos quickly get around and inspire people to do the same. Now, not all of the people so inspired *should* be, and Bill is therefore a bad influence.

So, Should I Do It?

Someone once said that to every complex problem there is a simple answer which is wrong. This is certainly true when trying to assess the ethics of free soloing: it's a complex issue with no easy answers. Each free solo can, and arguably must, be assessed in its particular context: What does the solo climber stand to gain – materially, psychologically, physically – from a particular free solo? What are his chances of success on the route? Who will be harmed if he fails? What example will he set for others?

No matter how hard one tries, I doubt that any universal answer will be the outcome. Of course, some cases will fail miserably even to come close to moral approval: for instance, free soloing over other people, free soloing while having ten kids at home depending on you, and free soloing while under the influence, to give a few examples. But most free solos aren't such obvious cases. Most cases are perfectly open for ethical deliberation; an ethical deliberation which is unlikely to yield a universal answer.

However, since I want to avoid ending my discussion on such a disappointing note, let me suggest one moral rule which, unless there is some kind of an emergency, the aspiring free soloist is required to abide by in order for the free soloing to perhaps be morally permissible: *every free soloist must, before embarking on a free solo, carefully weigh all the above considerations (if not others in addition)*. This is not to say that, hey, do whatever you like as long as you sit down and pretend to be an intellectual for a minute or two. It isn't the thinking itself which confers moral legitimacy, but the fact that honest and careful reflection upon these issues is likely to bring important considerations to mind; values important to ourselves, our family and friends, and society. Most of us aren't ethical illiterates; we all have, and share, quite substantial ethical views. Reflection is meant to bring them out. For sure, we don't always agree, and often we derive our opinions by different routes, but it's remarkable how we usually come to agree on what should actually be done, after sharing the relevant information and after careful reflection.

So perhaps free soloing is a risky activity in more than one way: not only do you put life and limb on the line, but you are also entering uncertain moral terrain in which there is no ethical beta to rely on. Paradoxically, to make it through such terrain you don't need to know all the right moves, but you do need to have drawn yourself at least a rough moral topo.

NOTES

1 This essay has benefited considerably from comments by Stephen E. Schmid, Martin Andersson, and Johan Tovetjärn.
2 Simone Weil, *The Need for Roots: Prelude to a Declaration of Duties Towards Mankind* (London: Routledge, 2001).
3 John Locke, "The Second Treatise of Government" in *The Second Treatise of Government and A Letter Concerning Toleration*, ed. Tom Crawford (Mineola: Dover, 2002).
4 For a good introduction to the optimistic bias (and to the psychology of risk in general), see Glynis Breakwell, *The Psychology of Risk* (Cambridge: Cambridge University Press, 2007).
5 Aristotle, *Nicomachean Ethics*, in *The Complete Works of Aristotle*, Vol. 2, ed. Jonathan Barnes (Princeton: Princeton University Press, 1995).
6 See Jeremy Bentham, *An Introduction to the Principles of Morals and Legislation* (Mineola: Dover, 2007) and John Stuart Mill, "On Liberty" and "Utilitarianism," in *On Liberty and Other Essays*, ed. John Gray (Oxford: Oxford University Press, 1998).

 MARCUS AGNAFORS

CHAPTER 13

MAKING MOUNTAINS OUT OF HEAPS

Environmental Protection One Stone at a Time

In a 1972 article published in the Chouinard Equipment catalogue, Yvon Chouinard and Tom Frost noted that there was increased worry in the climbing and mountaineering communities about the environmental destruction caused by expeditions in several popular climbing areas.[1] Chips and holes in rock faces caused by bolting and pitons as well as the general wear and tear due to climbers traversing mountainsides were leaving indelible scars on the terrain. Additionally, trash left over from expeditions and the more mundane debris of human activity were taking an increasingly large ecological toll on the land. All of the signs of environmental deterioration were starting to weigh heavily on the minds of climbers almost forty years ago, who not only took climbing seriously, but also were drawn to it by the aesthetic wonder of unspoiled wilderness. How does one compromise between, on the one hand, being drawn to and valuing natural beauty and yet, on the other, passionately engaging in an activity that militates against that very value? The recognition of these contradictory goals began with the fledgling environmental movement at the same time as climbing was becoming more popular.

Have times changed that much? There are more climbers now than ever before, and while some "alpine starts" have been made to protect fragile mountain ecosystems, there have been precious few ascents. What is an ecologically conscious climber to do? She might try to scramble over this difficulty by thinking that surely her *own* individual climbs are not so damaging and hence absolve herself from responsibility. After all, she is only one climber. How much damage could she really be doing? Perhaps more importantly, even if lots of other climbers contribute to preserving the environment by limiting their number of climbs or by only free climbing, is it rational for her to do so as well, since again she is only one of many, and it seems her contribution would be negligible?

I think it will be helpful to look at these questions in light of recent work done on three concepts philosophers discuss a lot: the free-rider problem, the sorites paradox, and vagueness. Lessening environmental damage that comes from climbing presents us with a genuine instance of what in political philosophy is called the free-rider problem. I will argue that the free-rider problem is just the sorites paradox applied to social situations. "Environmental degradation" is a vaguely specified term – at what point is it that we have reached "undesirable destruction" of a rock face or alpine terrain? Since all of our questions are related to all three of these concepts, we need to investigate the latest work on them all. So, *Allez!*

The Free-Rider Problem

What does the free-rider problem concern? It usually involves large groups of people, but it may be clearer to start with a smaller and easier case. Imagine that you are aid climbing with a group. You don't know any of the other climbers all that well. You do notice one guy (not a gumby, he's done A5 climbs) who doesn't really hoist any equipment, never leads the climb, never finds routes, and conveniently forgets to bring his ropes. We'll call him Freddie Free-rider. Why are we annoyed by him? The main reason is that Freddie isn't making a contribution even though he could. So, in philosophical lingo, he is free riding – Freddie is getting goods (benefits) from the efforts of others without doing any of the work or supplying any of the resources. How could we have avoided this scenario?

That is the worst part of it – it doesn't seem that there was a way. Neither you nor your fellow climbers knew that Freddie would fail to contribute before the climb. And of course, once on the climb, it is not really feasible to stop and retreat, since you have committed yourself to the point where finishing the climb is as safe and quick as bailing. So, at this point, simply not climbing with him wouldn't work. Unfortunately, you're stuck with him.

Also notice the types of goods involved in this case. The food and water, the ropes, the anchors, and other aid-climbing gear are all goods you can't really *exclude* him from using. Philosophers refer to this as the *non-excludability* feature of public goods. This means that without extraordinary effort, no one can be kept from using these goods even if some fail to contribute to them.[2] So free riding involves being in a group of people in which there are some goods that are available to all and that you can't easily exclude people from using even if they are not contributing.

Free riding can occur in the small-scale case just described and perhaps we can conclude that Freddie Free-rider is simply being a jerk. But this isn't the end of the story. Have we heard Freddie's side of it? What if Freddie tells you that he doesn't contribute because it is not rational for him to do so? And would this change if Freddie was part of a larger group?

As already mentioned, free riding usually involves large-scale collaboration of many group members, such as in the case of taxation for public benefits. As an individual, is it rational for me to pay taxes when I think many others will? I could imagine that in the whole scheme of a larger cooperative venture, my contribution will be so small in light of all other contributions as to be negligible. It's not that I don't want the benefits. For example, I would love to enjoy national parks that are well maintained or use community rock climbing walls funded by tax dollars. However, my failure to contribute will not likely adversely affect the construction of such projects. After all, it is not as if the benefit that I get from the national park system will vanish simply because I don't pay my tiny proportion of tax dollars to it. So, without some measure designed to *make* me pay, I will readily use these benefits despite my failure to contribute. It would seem, then, that given this description it is unreasonable for me to pay if I'm not forced to do so. Okay, we might still be annoyed by Freddie, and think that his contribution to our small climbing team would have been somewhat valuable had he chosen to contribute, but at least we can understand why he might think the way he does. In our small-scale case, the ascent was successful despite Freddie's free riding. And in fact it seems that the larger the group Freddie is in, the stronger is his claim that his single contribution is negligible and therefore it is irrational for him to contribute.

One interesting feature of the free-rider problem is that, according to political theorist Richard Tuck, it is a rather recent phenomenon.[3] Many prominent philosophers of the past were very concerned with how individuals ought to relate to others and to society at large. However, neither David Hume (1711–76) nor Jean-Jacques Rousseau (1712–78) nor John Stuart Mill (1806–73) thought that it was rational for individuals to fail to contribute to goals they would enjoy. In Tuck's historical analysis, it was not until the mid-twentieth century that economists began introducing models of perfect competition that made them consider rational choosers in a new light, as those who would experience better payoffs if they failed to contribute to large-scale cooperative ventures. These days it is virtually impossible to read a political philosophy journal without running into some instance of the free-rider problem being described. Yet this seemingly obvious issue went virtually untouched for about two thousand years – that is pretty odd.

I mentioned earlier that since one might think her contribution doesn't really make a difference and others might likely think in the same way, in order to get the collaboration needed to secure some benefit we must be coerced. So maybe a more interesting feature of the free-rider problem is that I need to be convinced to contribute to something that I already think is valuable. Think about it. I may want to climb, but I want to scale the unspoiled rock face. I also suppose that if all climbers, whether they are free or aid climbers, limited their climbing, this would go a long way toward diminishing the bad environmental effects of climbing. But I don't think it makes sense for me to contribute to the very thing I want. It also makes sense that lots of other climbers may think in the same way about their possible contributions. So, in order to make sure that enough contribute to get unspoiled climbing areas, I (like all other climbers) will need to be forced to do something that is not irrational for us to want. In sum, I have a goal but I am being rational in not contributing to it – to achieve that goal I need to be coerced. All of this is really weird.

The Sorites Paradox

In contrast to the free-rider problem, the sorites paradox (which is also called the paradox of the heap) is much older. What is a paradox? A paradox is a statement that seems to be self-contradictory but may still be true. When the Ancient Greeks first made reference to the sorites paradox, these thinkers noted the troubles of describing a number as "small" or a quantity as "few."[4] The classic heap case comes about at least by the time of Galen (131–201 CE), a physician and thinker, in his book *On Medical Experience*:

> Wherefore I say: tell me, do you think that a single grain of wheat is a heap? Thereupon you say No. Then I say: What do you say about two grains? . . . [A]nd if you do not admit that two grains are a heap then I shall ask you about three grains. . . . For the conception of a heap which is formed in the soul and is conjured up in the imagination is that, besides being single particles in juxtaposition, it has quantity and mass of some considerable size [that is, a "heap" is not simply a numerable set of grains]. . . . If you do not say with respect to any of the numbers, as in the case of 100 grains of wheat for example, that it now constitutes a heap, but afterwards when a grain is added to it, you say that a heap has now been formed, consequently this quantity of corn[5] becomes a heap by the addition of the single grain of wheat, and if the grain is taken away the heap is now eliminated. And I know of nothing worse and more absurd than that the being and not-being of a heap is determined by a grain of corn. And to prevent this absurdity adhering to you, you will not cease from denying, and will never admit at any time that the sum of this is a heap, even if the number of grains reaches infinity by the constant and gradual addition of more. And by reason of this denial the heap is proved to be non-existent, because of this pretty sophism.[6]

Another way to think about this is to imagine that you are on a long alpine trek and you're using cairns to guide your return. A cairn is a heap of stones used to mark a trail. As the trek proceeds you begin to wonder if the next time you build a cairn you will need to build one with as many stones. Imagine, then, that cairn-by-cairn you build your cairns with one less rock each time. For instance, you used 15 stones last time but it still seems reasonable to say that if you used 14 stones this time you'll still have a cairn. And if you were to do this each time you would still call the group of stones a cairn. So the principle you are following seems to be that your rock heap remains a rock heap even when you take away one stone.

All of this seems fine, but what happens when you get down to one stone? On the one hand, the principle that a cairn minus one stone is still a cairn seems right (it would be crazy to think that it is not a cairn just because it had, say, eight stones instead of nine). On the other hand, it seems like the principle doesn't work when we get down to the final stone. This is because it seems crazy to say that two stones minus one is still a cairn, or (even nuttier!) that *one stone minus one* is still a cairn.[7]

Notice that the instances of the free-rider problem noted in the previous section sound suspiciously similar to these cases of the sorites paradox. In the same way as we have trouble with what philosophers call "vaguely specified" terms such as "cairn" where it is difficult to say that one more or fewer stones define a cairn, we can wonder if one more climber really causes "undesirable deterioration" to the rock face. After all, at what point do we say that the rock face is undesirably deteriorated? It seems difficult to determine *a* precise point where this deterioration occurs. In fact, it appears fair to say that the free-rider problem is merely the application of the sorites paradox to social issues involving human actions. If this is true, it appears that if we can dig our crampons into the sorites paradox, we perhaps can scale the free-rider problem as well. At least we might be left with better reasons for why policies forcing us to climb less or in a different way may be morally right.

So the situation for many climbers seems to be that they wish that mountainsides remain unspoiled. Can we straightforwardly say that I (especially if I'm a free climber) am really going to make a difference by my individual climb? Is it rational for me not to climb to protect the pristine rock? Besides, if enough others (especially aid climbers!) refrain from climbing, I can still climb and enjoy the benefit of unscarred rock faces without any sacrifice.

For the past fifty years the vast majority of economists would think that if you said it is irrational to contribute, you're right. But is this true? Again, I want to climb in unspoiled wilderness. Let's say I refrain from the most destructive form of rock climbing, aid climbing, that involves driving lots of protection into the rock face (and is of course sometimes left in the rock). By free climbing I will cause some damage, but likely very little on my own. And what about that *forcing me* part? It doesn't seem right that I'm forced to do something (even if I have an interest in the goal), if it is irrational for me to think that my contribution matters. Besides, what about all of the other climbers? Won't they think in the same way I do and not contribute? If they don't contribute, I definitely shouldn't have to contribute.

So, in the background of all of this, I have to have reasonably good grounds for believing that others are going to contribute to the goal of maintaining natural beauty by their limiting their climbing. If I don't have this confidence, then I don't have any reasonable ground for thinking that my contribution matters.

However, even if I assume that others will contribute, is it rational for me to contribute? Is there a solution to the paradox? This brings us back to the issue of vagueness. One suggested solution comes from the work of Timothy Williamson on vagueness.[8] He thinks that there must be a threshold where a collection of grains becomes a heap even though he admits that we can't know precisely where it is.

Let's think about this carefully. If we were simply to specify a precise point at which some precise number of stones makes a cairn a cairn, and stick to it, this would be nuts. That is, if you say that I've failed to build a cairn unless I put together the *exact* number of stones, this is at least bizarre. One reason for this is that it seems as though, thinking back to the trek where we were using the cairns, intuitively there is a point at which we could say that we have "enough" stones for the cairn. It would be odd that we would add more stones after we thought we had enough just to meet some goal of precision.

Perhaps the solution to the sorites paradox must be strange in the same way that the paradox itself is strange. Indeed, the threshold will likely be unstable and complex, changing relative to the situation. While it appears that we can examine a pile of stones and have a notion that it will have enough to act as a guide, it also seems that the next time we build a cairn that we might determine that some different number of stones is sufficient.

With that said, let's now look closely at the case of environmental degradation caused by climbing. We can agree that there are climbs where we all think that what used to be a fairly pristine place is now unpleasant and in some sense spoiled. Yet there doesn't seem to be a point where climbing a route tipped the state of the rock face from being "acceptably pleasant" to "unacceptably unpleasant." There is no single climber who can be accused of being the one who trashed the route. What this means is that this case is genuinely a *vaguely specified* one.

First of all, even if you can't specify a point (is it the 999th assisted climb up Serenity Crack or the 1,000th that leads to the destruction of that route?), there is likely a vaguely specified range of ascents that we don't want to be on the wrong side of. And it may be that on other rock faces, fewer or more trips will be part of the range beyond which we reach destruction. But notice that this means that there is a vague threshold and that it can be different from case to case. This is precisely what Williamson and Tuck mean about the threshold of vaguely specified cases as being "unstable." In response, according to Tuck, we are left with the conclusion that we have to act "as if" there is a threshold and see that our contributions do matter.

So, is it Rational for Me to Contribute by Not Climbing?

Some of you may be thinking that not all climbers necessarily believe that pristine wilderness is a primary goal or value. For example, I might love climbing so much that I care about climbing more than about any rock face I ever scale. On this view, the rock face is, as philosophers say, only *instrumentally valuable* – a means to an end. So, if climbing comes into conflict with natural beauty, so much the worse for natural beauty. If I truly thought this way, I would not curtail my climbing for anyone or anything – not my wife, not my kids, and certainly not for preserving the prettiness of mountainsides!

I have a few things to say about this. First of all, the arguments I give here are limited. If it is true that you don't care about anything except climbing, you will not be convinced that there is any paradox at all. I (or someone else) will need to appeal to other reasons or passions to convince you to either take care in how you climb, or to sometimes refrain from climbing, or to submit to some system that issues permits to regulate climbing. Second, I actually think in my discussions with climbing friends and from reading the accounts of other climbers that the natural surroundings we climb in *are very significant* to many of us. Most climbers at least feel some tension between the values of climbing and environmental conservation.

So, under what conditions do we find ourselves with reasons for contributing? Of course, the interesting thing about what I would call a contribution in our case is that it usually simply means not doing something. That is, I shouldn't climb certain popular routes and/or I should only free climb instead of aid climb in vulnerable terrains.

From the work of Tuck, we are to believe that our contributions are not negligible under certain conditions. For instance, I have reason to contribute if I have some confidence that others will also contribute by refraining from climbing as well. If I have such assurances I have a reasonable expectation that my contribution (by not aid climbing) will be part of the effective set of those contributions that preserve the rock face. In fact, even if your contribution was not necessary, it is even more likely that someone else's is. So, if the goal is to preserve the rock face, it is still met whether or not *your* contribution was needed. You also have assurance that your climbing was not part of the set that degrades the terrain, which will be important to a point I make later.

  DALE MURRAY

What this suggests is that in vaguely specified cases such as environmental degradation, we might have a different understanding of causality. *Normally* we think that we are making a *real* contribution when we are the *necessary* cause of something – it is my solo climb instead of an aided climb that was *absolutely needed* in order to preserve this rock face. But to think that this is the only way to be an important contributor to a cause is shortsighted. Instead, couldn't we think that to be an important contributor means that you were one of those *sufficient* causes to bring about the preservation of the rock ridge? That is, I will have brought about the result even if my action is not necessary, in the sense that without it the outcome would not have happened.[9]

For example, think about Freddie Free-rider. When we were upset with him it wasn't because his failure to contribute doomed the trip to failure. Despite the fact that Freddie didn't help fellow climbers carry gear and failed to bring ropes and a chalk bag (or even serve as a belay monkey!), this didn't keep them from climbing. The annoyance with him came from his not making any contribution at all – not because he didn't make *necessary* contributions. The problem was that he was part of *neither the necessary nor the sufficient* group of contributors. Hell, even if he had offered to carry some of his partner's gear but wasn't taken up on the offer, we would have likely had a better opinion of him, as being a conscientious (and sufficient!) member of the team, even if his contributions were unnecessary.

The point of this is that to be an instrumental cause of some outcome, you don't have to be a necessary cause, just a sufficient cause. This lends support to the idea that as long as we are contributing with *enough* others, we will likely be in the group of people who sufficiently bring about an outcome.

This brings us to the question of motivation. Even if I recognize that I have good reason to believe that I am one of the set of climbers whose refusal to aid climb or commitment to low impact climbing is enough to stop the damage to rock faces or alpine terrain, what impels me to do it? For this, presumably we have to channel our inner Chouinards and Frosts. In other words, in the same way that Chouinard and Frost note in "A Word" that once we see that we, with the help of others, have control over our natural surroundings we have good reason to contribute. It isn't merely that I want to preserve mountainsides and that I can do so (with enough others), it is also that I want to be the kind of person who does the preserving. So, to bring about a greener and cleaner terrain, I will want to be causally responsible for this outcome.

Concluding Remarks and Implications

For some, it will seem as though I've shown little. The basic message is that it is rational to contribute to environmental conservation by limiting my climbing even though it seems as though my contribution is negligible. There may be a number of people who don't care about environmental goals. Besides, as I admitted, we have to have some assurance that enough others will also contribute to stop the deterioration of certain climbing areas. However, at least we have seen an argument for the many climbers who think protecting the environment is an important goal but who are skeptical that it is *ever* rational *for them* to do so (even if lots of like-minded climbers were to do so). Remember that for some time now many have thought free riding is the rational thing to do. I've endeavored to show that this way of thinking is not rational when we look at it closely.

Notice something else as well. Just because we have an argument for why it may be rational for me to only either free climb or not climb at all in certain vulnerable areas, this doesn't mean that the need for coercive ways to make me do what I want to do simply goes away. For one thing, even though my rational, moral climbing ideals may beckon, my will may still be weak, in which case having something to "keep me in line" may be necessary to get to the right outcome. It may be rational, then, to advocate for a system of climbing quotas, such as those used in national parks (for example, permits are required to climb Mt. St. Helens).

There is something else that comes out of this as well. I might think that "I am doing my part" merely in my willingness to curb and/or change my climbing habits. However, if I really think that the cause is worthy, I need to try to convince others to curb and/or limit their climbing habits. And I need to show those who don't why they should. In order to help others make sure that they are continuing to contribute, I should focus on being active in the larger climbing community, trying to convince them that if they share my ideals, they should not climb or minimize their impact.

NOTES

1   Yvon Chouinard and Tom Frost, "A Word," *Chouinard Equipment Catalogue* (1972): 2–3.
2   Richard Arneson, "The Principle of Fairness and Free-rider Problems," in George Sher and Baruch A. Brody (eds.) *Social and Political Philosophy: Contemporary Readings* (Orlando: Harcourt Brace, 1999), p. 175.

3 Richard Tuck, *Free Riding* (Cambridge, MA: Harvard University Press, 2008), pp. 156–204.

4 Ibid.

5 Note that "corn" was used during Galen's time as a general term for stuff, not merely to label the crop for which the American Midwest is known!

6 Galen, *On Medical Experience*, ed. and trans. R. Walzer (Oxford: Oxford University Press, 1944), pp. 115–16.

7 It is *possible* to build one-stone cairns (especially with long, narrow stones placed like a post on an out-cropping in which it is very unlikely for it to occur naturally). However, this happens very rarely and doesn't really affect the point of the example.

8 Timothy Williamson, *Vagueness* (London: Routledge, 1994).

9 Tuck, *Free Riding*, p. 100.

PART IV

MIXED CLIMBING

Philosophy on Varied Terrain

CHAPTER 14

FROM ROUTE FINDING TO REDPOINTING

Climbing Culture as a Gift Economy

Not too long ago I was sitting with a climbing friend at a new "secret" sport climbing area close to Honolulu, Hawai'i, listening to him express concern over the fact the area was no longer secret. The existence of the climbing area was due to my friend's love of climbing. He had found the small cliff line, figured out how to access it, built a trail, cleaned up the trash, purchased the gear necessary to bolt the climbs, invested hours of his time drilling and gluing the bolts, setting up the anchor systems, and recruiting friends to help him. He received no compensation for any of these activities, nor did the people who helped him.

My friend was upset because one of his friends, whom he had brought to the area under strict instructions to keep the place a secret, had instead told his friends. Of course, these friends, also keeping the area "secret," brought their friends. Soon enough, the area was seeing fairly heavy climbing traffic, despite its continued status as "secret." The area retained some level of exclusivity because its existence was not published and knowledge of the routes was passed from one climber to the next, but otherwise it had become a resource open to all and nobody gave much thought to who had worked to put up the routes they were using.

Liberal theorists from John Locke (1632–1704) and Adam Smith (1723–90) to the present assert that the public good exists as a byproduct of individual self-interest and that rational actors seek to secure for themselves the fruits of their labor. Climbing culture, however, defies the logic of a system premised upon maximizing self-interest. While often considered a sport attractive to radical individualists, climbing can also be interpreted as embracing the values of individual expression within a framework of mutual aid. Climbing exists because of the time donated by those who establish routes and trails, most often using their own money and the help of friends. This underlying gift economy, as best described by Lewis Hyde, makes possible the commercial layers of the culture that have been built around the sport, including climbing gyms, guiding services, and gear shops, as well as ancillary needs like camp grounds, food establishments, and local hang outs.[1]

From route finding to redpointing, climbing is an example of a gift economy that undermines traditionally held capitalist assumptions about property rights, competition, and self-interest. Instead, climbing fosters an understanding of mutual aid and self-organization associated with social anarchism. To investigate this argument, I will look at several layers of the gift economy that underlie climbing. First, I want to investigate the gift of route finding and route setting. Second, I'd like to look at climbing culture to better understand the self-organizing ethic of social anarchists in opposition to the individualism of American liberalism and the ways in which the gift builds a community. Third, I'd like to use climbing to challenge the notion of private property as the penultimate value and instead suggest that the value of culture does not rest in privatization but in what Carol Rose calls the "comedy of the commons." By exploring these layers of climbing culture, it is possible to test ideas about the possibility of anarchist alternatives to the status quo.

Route Finding and the Creation of a Commons

While it was difficult for my friend to articulate exactly what bothered him about other climbers coming to the new area, there could have been lots of possible reasons, at least according to prevailing political theory. For example, the time, money, and energy invested in the area belonged only to a small group of people. What right would others have to climb on routes they put no effort into building? Second, with no organized climbing community or dues-paying membership, climbers rarely if ever contribute anything to the establishment of new routes or the maintenance

  DEBORA HALBERT

of old ones. Despite the life-threatening implications if anchors or bolts fail, the vast majority of climbers happily pursue the sport as what economists would call "free riders"; those who benefit from the labor of others without giving much thought to the underlying infrastructure to which they trust their lives. To further problematize the issue, according to Locke's labor theory of value, my friend should rightfully understand these routes as his property.

John Locke, in the *Second Treatise of Government*, outlines the labor theory of value which goes something like this: from property held in common by all people, the individual is able to secure personal property through work. Locke states, "thus *labour*, in the beginning, *gave a right of property*, wherever any one was pleased to employ it upon what was common, which remained a long while the far greater part, and is yet more than mankind makes use of."[2] For Locke, it was labor that produced value and thus translated that which was not useful into something that could be owned.[3]

According to the Lockean labor theory of value, my friend had every reason to be upset that others had begun to use the climbing area he had established and that they did so without his permission or without contributing anything to the maintenance and development of the area. He should even consider their entry to be a form of trespass on what he had appropriately enclosed for himself. According to Lockean logic, wresting these climbing routes from an undeveloped state of nature and transforming the otherwise "fallow" land (or in this case, cliff line) into a useful climbing area was sufficient for him to claim a property right.

However, such a theoretical justification does not match the ethic of the climbing world. My friend wasn't upset that people were climbing "his" climbs. In fact, the entire point was to develop more climbing for everyone. Ultimately, the area was to go in the guidebook and be publically available. He was upset that his friend violated an unspoken norm of secrecy before access issues had been fully worked out and before the climbs had been completed, thus jeopardizing the sustainability of the area for all climbers, as well as posing possible safety issues if climbers were to lead unfinished climbs. Furthermore, the route setters had not been able to get the first ascents on the climbs yet and one of the other unwritten rules of climbing is that those who establish the route get to make the first ascent.

Modern climbing follows specific routes that have been established by the first people to climb a given area. In the mountains many first ascents were done decades, if not centuries, ago. These routes tend to be a fairly loose description of how the climbers reached the summit and most likely include no fixed protection left for future climbers. Mountaineering routes are primarily the information provided by past climbers and sometimes a rough topographical outline regarding the types of features found along the way. Sometimes anchors have been placed, but more often than not the gift provided by these route finders is the information future climbers can use in an effort to ascertain they are in the right area. Often, these descriptions are vague at best, such as "climb the west ridge along a prominent buttress." However, the underlying impulse to share remains intact.

In sport climbing, routes tend to be a single rope-length long and follow pre-placed expansion bolts. The prevailing sport climbing ethic is that until the first ascents by the route setters have been made, it is very bad form to climb the routes, especially if the interloping climber gets what is called an "onsight" or a "redpoint." Sometimes the first ascent is easy, sometimes it can take months, and I've heard of cases that have taken years.

For any first ascent, substantial labor is invested. In the mountains this can mean lengthy excursions and days spent following dead ends, sometimes competing against other climbing parties for the goal. For a sport climb, in addition to time invested in finding the cliff line and a route worth bolting, the route setter must also own a drill, as well as purchase the bolts and hangers that need to be placed. Some areas may have voluntary bolt replacement funds, but generally gear is supplied by the route setter, who can spend thousands of dollars establishing climbs.

The desire to complete an area in relative peace, get the first ascents, and sometimes have a place to go with only your friends is inherent in the sport and should not be discounted. Solitude is often understood as commensurate with climbing but because of the popularization of the sport, it is increasingly difficult to find uncrowded rock. Some climbers start route setting in new areas in an effort to get away from the crowds.

The problem is that the drive for secrecy and the countervailing urge to share the climbs are in constant tension. Ultimately, sharing wins. It is simply the case that climbers cannot keep secrets. First, with some exceptions, you need a climbing partner to climb. This means that any secret area must be known by at least two people. Unless you climb with the same person all the time and make a pact to never go to a secret area with anyone else, at some point others will know. Second, climbing is inherently social and the existence of a good line that can be shared with others, talked about, and then dissected move by move, is too tempting to avoid. The enjoyment is in climbing it yourself, watching others do it, providing "beta," and often collaboratively working out difficult sections. Further enjoyment is then derived by endlessly talking about the moves, the routes, and other climbers throughout the evening and whenever you meet. Third, even climbers who seek solitude and don't like climbing around large packs of people enjoy sharing an area with their friends. Thus, because secrets are hard to keep and climbers tend to share, the labor invested in creating a climbing area does not result in an enclosed field of private property, but instead leads to the creation of a commons itself.

What would motivate my friend to establish routes if the goal is not to secure for himself a private club for climbing? What would motivate him to keep setting routes knowing they would become common property? Within the climbing world, very few people actually engage in route setting, but despite the labor theory of value, the intended result of establishing a climbing route is ultimately to contribute that route to the climbing community for the enjoyment of everyone.

While Locke's theory suggests that the fruits of one's labor become personal property, climbing offers a complex alternative. While route setters may establish climbs for individual reasons, including having new things to climb themselves, the social nature of the sport means that inevitably more than just the first ascentionist will climb the route. Climbs are rated by the community and popular climbs will see lots of traffic if they have aesthetic "flow" that can be so important to a good route. Unlike private property that is valued because of the right to exclude associated with it, the value in a climbing area emerges from sharing.

The Red River Gorge in Kentucky is an example. The overhanging sandstone cliff lines throughout the region bring people from around the world to this rural and depressed part of Kentucky. The vast majority of the climbs have been put up by only a handful of route setters over the last thirty years, none of whom were paid for their work, all of whom donated their time and money to the project, all of whom placed no limitations on the climbs once the first ascent was achieved, and many of whom have entered the lore of the community despite having moved on. In the process, they built thousands of routes and created a place where untold thousands of people can enjoy climbing each year. The labor of the route setters created a climbing area with an international reputation, a gift that simply does not match the liberal argument of profit maximization and suggests that enclosure of land through the use of labor is at best only one way to improve the collective good.

Creating Value, Building Community

The importance of route setting for the construction of a climbing community leads to speculation about the creation of community itself. In classic economic terms, route setting cannot exist because there is not the sufficient economic motivation. Here is an activity that drains personal resources in time and money for the limited and intangible goal of achieving a first ascent. Furthermore, instead of capitalizing on the results of one's labor, the product of labor is given away freely. However, when a route setter is seen as part of a larger social and self-organizing community, their individual actions are less confusing.

Herein lies the relevance of social anarchism and Peter Kropotkin (1842–1921). Kropotkin wrote his classic work, *Mutual Aid,* in response to those who sought to adapt Charles Darwin's theory of evolutionary competition to human society. Social Darwinists, as they were called, argued that humans progress through competition and the survival of the fittest. They used this paradigm to justify the gap between the rich and the poor and to enforce the tenets of capitalism, which embraced competition, thrived on inequality, and whose logic had been instrumental in transforming the traditional commons into private property for the elite.

Unlike the Social Darwinists, Kropotkin sought to demonstrate that human progress was the result of mutual aid, not the war of all against all. Instead of supporting a political theory that justified radical individualism at the expense of the co mmunity, Kropotkin argued that only through the creation of social relationships did humans actually thrive. He writes of the village, a way of life destroyed by the nation-state, as a place where labor was freely given and community was created through mutual aid. In one story from Southern France, Kropotkin writes, "When many hands are required in a *métairie* for rapidly making some work – dig out potatoes or mow the grass – the youth of the neighborhood is convoked; young men and girls come in numbers, make it gaily and for nothing; and in the evening, after a gay meal, they dance."[4]

Thus, community is solidified around collective labor provided as a gift and the mutual aid one human seeks to give to another. Kropotkin continues, "These days of hard work become *fête* days, as the owner stakes his honour on serving a good meal. No remuneration is given; all do it for each other."[5] He goes on to describe examples from multiple cultures where the power of community to support and aid each other

DEBORA HALBERT

transcends the self-interest advocated by liberal political theorists who were consolidating their doctrine to support modern industrialization. As Kropotkin concludes:

> But the nucleus of mutual-support institutions, habits, and customs remains alive with the millions; it keeps them together; and they prefer to cling to their customs, beliefs, and traditions rather than to accept the teachings of a war of each against all, which are offered to them under the title of science, but are not science at all.[6]

Two examples help demonstrate the primacy of mutual aid over the assumed superiority of privatization and self-interest. The first is the creation of the Red River Gorge Climbing Coalition (RRGCC). As the popularity of climbing grew in the Red River Gorge area, access on both public and private land became a concern. In response, the RRGCC was created through the dedication of volunteer climbers. The leaders of the RRGCC began to engage the Forest Service in dialogue over access issues, hold fundraisers to purchase over 300 acres of cliff line (now known as the Murray Pendergrass Nature Preserve), and sponsor trail-building days and bolt replacement efforts. RRGCC fundraisers are now important social occasions that forge relationships between climbers and help raise funds to pay for the land purchase.

From a classical liberal economic perspective, one could argue that the fact most climbers do not belong to the RRGCC or support it monetarily means that it is a failed system where the many free ride off the labor of the few. However, the RRGCC remains inspired by the enormous success of building a local climbing community and the hundreds, if not thousands, of people who have donated their time and money to the cause. In other words, climbers support the community but do so voluntarily and in the way that best suits their own preferences and needs: some volunteer hours to organize fundraisers, some simply give money, others work on trails. Their gifts keep climbing available for everyone. In doing so, mutual aid is cemented and more climbers are drawn in each year. The outcome is the formation of a community that transcends economic relations.

If outdoor climbing were to become privatized as some might endorse, climbing would continue to exist. While privatized climbing may enhance the experience for the few that will pay to keep the cliff line from becoming too crowded, it would also destroy the culture created by climbers themselves, much like the imposition of the nation-state destroyed the village community described by Kropotkin. Despite attempts to privatize, however, the social aspect of talking about climbing and sharing routes with others would mean people would choose to climb in the popular areas close to other climbers, instead of the exclusive ones where fewer climbers might be. Upon the gift of a few route setters, a community is established.

A second example is the climbing development done through Climb Aloha in Hawai'i. While not a destination climbing area, Hawai'i has a small climbing community made possible by a few route setters. Most prominent of these is Mike Richardson, who runs the only climbing store from his home. While the business helps support Mike and his family, one of its primary objectives is to fund the purchase of titanium bolts for new projects as well as retro-bolting old climbs. Climb Aloha is both the name of a store and the team of volunteers and friends who work on trail maintenance, scout out new areas, clean and create new routes, and help create community for all those interested in climbing in Hawai'i. More than once, I have meant to cut the tall grass heading towards the most popular climbing area only to find the job had already been done by some unknown volunteer. Hawai'i is the only climbing area in the world where I have seen a string system that makes every climb capable of being top roped, strings that are slowly being replaced by yet another anonymous volunteer. Having moved to Hawai'i a little over a year ago, the gift of these route setters made it possible for me to become part of a climbing community immediately and establish new friendships that ultimately transcend the cliff.

Property Rights and Climbing

Often, advocates of private property tend to see the existence of property as such a valuable entity that they fail to see that too much property can hinder innovation as much as it can help, an argument recently made by law professor Michael Heller in his book *The Gridlock Economy*.[7] Keeping the underlying layer of climbing open and accessible actually makes the additional layers of for-profit activities possible. At one level, private entities thrive upon the appropriation of the free labor of others – "free" labor becomes the foundation upon which other entities can make their money. Better understanding the ways in which climbers

DEBORA HALBERT

relate to private property can help tease apart the many dimensions of property rights issues as they relate to rock climbing.

Issues of access have long been of concern to rock climbers. Climbing is rarely accessible on private land for fear of liability, though increasingly climbers are securing land privately to assure future climbing. Thus, climbing has long taken advantage of the vast public lands held in the United States by state and federal government agencies. Public lands also involve access issues for climbers. Endangered species, voluntary closures for the purposes of recognizing Native American traditions, legal definitions of wilderness, and possible overuse of fragile areas have all been reasons to limit climbing access on public lands.

Within these limitations, however, access to rock climbing in the United States is premised upon a commons of climbing that provides the structural foundation for numerous economic activities that occur on top of it. Guiding services, for example, require access to public lands and the climbing commons of routes discussed above. Guidebooks, which are published by private individuals, describe the routes in a given region that then opens them to all climbers. In many ways, whether the underlying property is public or private, the climbs themselves constitute a commons open to all and to which the notion of the tragedy of the commons seems not to apply.

Garrett Hardin's (1915–2003) classic essay "The Tragedy of the Commons" argues that common ownership of land inevitably leads to its destruction because everyone will exploit the commons, or land that is not privately held, for their own personal benefit. As he puts it, "ruin is the destination toward which all men rush, each pursuing his own best interest in a society that believes in the freedom of the commons. Freedom in a commons brings ruin to all."[8] This outcome, which is the result of rational actors seeking to maximize personal benefit, structures our relationship to land held in common.

Climbers, however, offer a much more complex understanding of the tragedy of the commons argument. Hardin is concerned that a rising population will have a deleterious impact on the environment because individuals seeking to maximize their personal interests will exploit the commons to its ruin. One might make a similar argument about climbing and the commons – there are limited climbing resources available and as the numbers of climbers increase one can anticipate a tragedy of the commons effect on existing resources. Property advocates suggest that the only way to deal with this tragedy is to privatize resources. Certainly, privatized climbing will limit access. However, climbing is far more demonstrative of Carol Rose's notion of the "comedy of the commons" than it is of its tragedy.

Rose critiques Hardin's thesis by suggesting that in many cases the construction of a public space adds value that simply cannot exist within the private space of property. The public square, the highway, the public path are all examples where public benefits transcend the private benefits of private property. As Rose points out, "at least within the limits of the community, the more who join the dance, the greater the enjoyment of each participant."[9] Climbing and the collective routes that make it possible are yet another example of the comedy of the commons. Rose continues to describe "interactive" activities as those "where increasing participation *enhances* the value of the activity rather than diminishing it."[10] Such is the case with climbing. The gift of land and routes for climbing defies conventionally held assumptions about the tragedy of the commons and instead embraces the possibility of transcending property rights by offering climbing as a gift to the community, enhancing the benefit of all, and instead demonstrates that the value is in the community and not in the isolated experience of excluding others.

The benefit of a commons in climbing can be found in the Red River Gorge in Kentucky. In the late 1990s, Rick and Liz Weber opened up Muir Valley, a 400-acre piece of land in Kentucky that they had purchased for retirement. As a gift to the climbing community, Rick and Liz built roads and trails and opened their over seven miles of cliff lines to climbing development. As a result, they have created one of the best climbing areas on the region, which sees hundreds of climbers each weekend.

While the Webers monitor who can set routes and the procedures for doing so, there are few restrictions on using the land, except to refrain from bringing dogs and staying on the trails. They invite climbers to support their efforts with trail days and they are active in local climbing initiatives. Their gift is a gift to a community of strangers brought together through the love of rock climbing. It is a gift that cannot be explained through the lens of property rights theorists or those who claim that as isolated individuals we seek to secure for ourselves private benefits that only create social goods as a byproduct. While we all understand public lands as publically accessible, it is very rare to find private property treated in such a way. However, climbers have as the foundation of their culture a gift economy that challenges the value of private property and instead supports the notion of the "comedy of the commons."

  DEBORA HALBERT

Conclusion

So what makes a highly paid fashion designer quit her job, buy a Eurovan and move to Kentucky to serve pizza and climb every day? What possesses an engineer to become a climbing guide? Why would a professional pilot or an entomologist spend thousands of dollars and hours of their time establishing climbs for no reward except the honor of a first ascent and the ability to name the route? Why, indeed, would anyone sacrifice what most Americans understand as the "American Dream" – a career, a house, and material wealth – to live in a tent or car, and have no permanent employment or discernable future goals?

I was having a discussion with a friend not too long ago which involved fantasizing about quitting our jobs and going on an extended climbing trip. He wasn't so sure he could put climbing as his sole focus for that long. After thinking about it, I said it isn't simply the climbing that is the attraction, though climbers are certainly obsessed enough that they could do it virtually full time. It is a way of life aligned with personal autonomy, freedom, and the escape from the alienation of wage slavery that draws people to climbing. Climbers who opt out of the mainstream economy do so because they value their autonomy and the sense of mastery that comes from focusing the mind and body on achieving a difficult climb. They also value the community created throughout the world whenever climbers self-organize to create a climbing commons for each other.

Given its existence as a self-organizing community, and the fact it tends to attract individuals who are most interested in forging a life outside the boundaries of late-capitalist America, climbing allows one to tap into a way of life that transcends the nine-to-five; to experience risk; to engage with the natural world; and to become physically empowered. However, climbing culture allows us to challenge the cherished values American culture holds dear – private property, radical individualism, survival of the fittest, and the maximization of personal profit. Instead, it suggests that mutual aid, self-organization without the force or power of the state, and the power of the gift creates a far more interesting and longstanding cultural commons. These are values worth climbing for.

NOTES

1   Lewis Hyde, *The Gift: Creativity and the Artist in the Modern World* (New York: Random House, 2007).

2   John Locke, *Second Treatise of Government*, 1st edn. (Indianapolis: Hackett, 1980), p. 27.

3   Ibid., p. 25.

4   Peter Kropotkin, *Mutual Aid: A Factor of Evolution* (London: Freedom Press, 1998), p. 194.

5   Ibid., p. 195.

6   Ibid., p. 207.

7   Michael Heller, *The Gridlock Economy: How Too Much Ownership Wrecks Markets, Stops Innovation, and Costs Lives* (New York: Basic Books, 2008).

8   Garrett Hardin, "The Tragedy of the Commons," in John S. Dryzek and David Schlosberg (eds.) *Debating the Earth: The Environmental Politics Reader* (Oxford: Oxford University Press, 1999), pp. 23–4.

9   Carol M Rose, *Property and Persuasion: Essays on the History, Theory, and Rhetoric of Ownership (New Perspectives on Law, Culture, and Society)* (Boulder: Westview Press, 1994), p. 141.

10 Ibid.

CHAPTER 15

ARE YOU EXPERIENCED?

What You Don't Know About Your Climbing Experience

So, are you experienced?
Have you ever been experienced?
Well, I have.

Jimi Hendrix

A far more common answer to the question why do you climb than George Mallory's famous "Because it is there" is "For the experience." A recent common variant on this theme is "Because it is fun." But, as one climbing friend of mine bluntly points out, "It is often not." The range of experiences associated with climbing include anxiety, terror, discomfort, and exhilaration; and on rarer occasions, just simple pleasure or enjoyment. Telling your climbing friends that you had fun on a route is often a completely inaccurate account of your experience. Given that climbing is all about the experience, it seems a little odd that we might not be in the best position to assess what we were experiencing at the time we were climbing. What I will argue is that this is to be expected and, further, that this disparity between what has gone on during a particular climbing venture and our account of that experience explains a lot. On the lighter side, the disparity can readily account for the climbing equivalent of fishermen's tales. On the darker side, we can appeal to the disparity to account for the tragic misjudgments of ability that can lead to climbing accidents.

The philosophical territory here lies somewhere around the area of self-knowledge. The problem of self-knowledge is the problem of whether or not my judgments about myself are true or justified. This is an odd philosophical problem (but they all are, or so it seems). You might think that your judgments about yourself are the ones you have the best handle on, but lots of philosophers disagree. Descartes (1596–1650) famously had to go to great lengths to argue for the conclusion that he knew his own mind better than he knew anything else. He did not take this conclusion for granted. Kant (1724–1804) was less sure than Descartes about the issue and erred in the other direction. Our problem is in this neighborhood but is slightly different; it is the problem of our access to our internal states. Think of a related epistemological problem to the self-knowledge problem: the problem of our knowledge of the external world. This is the problem of whether or not my judgments about the external world are true or justified. If our visual system could be relied on to bring us high-quality information about the external world, we could appeal to the fact that we have seen this or that to justify our judgment that this or that existed. Again, lots of philosophers disagree. Descartes also made a prominent contribution to this discussion, arguing that we should be skeptical about the powers of our visual system. Our problem relates to self-knowledge in the way that worries about the visual system relate to knowledge about the external world. What I will argue is that we do not have reliable access to our inner world, our internal states.

One striking illustration of this possibility comes from a very influential psychology experiment. Richard Nisbett and Timothy Wilson asked subjects to choose their favorite from an array of socks.[2] Subjects made their choice and then were asked to explain the choice. Subjects gave a range of reasons for their choices, including liking the texture or the color of their favorite. All the socks in the array were the same. Nisbett and Wilson concluded that all of the reasons given for choosing socks were *post facto* confabulations; in other words, they fabricated their reasons after they made their selection. This experiment was one of the earliest in a burgeoning tradition of experimentation in cognitive and social psychology. Many psychologists working within this tradition subscribe to a dual process theory of the mind. On this view, much of our everyday decision-making and other behavior is driven by fast, automatic processes that are inaccessible to conscious awareness, the first of the dual processes. The second process is slower and accessible to conscious awareness and handles higher cognitive tasks, such as playing chess or making complex calculations. The first process has been dubbed the

  STEPHEN M. DOWNES

"new unconscious," to distinguish it from the related Freudian idea. Many psychologists now agree that "conscious awareness . . . is not necessary for complex psychological functioning."[3]

Rock climbing is a good candidate for a complex human behavior that is produced by a suite of automatic unconscious mechanisms. Think of any part of the practice: if you have done it for long enough, you quickly realize that you do not know why or how you did it, you just did. For example, if you are a sport climber and have put months into working a route, the eventual redpoint is often disappointing. The route floats by, the moves come easily and you are at the top clipping the chains. If you say that you are so happy to have done the route, you are not basing this on any access to your internal states while doing the route. Often, you are expressing relief that all the hard work is over. If you are a traditional climber, you often experience clipping a piece, which you simply reached for, pulled off your rack, and plugged in. The process whizzes by without a millisecond's reflection. If you have to reflect on your internal states during a climb, it is often the sign of impending disaster. On long leads with rests available – or worse still, long slab climbs – stamping out self-reflection is an important part of a successful ascent. The process of self-reflection can sometimes be helpful but often involves accessing just the wrong kinds of internal states, beliefs about the route, your abilities, the potential fall, and so on. You are far better off trying to breathe more slowly during a hard lead to bring your heart rate down than you are trying to remember what piece to put in or what the next hold is like, or reflect upon whether you are strong enough to do the next move. Many readers may not be convinced, so I will use some examples to further examine the climbing experience and what kind of access we have to our internal states during our climbs.

Most of my first climbing adventures took place in North Wales. I grew up in Merseyside, the metropolitan sprawl surrounding Liverpool, and it was a short drive, a slightly longer hitchhike, or an unbearably long bus ride from there to the Welsh hills. The previous generation of Welsh climbers had pushed the standards of climbing in the area and also pushed the standard of boldness. In the early to mid-1970s, soloing was promoted as the pinnacle of the climbing experience. Anyone who was anyone wanted the experience that accompanies soloing a route. Alan Rouse relates the story of one day during this era: "One generation of climbers was here; the in-between generation who lacked a definite direction but enjoyed climbing immensely. The best protagonists, Cliff Phillips, Eric Jones, Richard McHardy, Pete Minks and Paul 'Tut' Braithwaite, were all soloing, a popular practice which indicated the dominant desire for thrills and freedom."[4] Rouse goes on to describe his own solo of the Boldest on Clogwyn Du'r Arddu (Cloggy) that day. His description includes the following account of his own state on entering into the crux section of the route: "Now I was committed and a real wave of pleasure accompanied precisely executed moves." He concludes by describing the experience with a bit of reflective distance: "Fifteen minutes on the thin red line is worth an awful lot of ordinary living. Mad? Probably, but what a superb form of madness to engage in."[5]

I wanted to engage in that form of madness when I was younger. Unlike Rouse, I do not have much to report about my soloing experiences. Looking back on them, I think this may be due to a concerted attempt not to have anything going on in my mind during the climb. I can muster up one fleeting glimpse of stepping across a groove above the sea on a pitch of Dream of White Horses at Gogarth, the sea cliffs on the coast of Angelsey, and then being at the top of the route. I tend not to engage in such activities any more, but on my frequent trips back to Britain I like to get out on the Welsh cliffs with my brother or old friends. On one such visit I returned to a table at a Llanberis pub to hear the end of a tale being recounted about me. Alan McSherry and I had been climbing at Gogarth a few days earlier. On this day, I joined Alan on one of his attempts to "tick" routes in the book *Extreme Rock*. We had dispensed with Winking Crack without much event, although we both found the route quite hard. Next up was a meandering venture across the Main Cliff taking in pitches of a few routes and finishing up the last pitch of Dinosaur. Alan was belaying as I led this pitch, our last of the day. I was out of sight. As Alan told the tale in the pub, he asked me how I was doing and I replied, in a very feeble voice, "I am very tired and very scared." This is a pretty typical condition to be in when leading a pitch at Gogarth. Of course, telling a group of climbers about someone admitting to it in the pub is guaranteed to produce gales of laughter at the protagonist's expense, mine in this case. What is my version of the story? I pulled off a bold lead in fine style, of course.

Let us focus in a little closer on our access to our internal states during a climb. Here is an oft-repeated scenario: you reach a point on a route, perhaps you have just clipped a bolt or a piece of gear, and confront a hard move. Ultimately, you hang on the piece and declare yourself not strong enough to do the move. What happens next also is oft-repeated. Either someone else leads the pitch or you get the rope to the top somehow and then, top rope in place, do the move easily, first try. You were

   STEPHEN M. DOWNES

plenty strong enough. Consider another familiar predicament: you reach the anchors of a route and while clipping them declare "That felt easy." Everyone watching, including your nervous belayer, witnessed a desperate, by-the-skin-of-the-teeth, wobbler of an ascent. Were you experiencing what it feels like for a climb to feel easy? Just so the climbing reader does not feel picked on, let me stress that I was a repeat offender of the wobbler-influenced ascent. In my teens and early twenties I would shake my way up pitches and in the process kick pieces of gear out and put undue stress on belayers. The whole affair felt fine to me. I would get to the top feeling a sense of achievement at my latest ascent, unaware that I had kicked out most of my protection. One of my climbing mentors and belayers on a number of these occasions, Leigh McGinley, had a way of dealing with these events – he simply paid out loads of slack and walked away from the base of the route. His explanation was that if I fell I was going to deck it and he did not want me to take him out in the process.

Remember that I want to argue that we do not have reliable access to our internal states. Let us assume that the default position is that we do have reliable access to these states and that our self-reports accurately reflect these states. Someone holding the default view might reflect on the range of examples I have just given and conclude that they are too disparate to support one conclusion. Surely, some kinds of self-report have to be accurate. Rouse's claim that he was experiencing pleasure on his climb could be an example. Just as my claim that I am in pain on a given occasion must be accurate. On the other hand, someone saying that they are not strong enough could easily be mistaken. The relevant difference here, so the objection might go, is that we have no reasonable expectation of having access to our forearms' muscle fibers but we do have access to whether or not we are in pleasure or pain. A number of philosophers, including Paul Churchland, have pointed out that we may not be entitled to the assumption that we have 20/20 access to pain and other such feelings.[6] Such feelings can be manipulated by changing context, or what psychologists call "priming." If we anticipate that something will cause pain – for example, a clothes iron about to be pressed on our skin (Churchland's example, not mine) – we will feel pain even if the iron is cold. If we can be mistaken about something this basic, the implication is that we can be mistaken about a whole range of our experience.

Maybe this is something you could get used to. Once you realize that there is this strong tendency to mistake your internal states, you could rely on others to fill you in, when the requisite feedback was required. But this might somewhat diminish climbing for you – you are in it for the experience but you have to ask others what you experienced! The predicament is reminiscent of the old joke about behaviorists: one behaviorist says to another, "How am I feeling?" The climber's predicament is not quite that bad. Let me use an analogy with another notoriously dodgy cognitive faculty – memory – to explain why.

There are plenty of occasions when my memory is pretty bad. Lately, I have been walking to work, riding my bike, taking the bus, and sometimes driving. If I get involved in a project late in the afternoon, I end up forgetting whether I have driven the car. I have two problems. The first is figuring out whether I have driven and the second, if I have, is finding the car. Our local worlds are full of scaffolding that supports cognition. We learn to use the scaffolding when our cognitive faculties fail us. If my car keys are in my pocket, that is a good sign that I have driven the car. Armed with the keys, I can go out into the parking lot and click the button on the keys and see if any of the remaining cars in the lot light up. If they do, problem solved, I drove. Failing to remember can easily be understood as an example of a failure to access an inner state. Is there any analogous scaffolding to help in the case of failures to access our other inner states such as those underlying the activity of climbing? If you are not sure if you grabbed a hold or grabbed it in the right way, you can ask your climbing partner or bouldering companions. They can point to the dab of chalk just to the left of the hold and you have a sense of what you did and also what you have to do on your next try. We have meticulously written guidebooks that can be used to prepare for an ascent but also to organize our account of our ascent. I would argue that it is almost inevitable that your account of your climbing experiences relies on these kinds of scaffolding. The richer the tale of the experience, the more the scaffolding has been relied on.

So far I have not touched on the ethical implications of our predicament. Before we do this, a brief detour into another area of philosophy is required. Discussions of self-knowledge are often accompanied with discussions of self-deception. The predicament I am describing for us climbers is similar to the way in which non-intentionalists characterize self-deception. They say that if you are self-deceived this is not something that you have intended to do to yourself. Rather, believing that your child is doing well in school when they are not can be a product of your desire that your child do well in school. Even if the evidence all points to the child doing badly, you can still maintain that she is doing well. You are self-deceived and the state is caused by your overriding desire. The belief that your child is doing well could also reduce anxiety and relate to a number of other emotional states.[7] In this situation you are self-deceived, but you are not intending to deceive yourself. In our climbing examples, we lack access to our internal states and as a result our self-reports are off base, but we do not intend for this to be the case.

Here are a few more climbing examples which we can use to work our way into the potential ethical implications of our failures of internal access. I was at an open-format bouldering competition recently. In these competitions boulderers have about two hours to complete as many problems as they can and they all carry around a score card. Problems are assigned a numerical value, which you add to your score card for a successful ascent. If you fall once on a problem, you dock a point, and so on. The whole scene is loads of fun but a bit of a mad house and the scoring is on the honor system. A young fellow started up one of the problems, a technical V6 or so with tiny footholds. On the second to last move, he put his foot on a huge foothold from another problem and reached right to the top. He was completely focused on the handholds and the top and said the problem felt easy for the grade. In this case, his self-report was pretty accurate. But the reason the climb felt easy was that he had used an extra foothold. So what did he do? He convinced some onlookers to sign his score card and support his claim that he had flashed the problem. In other words, he cheated.

Here is a related example: I was fighting my way up a crack climb in Yosemite some years ago. The climbing was in a dihedral, with jams in the crack in the back. I was getting pretty tired (so I thought) and found myself desperately trying to pull up on a jam. I seemed to be unable to move myself at all and started to panic and thrash even more. Inadvertently, I shifted my foot in the crack, resulting in me suddenly pulling up effortlessly, reaching for a sinker jam, and finishing the pitch. I had been standing on the rope and my foot was jamming the rope in the crack and, as a result, I could not pull up. No ethical implications here, at least so I thought, until I was talking about the incident with my climbing partner at the time and he mentioned the "old secret crack climbing rest trick." Imagine yourself replicating my maneuver but rather than trying to pull against the rope, you have a piece above your waist, sit back on the rope and you have yourself a no-hands rest. Done inadvertently in the heat of battle, this could feel strange and pass by quickly, but it could also be the difference between a successful lead and failure on a hard crack climb and amount to cheating.

One more example for all you boulderers: the dab. The secret crack rest could be classified as a dab, but the classic dab involves inadvertently touching the ground, the bouldering mat, or the off-routed wall opposite the problem. It is amazing how much help a short tap on the ground is for upward motion. Many times you are not the best person to ask about the dreaded dab. If your bouldering crew is attentive enough, they will let you know. The appropriate response is to say "No wonder that felt so easy" and rest up for the next attempt. If the dab is not registered and you claim the ascent, you have cheated. The most egregious bouldering dabbing case I ever heard of occurred at Morrison, a bouldering area just outside Denver. There are some very low-level roof bouldering traverses there and the footwork is very technical, as it is very hard to keep your feet off the ground. One (and maybe more) star of the circuit used to make this traverse look very easy because they were putting their feet on the floor all the time but doing a very good job of disguising the infraction – a highly technical dab and apparently a completely intentional one!

If I am right about our access to our internal states while we are climbing, you should expect not to know that you have added an extra hold, stood on the rope, or had your foot hit the bouldering mat during your ascent. As a result, sorting out valid versus invalid ascents comes down to your climbing and bouldering partners, their use of your report, and everyone's use of all of the scaffolding I mentioned above. Having unreliable access to our internal states may help explain the prevalence of inaccurate reporting of ascents by the ascensionist, but it does not justify it. If you are about to attempt the hardest climb or boulder problem you have ever done, take at least one reliable person along to witness the ascent or prepare to have the ascent disregarded.[8]

Social psychologists distinguish a huge variety of self-reports. So far I have concentrated on reports about our internal states that are most closely analogous to feelings, such as the feeling of being in pain. Now I want to return to the example of assessing our own strength to illustrate a related but different kind of failure of self-reporting. Study after study reveals that far more than 50 percent of us who drive report that we are better than average drivers.[9] Obviously, this makes no statistical sense. Why would we say such things? According to social psychologists, we make all kinds of self-attribution and self-assessment errors – saying that we are better than average at driving is just one example. When climbers say something like "I climb 5.12," this is self-attribution. When we say that we are ready to climb a route we have long aspired to, this is a self-assessment. Many of these climbing related self-assessments and self-attributions are as off base as our assessments of our driving ability.

Much of the time this is harmless and not much of a cause for concern, but there are cases we should be worried about.

Climbing is not a team sport and give or take some minor details, anyone can do it when they decide to; that is why lots of us like it so much. You can decide that you are up for the task and set off up pretty much any route or boulder problem you like (or even mountain for that matter). You cannot do that in organized team sports. If you are convinced that you would make a really good defensive lineman (in American Football), it is highly unlikely that you will end up in the starting defensive line for the Pittsburgh Steelers next Sunday, finding out what it feels like to be hammered by the opposing offensive line. If you have a similarly high regard for your abilities as a rock climber, you can easily end up over your head and perhaps end up badly injured any day of the week. There is nothing stopping you from rounding up a compliant companion and heading out to your doom. It is not a logical impossibility that you will be on the starting line-up for the Steelers, but the event is in a very distant possible world. Successfully climbing a hard and dangerous route is in a distant possible world, too – you just think that it is in a much closer one. The difference is that in one case a huge social organization consisting of many, many years of highly organized hoops to jump through stands between you and testing out your football abilities. In climbing, all that you need is the motivation to act on your self-assessment (and a ride to the cliff and a partner – but the point is clear).

An old friend of mine had a habit of saying "You're only as good as your last problem," and you could substitute "route" if you like. This might be a bit of a stringent requirement, but there is a lot of sense to the saying. The saying gives us a guide or a rule of thumb that we can use to temper our self-assessments. The psychology literature I have referred to simply reveals the shortcomings in our self-attributions, but philosophers see a problem that needs fixing.[10] The suggestion I give here is similar to the one I gave earlier when discussing cases where our self-reports rely on the available scaffolding. Setting off to do a climb involves a lot of practical reasoning. That reasoning will only be as good as the input it is based on. If you head off to solo a 5.12, onsight, and armed only with the knowledge that you think you are strong enough, good luck. My suggestion is that the "my last climb" rule of thumb is just one among many bits of information you should incorporate into your reasoning process. The more people whose lives hang on your decision to do the route, the more you should lean on the available information. I know that this may not be news to a fair number of readers. Many such rules of thumb are used by experienced climbers in the lead up to taking on a new challenge. For example, many folks planning to onsight a dangerous 5.12A or B traditional climb will make sure that 5.13A or B sport climbs feel very solid in the weeks leading up to the attempt. That kind of fitness is very helpful to fall back on in this kind of situation (so I am told, as that kind of fitness has always eluded me).

Coda: Getting Something Back

So what is left? "Have you ever been experienced?" One sense of experience we have not touched on is a looser sense of the term. In this loose sense, having been somewhere is to experience it. In this sense, I have experienced India; I have been there. This kind of experience is a hodge-podge of actual sensory inputs combined with storytelling, merging of our own stories with those of friends, and retelling the stories when we look at the photos together. In this sense, your whole life in climbing and around your climbing friends combines to produce your climbing experience – the routes you have done, the redpoints, the number of bolts placed, the countries you have visited, and the friendships you have made and lost. This rich personal history is your climbing experience – a mixture of memories, extrapolations, dreams, and retellings. What it *isn't* is a perfect recollection of all your perfect self-assessments of your climbing adventures. You may have been "experienced," but not in the way you think.

NOTES

1 I thank Cynthia Levinthal, Matt Samet, and Eric Wynn for their feedback on earlier drafts and I thank Stephen Schmid for his thorough editing job.

2 R. E. Nisbett and T. D. Wilson, "Telling More Than We Can Know: Verbal Reports on Mental Processes," *Psychological Review* 84 (1977): 231–59. For an accessible introduction to much of this psychological literature, see T. D. Wilson, *Strangers to Ourselves: Discovering the Adaptive Unconscious* (Cambridge, MA: Harvard University Press, 2004).

3 J. S. Uleman, "Introduction," in R. R. Hassin, J. S. Uleman, and J. A. Bargh (eds.) *The New Unconscious* (Oxford: Oxford University Press, 2005), p. 6.

4 Alan Rouse, "The Boldest," in K. Wilson and B. Newman (eds.) *Extreme Rock: Great British Rock Climbs* (London: Diadem Books, 1987), pp. 134–6.

5   Ibid.

6   Paul Churchland, *Matter and Consciousness* (Cambridge, MA: MIT Press, 1984).

7   The example is from Ian Deweese–Boyd, "Self–Deception," in Edward N. Zalta (ed.) *The Stanford Encyclopedia of Philosophy*, Fall 2009 edition; online at www.plato.stanford.edu/archives/fall2009/entries/self–deception/.

8   The closest analogue in the epistemology literature to the externalism I am advocating is Bishop and Trout's "strategic reliabilism." See M. A. Bishop and J. D. Trout, *Epistemology and the Psychology of Human Judgment* (Oxford: Oxford University Press, 2005).

9   These and other related studies are documented in Tom Vanderbilt, *Traffic: Why We Drive the Way We Do (And What It Says About Us)* (New York: Alfred A. Knopf, 2009).

10 This is very much Bishop and Trout's approach to the literature.

RICHARD G. GRAZIANO[1]

CHAPTER 16

WHAT *IS* A CLIMBING GRADE ANYWAY?

We climbers are drawn to the vertical places. Although we each have our own reasons for this, one shared reason is that such terrain presents us with a variety of challenges and we value overcoming them. Unlike Superman, the rock climber gets to the top of a climb by finding and climbing the weaknesses that he finds in the rock; for example, cracks, edges, pockets, etc. Interestingly, we don't question whether these weaknesses are actually part of the rock. Cracks and pockets are *there*, we can see them and touch them – we discover them as we climb the rock. To say that these cracks and pockets can be seen and discovered is to say that these features are real properties of the rock. But can I see that Serenity Crack is 5.10d? Is this route's climbing grade something I discover? Is it a real property of the rock?

On the whole, climbers answer such questions negatively; a climbing grade, we are told, is not a real property of the rock.[2] According to received tradition, climbing grades are like beauty: they are subjective. Climbing grades are, so to speak, in the eye of the beholder. This view, that climbing grades are subjective, is so commonly accepted, so entrenched, so unquestioningly assumed to be true, that climbers are almost dogmatic. I'll call this beauty-in-the-eye-of-the-beholder view about climbing grades the *orthodox view*. Is that view right? I will argue it is not. My view is that we should be realists; that we should take climbing grades to be real properties of the mediums we climb, just like the cracks and pockets we use to climb the route. To show this, I will argue for a particular realist view called *relationalism*. Relationalism, I will argue, better explains climbing grades than does the orthodox view. But first, let's get clear on what I mean by a climbing grade.

The Climbing Grade Question

To answer the question of what a climbing grade *is*, I'll use the classic Yosemite climb, Serenity Crack. Serenity Crack is rated 5.10d. This rating tells a climber how difficult that route is. Climbers have devised standardized rating systems by which we can classify the difficulty of a route, the Yosemite Decimal System being one of those rating systems.[3] These systems are *scaled* in the sense that difficulty is rated in degrees (some climbs are more difficult than others) and are *standardized* in the sense that a rating system is (ideally) uniform and consistently applied across locales.[4] Accordingly, a climbing grade is an assigned value, according to a standardized scale, that describes the degree of difficulty (and possibly the danger) that a climber will face were she to ascend that route. However, this answer is not helpful in answering what a climbing grade is because it only tells us how we *classify* climbing grades. If we are going to answer the question of what a climbing grade *is*, then we need to discover the *nature* of climbing grades. The Climbing Grade Question, as I'll call it, seeks to discover the nature of the thing we seek to classify with the 5.10d rating. The Climbing Grade Question, then, is concerned with what that degreed property is exactly and not how we classify it.

To help us answer the Climbing Grade Question, let us consider the following sentences about Yosemite's Serenity Crack:

1. Serenity Crack is pin-scarred in many identifiable locations.
2. Serenity Crack is in Squamish.
3. Serenity Crack is beautiful.
4. Serenity Crack is 5.10d.

The first statement gives a brief description of Serenity Crack. Originally used as a training route for aid climbers, Serenity Crack bears the scars from hundreds of pitons being hammered into and removed from its narrow crack. Today, climbers free climb the route using these pin scars. As a general description of Serenity Crack, we would say (1) is true. (1) is true because the properties the description attributes to Serenity Crack are really there. If we wanted to get really specific, we could count, measure, and map all the pin scars along the crack. The detailed description is true because Serenity Crack has the properties (pin scars) the description says it does. We can compare the description to the route and see that the two match up.

Now compare (1) and (2). "Serenity Crack is in Squamish" is false. The property being attributed to Serenity Crack is not one that Serenity Crack possesses. Serenity Crack is in Yosemite and not in Squamish. So (2) is false because it doesn't accurately describe the world. Simple enough.

What about (3), the proposition that Serenity Crack is beautiful? Is (3) true or false? According to many people, beauty is in the eye of the beholder. That is, beauty is a property someone attributes to an object based on their own tastes and preferences. For example, I love a nice pint of Guinness. My wife, however, cannot stand it; she thinks it's like drinking sludge. My love of Guinness reflects my personal preferences and my wife's dislike of it reflects her personal tastes. Many consider attributions of beauty to be like this; it is a reflection of one's personal preferences like my preference for Guinness. Now, if beauty is like this (a view I don't accept), then it doesn't really make sense to ask whether "Serenity Crack is beautiful" is true because the property being attributed to Serenity Crack is not something that route can possess – beauty is a personal preference that reflects *my* tastes. Rather, "Serenity Crack is beautiful" is really attributing something to *me* and not to Serenity Crack at all. This way of characterizing (3) is what I earlier called (when I was talking about most climbers' views of climbing grades) the orthodox view. It is the view that some things are neither true nor false; they're really about my subjective states or preferences.[5]

Now for the important question of this essay: is (4) more like (1) or (3)? Is the property of *being 5.10d* like the property of *being pin-scarred* or is it like the property of *being beautiful?* The orthodox view holds that 5.10d is like beauty, it is in the eye of the beholder. I think 5.10d is like *being pin-scarred*. Just as *being pin-scarred* attributes to Serenity Crack properties it really does possess, so too *being 5.10d* attributes to Serenity Crack a property it really does possess. Both *being pin-scarred* – as (1) asserts – and *being 5.10d* – as (4) asserts – refer to *real* properties of Serenity Crack. In short, Serenity Crack's climbing grade, or the climbing grade of any other route, is a real property of that route. In the next section, I will give an account of climbing grades that makes this case.

  RICHARD G. GRAZIANO

But first, let's compare statement (4), "Serenity Crack is 5.10d," with statement (2), "Serenity Crack is in Squamish."

Remember that (1), "Serenity Crack is pin-scarred," is a true claim and (2), "Serenity Crack is in Squamish," is false. (2) is false because the property being attributed to Serenity Crack – namely, *being in Squamish* – is not a property Serenity Crack actually possesses. But Squamish really exists and *being in Squamish* is true of some routes; it just isn't true of Serenity Crack. So, if we were to ask if (4), "Serenity Crack is 5.10d," were like (2), then we would be asking whether (4) is false and we would have to assume that *being 5.10d* is a property that Serenity Crack could really possess, like *being in Squamish*. But assuming this means that we think that *being 5.10d is* a real property, like Squamish, and we want to know if Serenity Crack actually possesses it.

So the Climbing Grade Question is at core a question of whether climbing grades are real properties of objects about which we *could* say something true or false. In the next section, I will give an account of climbing grades that gives one reason to think that climbing grades are real properties of objects and thereby about which we can say something that is either true or false.

Relationalism About Climbing Grades

According to relationalism, climbing grades are like the cracks and edges we discover on a route: they are real properties of the rock we climb. So relationalism is a form of realism: it tells us that climbing grades really exist and that is so whether we are aware of them or not. Accordingly, they are something we discover and don't make up. What do these real properties turn out to be? They are dispositions of sections of rock that challenge climbers to some degree of difficulty or another. This account of climbing grades is similar to the account of dispositional properties advanced by the philosopher John Locke (1632–1704). In particular, a route's climbing grade is similar to the hardness of an object: it's a disposition.

Before we take a closer look at that idea, however, there are two things we should note that follow from relationalism being a form of realism. First, if a climbing grade is a real property, then it is possible to assert true or false statements about the difficulty of a route in the same way that it is possible to assert true or false statements about a route's location, length, etc. That does not mean our assertions are always right.

Like (2), if I were to assert that Serenity Crack is a third-class route, I'd be wrong. Even so, such properties being real make it *possible* that it be true or false that Serenity Crack have a climbing grade. Second, relationalism and the orthodox view cannot both be true. The orthodox view is a form of *anti*-realism; it tells us that climbing grades are subjective, hence not real. So, if relationalism is correct, then the orthodox view is false, and vice versa. As I will argue in the next section, we should accept relationalism.

Let us state the relationalist view of climbing grades as follows:

RCG A climbing grade is the real disposition of a route to challenge a climber to some degree and that disposition emerges when a standard climber climbs the structural features of a route in normal climbing conditions.

How are we to understand RCG?

Climbing Grades as Emerging Real Dispositions

As I will explain shortly, I take climbing grades to be importantly similar to Locke's dispositional account of hardness. But first, what is a disposition? To understand this, we need to understand Locke's primary–secondary quality distinction. According to Locke, there are two types of properties: primary and secondary qualities.[6] Simply put, primary qualities are real properties of objects, they really exist in those things; secondary qualities are not real, they are not really in those things. To say that the primary qualities are real is to say that they exist whether we are aware of them or not. They are something that we discover about objects in the world. My climbing shoes, for instance, have a number of primary qualities: they have a certain shape, they are located somewhere, they have a size, etc. These are *primary* qualities given that my shoes would still have those properties even if they were forever lost. My shoes have a number of secondary qualities as well. For instance, they are red colored, they smell like leather, they are cold when I put them on for the old 5:00 a.m. alpine start, etc. These *secondary* qualities – colors, odors, and temperatures – do not really exist in the way that we commonsensically think they do. According to Locke, the secondary qualities actually emerge, that is, are caused to exist,

  RICHARD G. GRAZIANO

when and only when human beings – or a relevantly similar species – are rightly related to an object's primary qualities. In other words, they exist when the right sorts of creatures come into *contact* with an object's primary qualities in the right conditions. This being so, the primary qualities are dispositions to create certain experiences such as seeing colors, smelling odors, feeling temperatures, etc. Again, the secondary qualities are not real; they only exist in the minds of creatures such as humans when humans experience the primary qualities of objects in the right conditions.[7] But the dispositions are real; they are there whether we are or not. They are the causal ground of the secondary qualities; they cause them to exist.

On this view, a disposition is the capacity of a thing to have certain properties when and only when it's in the relevant conditions. In other words, a disposition is the way a thing will be just in case certain relevant conditions are actualized. Consider my climbing shoes again. Not only does the material make-up of my climbing shoes give them the disposition to cause experiences of color, smell, and temperature, but the sticky rubber has the disposition to provide enough friction to help me climb. It doesn't provide that friction when the shoes are in my pack, but does when I'm wearing them on a climb. Accordingly, dispositions are relational: they bring about certain properties when the disposed thing stands in the right kinds of relations. RCG states that a climbing grade is just such a property: it is a disposition of a route to affect climbers in certain ways. In particular, a climbing grade is the disposition of the rock to produce a certain challenge given the right kind of climber and standard environmental conditions.

As I said, I take climbing grades to be similar to what Locke calls hardness. What is hardness, and how are climbing grades like it? Locke says that hardness is the property of an object that causes it to retain its shape. Is it a primary or secondary quality? It's a primary quality; all matter has it. But his discussion suggests two important things about hardness. First, it's a property that emerges from other primary qualities; in particular, it's caused by the object's molecules and how they're organized. Second, hardness is a disposition. This is because it's the capacity – the propensity – of an object to retain its particular shape when it collides with other objects in the world. Given this, we can see that it's a property that comes in degrees: different material objects have different degrees of hardness. One object can be *more or less* hard than another. Whether an object will keep its shape when it collides with another object depends on the relative hardness of each. Consider an example.

Imagine we have three 4-inch cubed objects: one of molding clay, one of pine, and one of granite. (Let us name the objects Plato, Woody, and Rocky, respectively.) Plato, Woody, and Rocky are all hard objects. Each can be held; each is firm to the touch. But the firmness of each varies; it comes in degrees. Each has some capacity to retain its respective shape. I cannot change Woody's or Rocky's shape with my bare hands, but this is not the case with Plato. I can compress Plato and change its shape from a cube to that of some other shape (say, an orb). Again, hardness is a dispositional property that an object has in relation to other objects. So our inspection also reveals that Plato is less capable of retaining its shape than are Woody and Rocky in relation to human hands. Of course, although I cannot easily change the shape of Woody or Rocky, that is so if I attempt to do so *with my hands*. I can change both Woody and Rocky if I use something *other than* my hands. Were my hands replaced – say, with tungsten carbide robotic prosthetics – or were I to use a chisel, then I could change Woody's or Rocky's shape. For Woody and Rocky are not as hard as such things.

If the foregoing discussion is correct, then this tells us that hardness is in fact a disposition of an object to retain its shape when related to some – though not necessarily every – other material object. It's a property that material objects have in relation to each other. In the same way, a climbing grade is a disposition to have certain characteristics in relation to climbers in the relevant conditions. As such, it would be wrong to think that climbing grades depend on there being minds in the way that Locke said that colors, odors, and temperatures so depend. Moreover, if this is right, then this explains why the difficulty of a climb comes in degrees. For it emerges when a standard climber climbs the structural features of a route in normal climbing conditions. Were we to fix the notion of a standard climber and standard climbing conditions, but make enough structural changes to the rock, then the climbing grade would change: the route will be differently disposed. Think of climbs that have had a rating change given an important change to the structure of the route. An example that comes to mind is Pinched Rib in Joshua Tree. The route was originally rated 5.7. But when an important hold broke off, the climbing grade increased to 5.10b. We could come up with countless other examples. The same point follows: a climbing grade is a real dispositional property of a route that emerges – that is, is caused to be – when a standard climber climbs the route in standard conditions and that property poses certain challenges for the climber.

Standard Climbers in Standard Climbing Conditions

Throughout the discussion of dispositions I have been talking about this disposition as a property that emerges when *standard climbers* climb a route in *standard conditions*. What does that mean? What are standard climbers and standard climbing conditions? Let us begin with the idea of a standard climber.

You and I have an innate climbing ability. As little children, we naturally try to climb a variety of objects: trees, rocks, fences, etc. As we get older, some of us continue to pursue the vertical terrain. We not only continue to climb, but we work to improve our abilities so that we can climb better, harder routes. We seek to be more efficient, have better technique, be stronger, be more flexible, etc. Yet, at the end of the day, there is only so much we can do; we only have certain abilities. Why? This is because we are human beings. We have a specific biology and that limits what we can do physically. We may or may not be near those limits at this point in our history, but there are limits nonetheless. Some humans may be able to climb 5.15 (or harder), but even the most capable human climber can only do so much! This is relevant to a route's climbing grade and why RCG tells us that a climbing grade is a dispositional property that emerges not *only* from the structural features of the route, but from how capable a species of climbers is at negotiating those structural features. So, to speak of standard climbers is to speak of this fact. Human beings have an innate climbing ability, but that ability is ultimately limited by biology.[8] So a climbing grade is fixed in part by the biological make-up of the kinds of creatures that climb the route. If that is so, then Serenity Crack has a degree of difficultly for me *as a human*. I may be able to improve my climbing abilities, say, by doing yoga or by being deliberate in my efforts to improve my crack climbing technique. But, at the end of the day, I am still only human. Of course, were I suddenly to gain superhuman abilities, say, those of Spiderman, then Serenity Crack would no longer be difficult *to any degree* for me. So relationalism tells us that climbing grades are dispositional properties that are ultimately relative to a species and to speak of standard climbers is to talk about the abilities of a species.[9] Of course, saying that climbing grades are relative to a species does not mean they are not real properties. Climbing grades may be species relative, but the properties still really exist. Accordingly, statements like (4) – "Serenity Crack is 5.10d" – can still be true; Serenity Crack can possess that dispositional property. Now to the idea of standard conditions.

Standard (or normal) conditions are simply those environmental conditions that are relevant to the goings-on in question and importantly similar across the board. Let's think of the idea of standard conditions once again using Locke's dispositional account of colors. Recall that Locke advances the view that colors are secondary qualities. Colors are not really in the objects; they actually exist in the minds of those who see those objects. Again, climbing shoes are not actually red. What *is* really in my climbing shoes are the primary qualities – such as the physical structure that reflects light – and these properties have the disposition to cause humans, or a relevantly similar species, to have color experiences. The primary qualities of my shoes cause me to see them *as* red, but they are not *really* red. Yet seeing them as red requires that they are viewed in standard – that is, normal – lighting conditions. They will not appear red unless they are illuminated by the right light. Were we to view my shoes under green light, they would appear black. So the Lockean theory of colors "ties" colors not just to a species' sensory faculties, but also the lighting conditions under which the objects are viewed. In the same way, relationalism "ties" climbing grades to the physical conditions under which a climber attempts a route. By "physical conditions" I don't mean the kinds of environmental goings-on such as the weather. There is no question that the weather can affect a climber's ability to negotiate a route, but climbing ratings are not thus affected. It may be more difficult to climb Serenity Crack in the rain, but if Serenity Crack is 5.10d, it is 5.10d *rain, snow, or shine!* No, I'm thinking of such environmental factors as gravity. Gravity affects a climber differently when it comes to climbing low-grade slabs, vertical splitter cracks, or 30-degree overhanging faces. It's the same with a wide range of physical considerations. As we know, there are other places than Earth such that were we climbing there, gravity would affect us differently; we would be differently challenged in those places. As such, were I climbing Serenity Crack in an environment that is gravitationally different – say, on the moon – Serenity Crack would have a different climbing grade. Alternatively, if we assume that the laws of nature could have been different, a route's grade *on Earth* would have been different. If that is so, then such conditions have relevance to a route's climbing grade; a climbing grade is indexed by the physical goings-on. That is not to say that had gravity been different on Earth or we were living on a different planet, we would not classify Serenity Crack as 5.10d. Relationalism is not a view about our current use of a rating system. It's a view about what a climbing grade actually *is*.

Relationalism: The Better Theory

In the last section I sketched the form of realism I call relationalism. Again, it tells us that a climbing grade is a real disposition and it emerges when a standard climber climbs the structural features of a route in normal climbing conditions. It is undoubtedly a first approximation and needs refinement. Even so, we should accept relationalism and reject the orthodox view. Before I close, I want to give some reasons why. Relationalism not only explains why (4) – "Serenity Crack is 5.10d" – *is* true, but why it *can* be true. The orthodox view cannot. As we saw, relationalism tells us that climbing grades are real properties; they are dispositions that really exist. As such, they are properties like *being pin-scarred, being located in Yosemite*, etc. They are properties that Serenity Crack and other routes can actually possess. Yet the orthodox view can't explain this. Recall it says that climbing grades are subjective; they're really descriptions about a climber's personal preferences and tastes. Given that view, (4) is said to be like (3), the proposition that Serenity Crack is beautiful: it *cannot* be true of Serenity Crack. It's not that it *isn't* true; it *can't* be true. Why think that (4) *can't* be true? Those who advocate the orthodox view need to give us an argument for this. To be successful, that argument must show either that dispositions aren't real or that climbing grades aren't dispositions. Given that it's relatively uncontroversial that dispositions are real properties, supporters of the orthodox view have to show us that climbing grades aren't dispositions. I don't think that they can make that case. That climbing grades are real dispositions best explains why routes such as Pinched Rib can change from 5.7 to 5.10b simply because the properties of the rock changed. This is similar to how we explain the change in the hardness of water. H_2O molecules are disposed to make water more or less hard depending on how "bunched up" their structural organization is. When a cup of water is frozen, the molecules are really bunched together in rigid structures like a lattice fence. However, as those lattice structures break and the molecules begin to get less bunched up, the ice melts and the water becomes a liquid. If the molecules continue to spread out, the water turns into a gas or vapor. Ice is obviously harder than gas; that's explained by the disposition of certain organizations of the molecules.

There's also a reason to reject the orthodox view. It seems to me that the intuitive pull of the orthodox view – its persuasiveness – is due to a fundamental confusion between two things: what a climbing grade *is* – its nature – and how we *determine* what grade to assign a route. What something *is* and how we come to *know* what it is are related, but importantly different. There may be things that we are unable to know about the world, but that does not imply that there is no way the world actually *is*. We may never know, for instance, whether Mallory and Irvine reached the summit of Everest; but that does not affect whether they did or not. What the world is actually like is independent of our knowing or not knowing what it's like. I agree that it's difficult to determine a route's climbing grade; it may be that we cannot know what a route's climbing grade really is. But that does not imply that climbing grades are not real.

Let me lastly mention and address a possible objection to my argument for relationalism over the orthodox view. Someone might argue that climbing grades need be neither fully subjective properties, as beauty is thought to be, nor fully objective properties, like *being pin-scarred*. There is a third option. Climbing grades are like the property *being money*; they are *weakly objective properties*. For instance, a dime's being money is not in the eye of the beholder, yet we do not discover that property. Money is a socially constructed thing; it emerges from the decisions of social institutions. Were societies to cease to exist, so would money. The objects that are *used as* money would not cease to exist; but those objects would not have that property. So, the objection goes, my argument relies on a false distinction; there's another way to understand the orthodox view.[10] Let us call this the *weak orthodox view*.

I don't believe that those who espouse the orthodox view actually have the weak orthodox view in mind. Yet, even if they do, I believe that the weak orthodox view fairs no better than the orthodox view with respect to the nature of climbing grades. It is true that the properties *being money* and *being 5.10d* have an important similarity: in the same way that money wouldn't exist if there were no social institutions, climbing grades wouldn't exist if there were no climbers. Relationalism does not deny that similarity. However, that is the only *relevant* similarity. The two are subtly, yet importantly, different. What money *is* causally depends on its having a certain use; as we saw, what climbing grades are is *not* like that. It's true that *rating systems* causally depend on their having a certain use. But that is not the case with climbing grades, that is, the real disposition that we classify with a rating system. That disposition is there whether we notice it or not. Again, climbing grades are discovered, not created. Accordingly, I remain unmoved: relationalism better answers the Climbing Grade Question than either version of the orthodox view. Climbing grades really exist – it's *true* that Serenity Crack is 5.10d.

  RICHARD G. GRAZIANO

NOTES

1   I am grateful to Stephen Schmid, Deanna Graziano, Ryan Matteson, and Sean Choi for their helpful comments and generous feedback on earlier drafts of this essay.

2   While I focus on rock climbing in this essay, the same view follows – with any necessary changes – for any other medium we climb.

3   Although a climbing grade is usually distinguished from the difficulty rating, I will use the terms interchangeably.

4   While the ratings systems currently in use only give us an approximation, and fail to be uniform and consistently applied, that does not imply that an ideal rating system is impossible.

5   Notice that saying "It's true for me" doesn't meet the demands for truth required by realism; those conditions for truth demand that things actually possess that property *independently* of the mind.

6   See his *An Essay Concerning Human Understanding* (1689), Book 2, Ch. 8. Locke distinguished a third type of quality – tertiary qualities – but I'll leave that aside since that category isn't relevant to our topic.

7   I will explain what "the right conditions" means below.

8   While I believe that psychological states can also affect a climber's ability, such states are neither relevant to nor affect a route's climbing grade.

9   I recognize but am not bothered by the fact that relationalism implies that there are climbing grades for non-humans such as squirrels, lizards, etc.

10   I thank Sean Choi for the example and bringing the objection to my attention.

CHAPTER 17

THE BEAUTY OF A CLIMB

When we climb, we describe routes as beautiful, outstanding, or even perfect. Guidebooks also pick out some routes as "classics" or label the best routes with stars. These are two cases where some climbing routes are taken to be "better" than others, meaning that these routes are held to have outstanding qualities which are available to other climbers if they try the route. So, when we claim that a route is beautiful, we do not only mean to communicate a subjective experience like "I enjoy this route." We also expect other climbers to share our opinion and share our judgement that "the route is beautiful." In philosophy, such commonly available qualities are often termed "objective." The branch of philosophy concerned with the nature and appreciation of beauty is called aesthetics. In aesthetics, there is a long tradition, based on this divide between the subjective and objective, of distinguishing between the merely agreeable and the truly beautiful, the former of which may include a variety of objects, such as wine, food, and climbing routes.

In this essay I will argue that judgments made by climbers about some routes should be considered aesthetic judgments and that climbing routes are aesthetic objects. Climbing routes are something that we can legitimately characterize as beautiful. To approach this question, two related and more fundamental philosophical questions need some clarification. First, what are aesthetic objects; that is, what objects can possibly be given aesthetic evaluation? And second, what is required for a judgment about such an object to be an aesthetic judgment? After a brief overview of this classic problem in philosophy, I will return to the main topic, climbing routes.

A short remark is also required on the types of climbing I will discuss and the corresponding use of examples. Climbing is a diverse activity, ranging from the highest mountains in the world to 3-meter-high boulders. I will delimit the discussion only to free climbing, like multi-pitch routes, sport climbing, and bouldering. The reason, which will emerge from my argument, is that bodily movements of the climber are most pronounced in this type of climbing. At the end of the essay I will briefly indicate how my main point relates to other forms of climbing, like big walls and high mountains.

What Are Aesthetic Objects?

The domain of the aesthetic is often taken to be art, like we find it in galleries, museums or, in the case of music and dance, concert halls. This institutional theory of art fails for the following reasons.[1] Many things can be given aesthetic evaluation (considered as beautiful) without being works of art. For example, take how we think of other people as beautiful or how we find beauty in nature: as in beautiful scenery or a melodious birdsong. The domain of the aesthetic is wider than the domain of institutional art. As Frank Sibley (1923–96) has remarked, if an object is capable of aesthetic appreciation, it is irrelevant whether or not it is an artwork.[2] If we find beauty in nature, as Immanuel Kant (1724–1804) forcefully argued and the above examples indicate, why should we not also find it in rocks and mountains? Thus, there is in principle no reason to prohibit climbing routes, considered as objects in nature, from being aesthetic objects. Climbing routes can appeal to us aesthetically much in the same way as other objects we experience in nature. Some may here want to object that even though routes are not objects of art in a traditional sense, neither are they pristine objects of nature. Many sport routes are created by being cleaned of vegetation and loose rock, bolts are placed, and holds are chalked. This need not imply, however, that the creator of the route is an artist. Rather, route setters prepare the conditions in which a climber can appreciate the aesthetic nature of the rock.[3] The point that will be made in this essay is also independent of whether a route is an artifact or a pristine object found in nature.

Given that climbing routes are possible aesthetic objects, the question that remains is how we can possibly judge a route to be beautiful. By what means do we come to our verdict? For even if climbing routes can be aesthetic objects, it is not clear how we are entitled to conclude from the observation that climbers respond to and describe some routes using aesthetic terms that these routes are aesthetic objects. Even though we use the same words and expressions, one might argue that what we really mean when we talk about routes is that they please us. If the experience of climbing a route results only in pleasure, we have misunderstood conceiving a route as aesthetically beautiful with merely being enjoyable.

To answer this question about the beauty of a climb, we will need to acknowledge that our understanding of the aesthetics of climbing routes depends on sense perception. In the case of pictures, we see them. With music, we listen. But with climbing, we engage the object with multiple sensory perceptions – we *see* the route from the ground, *feel* the holds when we climb it, and *experience* the bodily movements the route produces in us. This description contrasts with an established view in philosophical aesthetics, going all the way back to Aristotle (384–322 BCE), which holds that senses like taste and touch can only give us experiences of pleasure and not objective properties of objects, like their beauty. The question of the beauty of a climb is thus not only interesting in itself, it also provides a fruitful case for challenging an established view about the aesthetic senses in general. My argument will be that once we look closer into the experiences we have while climbing, we will see that vision – only seeing the route as beautiful – cannot be sufficient for making an aesthetic judgment about a climb.

Lines and Routes

The beauty found in nature is most often visually perceived. In the case of climbing, how a climb looks from the ground plays a considerable role in how it is assessed aesthetically. Beautiful climbs are, usually, also prominent lines. Just think of a finger crack that splits an otherwise blank wall, a series of pockets up a blue streak of limestone or a prominent arête. When referring to this aspect of a climb – how it looks from the ground – I will use the term "line." A line is a climb that the person who makes the aesthetic judgment need not even have climbed herself; in fact, it may not have been climbed at all. Most climbers agree that conceived as lines, climbs like The Nose on El Cap in Yosemite, Master's Edge at Millstone Quarry in Great Britain, or Realization in Ceüse in France are beautiful and that they were so even before they were first ascended.

But the visual properties of the rock by which we assess the line are not alone sufficient to judge that the climb really is beautiful. For it is conceivable, and sometimes it happens, that even the most beautiful looking line is experienced as the opposite once one starts to climb it. Cracks and dihedrals may look beautiful but provide awkward movements, and the blue streak with pockets may offer only sharp holds and uninteresting climbing. Consider the following statement from the Italian climbing legend Manolo, describing an 8b+ route at Kalymnos:

> It's a magnificent wall of excellent rock, 40 m high. The first section is slightly overhanging up small edges and is relatively easy, then it becomes vertical and compact on small edges almost all the way to the belay. A match made in heaven.[4]

The description of the beauty of the route includes reference to the climbing itself, and it is not as a line alone that this climb is taken to be beautiful. Once we include the experiential aspect of a climb – *how* it is experienced when it is climbed – we are no longer considering it as a line only but also as what I will mean by a "route." A route is a line that has been climbed by the person who makes the judgment that it is beautiful (or not). Even if we know a lot about a climb by watching the line or even watching other climbers on it, we are not in a legitimate position to judge it as beautiful until we have actually tried it ourselves.

What about the other way around? Can the experience of the climbing alone be sufficient? Or said otherwise, can an unimpressive, messy, or even ugly line be a beautiful route? If we agree that the look of the climb can be overruled by our experience of climbing it, the answer to this question should be affirmative. But here we also need to include another important issue that must be taken into account when we ask what determines the beauty of a climb; what are the qualities of a route that we appreciate when we climb it? While the seen properties of a line are commonly agreed upon, it seems that climbers prefer different kinds of routes, and how do we avoid a view where everyone adheres to their own standard alone?

Preference and Personal Taste

The aesthetic appreciation of a line as beautiful when it is seen from the ground can, to a certain point, be shared by climbers and non-climbers alike; it doesn't take a trained eye to see that The Nose on El Capitan is a line that looks beautiful. It stands out, so to speak. But knowledge of climbing also makes a substantial difference. Only the experienced climber can truly appreciate the feat of finding a route up such an immense wall. And most climbers have experienced how non-climbers judge short sport-climbing routes' difficulty by their angle of steepness alone.

Do climbers themselves agree on the criteria by which they judge a route to be beautiful? When two experienced climbers see the same line, then climb it and feel the same holds and do the same movements, we must assume that there is sufficient mutual experience for a discussion to be possible about the route's aesthetic value. What will generate disagreement is each climber's standard of taste, and not the very experiences. Normally, these perceptual experiences will vary a little from climber to climber, depending on factors like differences in bodily height, weight, strength, and reach. But insofar as two climbers perform most movements and sequences on a route in the same way, they also share a sufficient amount of information about the route's qualities. Disagreement normally takes place over which of these qualities should be appreciated.

Consider now the following reply from Chris Sharma when asked to characterize what makes a route special:

> The routes that inspired me . . . *Just Do It* at Smith Rock, that was a king line for sure. It was a line that was big and hard and beautiful. *Necessary Evil* at the Virgin River. *Super Tweak*. Those were all king lines. In terms of boulder problems, *Midnight Lightning*, *Thriller*, *The Force*. Those were all very inspiring. They were big lines, highball. They were full-value boulder problems.[5]

Sharma here attends to some features that characterize his favorite routes; they are "big, hard and beautiful." One understanding of this claim is that some climbs are beautiful *because* they are big and hard. "Big routes," those that are long and pumpy, are Sharma's personal preference. A route being at the limit of one's skills is a criterion that I think is valid for most climbers. Hard routes make the movements more pronounced to the climber, either alternative sequences don't exist or the difficulty of the movements you choose really requires your attention. A consequence of this view is that very easy routes with a myriad of holds and sequences are not primarily evaluated for beauty on the basis of the movements they produce, but depend more on properties like the quality of the rock and the look of the line.

I believe there are certain standards against which we, as climbers, evaluate both how a line looks and how we experience the climbing. Trying to make a complete list seems problematic, but I think most climbers will agree that obvious ingredients include the quality of the rock, the feel of the holds (as not being sharp and painful), the variety of movements, and the placement of footholds in relation to handholds. In addition, there are more disputable criteria, like Sharma's requirement that the climbing be sustained and the possibility and placement of protection, and even more controversial issues like chipped holds.

Neither is a shared standard like this, based on a selection and valuation of properties of routes, in itself fixed, but it changes over time. Buoux in Southern France, once the major scene of hard rock climbing with the world's first confirmed route of grade 8c, is now a quiet place. Pulling hard on one-finger pockets is no longer the type of climbing preferred by those who push their limits. Instead, we see that steeper rock with longer, more sustained routes and bigger holds are in fashion. Although the issue of preferences deserves a more thorough treatment, I do not think we should be misled into some kind of relativism about the aesthetic qualities of a route. There seems to be sufficient agreement among climbers about which experienced properties of the route are to be part of the standard. Even when one's personal preferences are different, we are capable of seeing beyond these. A boulderer will normally be able to recognize the qualities of a long and sustained route, although she will not have a preference for this type of climb, and vice versa.

A consequence of the above view is that knowledge of the standard is required for aesthetic assessment of movements and routes. A novice climbing an easy and beautiful route will not have the means, in terms of conceptual knowledge based on previous experience, to properly evaluate the route. He will simply lack the necessary ground for comparison. Previously climbed routes of the same type and difficulty form part of the background against which we evaluate new routes. And finally, if the experience of climbing the route is a necessary condition for making the aesthetic judgment, you have to be able to climb the route, or at least do its movements or sequences. A route far beyond one's level is also outside the scope of what one can assess aesthetically.

So, if we disagree about whether a route is beautiful, the root of the disagreement should be found either in a difference in the standards against which we evaluate the route or in a difference in the way we perceived the climb, in the sense of how we performed and experienced the various movements. The judgment that a route is beautiful is formed when our standards and knowledge are measured against our bodily experiences had while climbing the route. This latter experience is largely given by two sense modalities, touch and our internal monitoring of the body – what is often referred to as our proprioceptive system. Let us therefore turn to a discussion of how the proprioceptive experience one has while climbing plays a role in the aesthetic judgment. To do so, we need to understand what proprioception is and how it can provide aesthetic experience.

Is Proprioception an Aesthetic Sense?

Our senses are the means for providing us experience and knowledge of the world as it exists outside our body. Aristotle famously argued that human beings have only five senses – vision, touch, hearing, smell, and taste – at their disposal for this purpose.[6] For reasons I will return to, he denied that our inner sense of the body could play any role in providing us such knowledge. Proprioception is usually understood as just this inner sense – the inner perception of bodily position, posture, and movement in space. We immediately experience where our hands are in relation to the rest of the body, if our legs are crossed, and if we are standing upright or bending forward. All this can take place without the means of other sensory faculties. Proprioception then works much in the same way as other sensory faculties. It gives us experience and knowledge of an object in the world, namely our own body,[7] and it plays a basic role in how our body perceives objects external to and other than itself. So although his view has been dominant within much of the philosophical tradition, I think Aristotle was mistaken in the way he listed the senses.

The philosophical tradition of aesthetic appreciation has, however, held a strong bias against the so-called "bodily senses" (proprioception, as well as touch, taste, and smell), emphasizing instead the "intellectual senses" (chiefly sight and hearing). The way in which we perceive objects through these intellectual senses usually allows us to perceive them with

  GUNNAR KARLSEN

some kind of detachment from our own body and our own purely subjective experiences; a kind of detachment that is held to be necessary for experiences to be truly aesthetic. This is Kant's famous view when he claims that aesthetic judgments demand a special form of universal validity and to have such, the objects perceived must be "detached" from the perceiver.[8] Objects perceived by senses other than sight and hearing are experienced within or in immediate contact with one's own body. Therefore, they cannot be called "beautiful," they at best only "please" us. Hence, proprioception can be only subjective, thinks Kant. It is taken to be a sense that yields information only about the inner states of the body, not of objects and properties that exist out in the world.

If aesthetic senses require this distinction between objects perceived and bodily sensations, how can my proprioceptive experience of a climb have any universal validity and be more than just a subjective, sensory experience of my body and its movements? The problem we are facing can be expressed by the difference between uttering "I like this climb" and "This is a beautiful climb." The first is a report about myself, while the second is about the route and includes more than just its effect upon me. The second claim also demands universality in the sense that we expect other climbers to share our view. Contrary to what Kant likely would have held, I think we can claim that there are beautiful climbs.

Beautiful Movements or Beautiful Routes?

A way to answer this question about subjective experiences is by trying to sort out whether, in the proprioceptive climbing experience, it is *the body* that is experienced as moving in a way that is beautiful or *the route* that is experienced as beautiful. The aesthetic judgment climbers make is about an object – the route – but this judgment seems to be dependent on a particular series of bodily experiences, which in turn could be taken as beautiful. At the same time, the movements could not in the first place be performed without the route, which is the final cause of the experience. The question we are discussing is how to identify the *object of experience*; is it the movement or the climb? Correspondingly, either we conclude that the route is beautiful based in part on the fact that we experience movements or sequences of such as beautiful, or we directly experience the route as beautiful. This distinction, between the experience as beautiful and the route as beautiful, is not always easy to draw. To see why, let us try to analyze the experiences we have while climbing a route, which in turn leads to an aesthetic judgment.

On the first alternative, there are at least two ways in which proprioception can play a role in giving rise to aesthetic appreciation of climbing moves. First, each single move could in itself be experienced as beautiful. The route is then held to be beautiful if enough movements are experienced to be so. In principle, a route can be beautiful if only one move is beautiful, and some boulder problems are instances of this case. But more often we see that it is a sequence of moves that results in the aesthetic assessment, and this is how I believe most climbing routes are experienced. We evaluate sequences of movements as a whole. Instances of this type, where the aesthetic judgment is about the very movements, are also found in activities other than climbing, like when a football player makes a single feint or a ballet dancer an arabesque.[9]

But in contrast to activities like football or ballet where it is clear that the movement itself (which again belongs to the body) is the aesthetic object, in climbing it is the route itself that is the real aesthetic object. It is not the move but the route that produces them that in the end is judged to be beautiful. So it seems that climbing provides another type of case where proprioception reveals beauty. Climbers both experience that their bodily movements are beautiful and that the climb is beautiful.

In this second type of case, proprioception provides information about objects outside the perceiver's body. The idea that proprioception is a sense that yields knowledge about objects outside one's body may seem strange – it was after all introduced as the sense that gives knowledge about the body as such. But in combination with other sensory faculties, most often touch, proprioception adds substantially to our knowledge about ordinary objects. While vision tells us that it is a route we are ascending, proprioception contributes substantially to the total experience of the object. Without the felt experience of climbing the route, we would be lacking vital information about that route.

This view, that it is the route and not only the movement that is experienced as beautiful, also finds support in phenomenology, which is the systematic reflection on our conscious experience. For here we can make use of the insight that we more often than not find it impossible to separate the experience from what it is an experience of; a phenomenon known as transparency of experience. If you look at the blue sky, and have an experience of blue, it seems impossible to describe this experience of blue separate from its object; *it is the sky that is blue, not the experience*. Perceptual experiences appear in general to be transparent in the sense

GUNNAR KARLSEN

that we see "right through them" to the very object they are of.[10] In the same way, we can ask if we really can separate the experiences of climbing moves and the experience of the route. The phenomenon of transparency challenges the view that it is possible to give a description of the beautiful sequence of movements of a route without at all making any reference to the route itself. If this is a correct observation about the phenomenology of perception, it provides an argument for the case that proprioception also yields information about objects outside the perceiver's body.

So, I propose that in activities like climbing, proprioceptive experiences cannot be purely subjective, as they do refer to objects independent of our subjective experience. A point that further strengthens this conclusion is the fact that the aesthetic object, the route, will still exist after we have climbed it. The problematic subjectivism where experiences only are inner, private sensations – the kind that threatens objectivity – is one in which *there is nothing independent of our opinions* to which the experiences are answerable. This form of subjectivism has formed a strong argument for why perishable objects like food and wine cannot in principle be aesthetic, but only gives each consumer a personal experience of pleasure. But in climbing, we may return to the route and climb it again, and so may others as well. Even if climbing is not unique in this respect – objects as diverse as cars and ski slopes may be evaluated aesthetically in the same way – climbing does provide a very good case for analyzing the role of proprioception in aesthetic assessment.

Summary

If I am right in claiming that proprioception also yields information about external objects, objects outside the body, and that such information has the necessary "distance" to form an aesthetic judgment, we have a case for a revised view of the aesthetic senses.

The distinction between a line and a route has been important for reaching this conclusion. Although the discussion has focused on free climbing on rock, I think this distinction is necessary for analyzing the beauty of all types of climbs. Just to give a brief outline of my view, take the following parallel between a free climb and an aid route on a big wall: they both can be visually perceived as beautiful lines. However, they both also need to be climbed – actually experienced – in order to qualify for the status as beautiful routes. In the case of free climbing, proprioception is the sensory faculty that delivers much of the information that forms a basis for our aesthetic assessment. In the case of a big wall, other senses are more prominent. But as proprioception was in the case of free climbing, we need to include all the sensory information relevant to the route. In the case of a big wall, those experiences that inform us about the route's exposure, rock quality, the possibility of good bivies, and the existence of rock features, like thin seams, are just a few of the relevant features.

Finally, consider one single element which is, I think, shared among all types of routes when we appreciate them aesthetically. When a line looks impossible or challenging from the ground and then to be experienced as feasible when we climb it, we have a feature climbers in particular value. Whatever level we climb at, we seek the lines that look impressive and challenging, hoping both that we can succeed in climbing them and that they give us a memorable experience. When this expectation is fulfilled in the right way – proprioceptively, among other factors – the route is judged as beautiful. If other climbers, then, also have the same experience, the route's beauty will be widely acknowledged; it will become a *classic climb*.

NOTES

1 According to the institutional theory of art, art is roughly speaking anything which is in an art museum, gallery, or concert hall, and nothing else.
2 Frank Sibley, "Aesthetic Concepts," in *Approach to Aesthetics: Collected Papers on Philosophical Aesthetics* (Oxford: Oxford University Press, 2001).
3 This process of creation may of course go too far. Intentionally and radically altering the nature of the rock may change the status of the route from an object in nature into a created object. The ethical problems of creating routes by chipping holds are outside the scope of this essay.
4 Vincio Stefanello, "Manolo 8b+ on-sight at Kalymnos," interview with Manolo; online at www.planetmountain.com/english/News/shownews1.lasso?l=2&keyid=36828 (accessed June 25, 2009).
5 Fitz Cahall, "The King of Kings – The Complete Chris Sharma Interview," *Climbing Magazine*, online at www.climbing.com/exclusive/features/threedegrees/index.html.
6 Aristotle, *De Anima*.
7 See also José Luis Bermúdez, *The Paradox of Self-Consciousness* (Cambridge, MA: MIT Press, 1998) for a defense of this view in terms of the idea that the proper object of proprioception is the embodied self.

8 Kant does not discuss proprioception, but from his discussions of other bodily senses like taste and smell it seems unlikely that he would grant proprioception the role of providing pure aesthetic judgment. It would be a faculty without freedom from practical desires and, hence, cannot transcend individual whim and idiosyncrasy and lay claim to universal agreement.

9 For a discussion and defense of the view that dancers can perceive their movements as beautiful by way of proprioception, see Barbara Montero, "Proprioception as an Aesthetic Sense," *Journal of Aesthetics and Art Criticism* 62, 2 (2006): 231–42.

10 The description of the phenomenon of transparency is often traced back to G. E. Moore's discussion of "diaphanousness" in his book *The Refutation of Idealism* (1903), reprinted in *Philosophical Studies* (Totowa: Littlefield, Adams, 1965).

CLIMBING GLOSSARY

Most of the climbing terms included here are from or are modified from rockclimbing.com and are used with their permission.

ABSEIL – UK English for rappel. *See* rappel.

AID CLIMBING – Originally called direct aid or artificial climbing, aid climbing is a means of ascent where the climber's weight is supported primarily, or entirely, by slings attached to a device attached to the rope and/or rock. Weighting the rope or resting on gear is aid. Contrast with free climbing.

ALLEZ – French for "Go!" Used to encourage climbers to push on.

ALPINE START – The set-off time on an alpine route to enable a summit and return journey without the worry of the snow and ice melting in the day's heat or getting lost in the dark. Generally very early in the morning; e.g., 3 a.m.

ALPINE STYLE – Doing a mountain route without pre-placing fixed lines or using presupplied camp sites for any stage of the journey.

ANCHOR – That which attaches the belayer to the rock, or otherwise prevents the belayer from being pulled off the belay stance if the leader falls. In roped technical climbing, one climber moves at a time, while the other belays. The belayer must be securely attached to the rock by means of protection devices (cams, nuts, bolts, pitons) or tied to an immovable object like a boulder or sturdy tree. The attachments are called collectively the "anchor."

ARÊTE – A narrow ridge, or corner, of rock or snow. Derived from the French word for "stop."

BAIL – To give up and rappel or otherwise get off the route because of weather, darkness, or difficulties.

BASE CAMP – The lowest fixed camp on a long route or other journey.

BELAY – (1) The process of paying out the rope to the lead climber, or taking in rope for a follower, while he/she climbs, and of protecting the climber in the event of a fall. Belaying allows a climber to fall and live to try again. (2) The place where a climber belays and the anchor is set up attaching the climber to the rock, normally at the beginning and end of each pitch. Also, a session of belaying.

BELAY MONKEY – Any person recruited for the task of belaying for long periods of time. Similar to Belay Betty; usually a non-climbing female recruited to belay a significant other.

BELAYER – A person who is belaying a climber.

BETA – Information about a route.

BIG WALL – A large expanse of steep rock taking a minimum of three days to climb with conventional methods (free and aid climbing, hauling a bag with food, water, and shelter). El Cap and Half Dome in Yosemite Valley are big walls though both have routes that have been climbed in less than a day. The majority of routes on both require three to eight days to climb.

BIVOUAC – (1) A place to spend the night. (2) To spend the night, often in an unexpected location. Slang: Bivy

BOLT – (1) A permanent anchor in the rock installed individually as a protection device, or with other bolts or protection devices as an anchor. (2) To drill and place expansion bolts into rock to protect a climb.

BOULDER – (1) A big rock typically climbed without a rope. May be head high to over 30 feet. Each boulder may have many distinct routes. Boulder problems are often top roped, but climbing without a rope is thought to be better style. (2) To boulder or to go bouldering is to climb boulder problems.

CAIRN – A pile of rocks. Cairns are placed at intervals to mark a trail.

CAM – Short for camming device; removable, portable protection that helps arrest a climber's fall.

CHIMNEY – (1) A parallel-sided constriction wider than body width. (2) To climb a chimney.

CHOSS – Loose, bad-quality rock.

CRACK CLIMBING – The act of climbing continuous cracks in the rock often requiring specific techniques and protection methods.

CRAMPONS – Metal spikes which attach onto climbing boots to allow a firm grip on snow or ice.

CRUX – The most difficult spot on a climb.

DAB – The act of touching the ground or an out-of-bounds hold or area (usually with a foot) while climbing a route.

DECK – To "deck" or to "deck out" or "hit the deck" is to take a fall resulting in impact on the ground, often resulting in serious injury or death.

DISCO LEG – Also known as "sewing machine leg" or "doing the wild Elvis." Refers to the uncontrollable shaking of the leg(s) while climbing. Result of tired leg muscles or fear.

DOWN CLIMB – To climb downward rather than upward on a climb.

DYNO – (1) Abbreviation for "dynamic movement," a move that requires some use of momentum. (2) To perform a dyno.

EXPOSURE – Being very far above your last piece of protection or being in a situation in which you are very aware that you are high off the ground or in a remote location.

FIXED PROTECTION/PRO – Protection that is attached to and left on the rock for future use.

FIXED ROPE – A rope fixed to a route by the lead climber and left in place for all who follow. Also refers to ropes left on sections of alpine climbs in order to aid the next party to attempt the route.

FLASH – (1) Completion of a climb first try with no falls after having received beta about the route. (2) To perform a flash.

FREE CLIMB – The act of making upward progress using only your hands, feet, and other body parts for purchase on the rock, and none of your weight is supported by slings or the rope. When free climbing with a rope, the game is to never rely on the rope for assistance: it is there to catch you only if you fall. Contrasts with aid climbing.

FREE SOLO – To free climb without a rope and without protection. A fall is likely to result in serious injury or death. Usually distinguished from climbing high boulders in that free soloing implies a climb of a pitch or more. Contrast with highball.

GREENPOINT – To flash a route on top rope.

GUMBY – A name (often derogatory) for a novice climber.

HEADPOINT – To lead a trad route, without falling, after top-roped practice. Headpointing is a style of ascent used on difficult, and usually very dangerous, routes. Headpointing differs from redpointing in that the former is reserved for trad climbs and the latter for sport climbs.

HIGHBALL – A very high boulder problem, often with a hard landing. A high boulder problem with a sandy or otherwise soft landing may not be considered a highball. Of Planet X in Joshua Tree, John Bachar said: "That's not a f@#%in' highball."

HIP BELAY – To belay by wrapping the rope around one's waist.

JAM/JAMMING – Placing and wedging a body part (finger, hand, foot, etc.) into a crack in order to hold yourself on the wall.

JUG – (1) A big hand hold, usually a great relief to find. (2) A verb meaning "to jumar" or the act of ascending a fixed rope with jumars.

LEAD – To climb starting with the rope on the ground clipping into protection points on the way up.

MIXED CLIMBING – Climbing on both ice and rock and transitioning between the two in a single climb.

MOVE – Refers to the motion between holds.

MULTI-PITCH CLIMB – A climb with more than one pitch, or rope length.

NATURAL PROTECTION – (1) Protection (gear: cams, nuts, hexes, etc.) that is placed in cracks or pockets which can be removed with no harm to the rock. (2) Non-manmade features on a climb (trees, roots, chickenheads, etc.) around which a sling can be placed for protection.

NUTS – A flared piece of metal placed into a bottle neck constriction as a means of protection.

OFF-WIDTH – A crack that is neither wide enough to fit the whole body (chimney size) nor narrow enough to hand jam. Notorious for the necessity of awkward technique to climb.

ONSIGHT – A clean ascent with no falls, first try, with no prior knowledge of the route.

PENDULUM – (1) To swing in an arc on the end of a rope to gain access to an anchor or rock feature to one side of your current position. (2) A dangerous situation that may occur during a fall, if the top piece of protection is off to one side of the fall line.

PIN SCAR – The remaining damage to a crack after a piton (or pin) has been removed.

PITCH – Generally a rope length between belay stations on a multi-pitch climb.

PITON – A long-nosed, spike-shaped piece of metal driven into cracks for protection or aid.

POCKETS – An indented climbing feature that requires insertion of appendages to use.

PRO/PROTECTION – Gear (nuts, pitons, cams, bolts, quickdraws, etc.) placed on a climb through which the rope is threaded to protect the climber in the event of a fall.

PSYCHOLOGICAL PROTECTION – A very poorly placed piece of protection that will never hold a fall but makes the climber feel better about having pro beneath him.

PUMPED – Tired. Referring to the state of forearms in a desperate state of swollen unresponsiveness.

R-RATED – A protection rating given to a route or a runout section of a pitch with limited protection for the lead climber, where a fall will injure the leader even when properly protected.

RAPPEL – The act of self-belaying down the length of a rope to descend.

REDPOINT – To lead a free climb with no falls, accomplished after failing an onsight. Redpointing applies to sport routes with fixed protection already in place.

RETROBOLTING – The process of replacing old, small, loose, or worn bolts.

RUNOUT – A section of rock without adequate protection for the lead climber.

SCREAMING BARFIES – A term used by ice climbers to describe the screaming pain felt in the hands or feet as they warm from being cold and numb.

SECOND – (1) Following the leader on a multi-pitch route, and typically cleaning any protection that was placed on the pitch. (2) A person (one or more) who is seconding a climb.

SEND – To complete a route successfully.

SHARP END (OF THE ROPE) – The end of the rope a lead climber ties into.

SHORT-ROPE – A mountaineering scenario in which the rope attaching two climbers has been shortened where the intent is for one climber to hold up, assist, or haul the other climber up the mountain.

SIEGE TACTICS – A method of mountaineering employing large teams to transport supplies up the mountain to stock a series of linked, successively higher camps from which a summit attempt can be made.

SLAB – Any climb that is less than vertical, especially those devoid of features requiring smearing of the feet.

SLING – A loop of webbing or rope used for protection.

SOLO – Climbing alone, without a partner. *See* free solo.

SPORT CLIMBING – A school of climbing that generally emphasizes shorter routes, physically difficult movement, and bolted protection. This includes gym climbing and competition.

TOP ROPE – A climb that has the rope anchors preset at the top of the climb. In general, this results in shorter falls than a "lead."

TRADITIONAL/TRAD CLIMBING – Climbing that emphasizes longer routes and removable protection.

X-RATED – A protection rating given to a route or a section of a pitch with little to no protection for the lead climber, where a fall will likely result in death even when properly protected.

NOTES ON CONTRIBUTORS

MARCUS AGNAFORS received his doctoral degree in the Department of Culture and Communications at Linköping University, Sweden. He regularly teaches courses in moral philosophy and is currently doing research on social justice and the relation between state and religion. When the temperature drops, he is most likely to be found swinging his ice axes on whatever ice he can find. His favorite climbing destinations tend to be Chamonix (France) and the ice-climbing mecca, Rjukan (Norway).

PAUL CHARLTON is an MA candidate in Conflict Resolution at Georgetown University in Washington, DC. He worked for many years as a lead climbing ranger for the US National Park Service at Mt. Rainier National Park in Washington State, where he earned the nickname "Epic Man." Like many alpine climbers, he has a penchant for suffering, which he particularly enjoys doing in the Karakoram Mountains of Pakistan.

STEPHEN M. DOWNES is professor of philosophy and chair of the Philosophy Department at the University of Utah. His main area of research is the philosophy of biology with a special focus on the biology of human behavior. He recently stepped down from an eight-year stint as the board chairman of his local climbing organization, the Salt Lake Climbers Alliance. He is happy to live in Salt Lake City, where there is an abundance of rock to climb close to home and plenty more within four or five hours drive.

PHILIP A. EBERT studied philosophy and mathematics and graduated with a PhD in 2006 from the University of St. Andrews with a thesis in the philosophy of mathematics. Since 2007 he holds a lectureship at the University of Stirling, Scotland. His spare time is spent mostly climbing, be it sport climbing, trad climbing, bouldering, mountaineering, deep-water soloing or just pulling plastic. Sometimes, he can also be found paddling about in the North Sea attempting to catch some waves.

JOE FITSCHEN, MA, taught philosophy, writing, and skiing at Lassen College in northeastern California before he retired and moved to New York. During his teaching career he received four NEH grants. During the last one he fell in love with a philosopher, Rosamond Rhodes, who happened to live in New York. In his youth he did a number of big wall climbs in Yosemite Valley with Royal Robbins, including the first continuous ascent of El Capitan in 1960. With Robbins and Charlie Raymond, he also made three first ascents in the Kichatna Spires in Alaska in 1969.

HANS FLORINE has climbed for 27 years on six continents. He won the first ever World Championships in Speed Climbing in 1991. Hans has won the National Speed Climbing title a dozen times and the ESPN XGAMES title three years consecutively. He holds the speed record time of 2:37:05 on the 3,000-foot Nose Route of El Capitan in Yosemite Park, California. The first and only blind climbs of Mt. Kenya, Carstenz Pyramic, and The Nose of El Capitan were completed with Hans on the team. Hans has a BS in economics, has given hundreds of public presentations, and authored a book, numerous magazine articles, book chapters, and two audio programs. Hans is happily married to Jacqueline, and Papa to Marianna and Pierce.

RICHARD G. GRAZIANO, PhD (ABD), is a lecturer in the Philosophy Department at California Polytechnic State University, San Luis Obispo and a doctoral candidate in philosophy at the University of California, Santa Barbara. His primary research interests are in episte-mology, philosophical skepticism, and the nature of perceptual content. When not teaching or working on research, Rich is usually on the "sharp end" of a rope climbing the many classic routes of Yosemite, Joshua Tree National Park, and the high Sierra Nevada. He is also an American Mountain Guide Association certified Single Pitch Instructor and has worked as a mountain guide in the eastern Sierra Nevada.

DEBORA HALBERT is an associate professor of political science at the University of Hawai'i at Manoa, where she teaches courses on law, public policy, and futures studies. Her research focuses on intellectual property and she has published two books and numerous articles on the subject. Her book *Resisting Intellectual Property* (2005) discusses the resistance to the concept of intellectual property that has emerged around the world. She is currently working on a project that investigates the relationship of intellectual property to creativity and another more theoretically oriented project on anarchism. She is an avid rock climber and has been climbing for over twenty years, first in the mountains of Washington state and then on the sandstone of the Red River Gorge in Kentucky. While Hawai'i is not known as a destination for rock climbing, there are still a few places to climb and she gets out about once a week. However, she has also taken up competitive sailing, since there is limited climbing but there is lots of water.

GUNNAR KARLSEN, PhD, teaches philosophy at Bergen University in Norway. His main research areas include epistemology, philosophy of perception, and phenomenology. Being an active climber for the past twenty years, he has put up a series of first ascents in Norway, ranging from sport climbs to big walls, and climbed throughout the world. He believes he has spent more time climbing than doing philosophy, although a full-time job and family is about to change this proportion.

KEVIN KREIN, PhD, is an associate professor of philosophy and the academic director of Outdoor Studies at the University of Alaska Southeast, where he teaches courses in philosophy, mountaineering, and backcountry skiing. He also owns and guides for Alaska Powder Descents, a heli-ski company based in Juneau, Alaska. In the summers, he guides on mountains and glaciers in Southeast Alaska and has served as lead guide for film crews from PBS, Discovery Channel, and the BBC. Specializing in ski mountaineering, he has climbed and skied around the world, skied from the summit of Denali, and completed several first descents.

BEN LEVEY is a manager and climbing instructor at The Castle Climbing Centre in London and has climbed for over twenty years (mainly in Europe and the US). In between climbing trips, Ben received his PhD from University College London and served as an editorial assistant for *Mind* (2004–5). He has taught at both Heythrop College and University College London, and has been published in *International Philosophical Quarterly*.

HEIDI HOWKINS LOCKWOOD received her PhD in philosophy in 2009 from Yale University. She originally started graduate work in philosophy at MIT in the 1990s and returned to philosophy after a long hiatus during which she attempted to acquire a better grasp of reality through expeditions to Himalayan 8,000-meter peaks such as K2, Kanchenjunga, and Everest, with support from the National Geographic Society. Although the expeditions didn't improve her understanding of reality, they did lead her to the realization that the "wilderness" describes not just a specific type of place, but the way in which man interacts with such places. Her book describing the expeditions, *K2: One Woman's Quest for the Summit*, was published by National Geographic in 2001. She is currently an assistant professor at Southern Connecticut State University and writes on questions related to the metaphysics of modality, the individuation of possible worlds, consistency and completeness, and models of spacetime.

DALE MURRAY is an assistant professor of philosophy and holds a joint appointment at the University of Wisconsin-Baraboo Sauk County and University of Wisconsin-Richland. He is the author of *Nozick, Autonomy and Compensation* (2007), in addition to several articles and reviews. His research is mainly in social and political philosophy and applied ethics. He also finds himself fortunate to teach near some of the best climbing terrain in the Midwest.

WILLIAM RAMSEY got his doctorate in philosophy and cognitive science at University of California, San Diego in 1989 and accepted a position at Notre Dame University. Most of his work is in the philosophy of mind and cognitive science, and he recently published a book entitled *Representation Reconsidered* (2007). He started climbing at Smith Rock in the mid-1970s with his high school buddy Alan Watts, but quit for several years to focus on writing and teaching. Returning to the sport in the mid-1990s, he has climbed extensively throughout America and has made first ascents of such classics as Omaha Beach and Transworld Depravity at the Red River Gorge. He recently left Notre Dame for a job at the University of Nevada, Las Vegas, where he is enjoying the nearby sandstone and limestone cliffs. He enjoys discussing philosophy with fellow climbers around the camp fire, but only when there is plenty of beer.

SIMON ROBERTSON is a postdoctoral research fellow in philosophy at the University of Southampton, UK. His research lies mainly at the

    NOTES ON CONTRIBUTORS

intersection of ethics, metaethics, and practical reason. Outside philosophy, Simon's abiding interests are in various mountain pursuits; he has climbed throughout Britain, the Alps, Dolomites, Norway, the Pyrenées, and beyond.

PAM R. SAILORS, PhD, is an associate professor of philosophy and associate dean of the College of Humanities and Public Affairs at Missouri State University. Her research interests are in applied ethics and the philosophy of sport. In her spare time, she runs, as close to sea level as possible, confining her mountaineering efforts to climbing out of bed each morning.

STEPHEN E. SCHMID is assistant professor of philosophy at the University of Wisconsin-Rock County. His doctoral work was in philosophy of mind and his current research focuses on motivation in sport and education. He started playing in the mountains in the mid-1980s but didn't escalate his commitment to mountains and rock until graduate school and the UW Hoofers. In both philosophy and climbing, he finds himself awed by those who have risked much to challenge and satisfy their curiosity.

DANE SCOTT is the director of the Center for Ethics at the University of Montana and an associate professor in the Department of Society and Conservation in the College of Forestry and Conservation. Dane teaches courses on environmental ethics as well as ethics and climate change policy. His research and writing focus on ethical issues arising from science and technology. He started rock climbing in southern California as a teenager in the mid-1970s and on most weekends today can be found in the Bitterroot mountains of western Montana trying to put up hard routes with old friends.

ERIC SWAN, M.Ed, has a post-master's certificate in spiritual and existential counseling from Johns Hopkins University. He has a deep affinity with the wilderness and wisdom traditions of the East, and first learned to rock climb in southern Thailand. He is a professional counselor and songwriter and lives with his lovely wife where the rivers flow from the mountains. He looks forward to earning a doctorate degree in psychology and to one day deep-water soloing off the coast of Spain.

BRIAN TREANOR is an associate professor of philosophy at Loyola Marymount University. He has published widely on environmental ethics, philosophy of religion, ethics, and hermeneutics, and is the author of *Aspects of Alterity: Levinas, Marcel, and the Contemporary Debate* (2006). He began climbing 27 years ago at Stoney Point, CA, though he didn't become obsessed until the mid-1990s. Brian is the consummate punter, having achieved advanced intermediate ability in most climbing disciplines. He prides himself on climbing challenging routes in reasonably good style, but, as a punter, sticks mostly to the challenges of the previous generation. He often finds himself in trouble after uttering the phrase, "I'm just going to have a quick look."